Sigmund Freud

A CRITICAL INTRODUCTION TO MEDIA AND COMMUNICATION THEORY

David W. Park
Series Editor

Vol. 13

Debra Merskin

Sigmund Freud

A Critical Introduction to Media and Communication Theory

PETER LANG
New York - Berlin - Bruxelles - Chennai - Lausanne - Oxford

Library of Congress Cataloging-in-Publication Data

Names: Merskin, Debra L., author.
Title: Sigmund Freud: a critical introduction to media and communication theory / Debra Merskin.
Description: New York: PeterLang, [2024] | Includes bibliographical references and index.
Identifiers: LCCN 2024015383 | ISBN 9781433131202 (hardback) | ISBN 9783034349932 (paperback) | ISBN 9783034350112 (ebook) | ISBN 9783034350129 (epub)
Subjects: LCSH: Freud, Sigmund, 1856-1939—Influence. | Mass Media—Research. | Communication—Research. | Mass media—Psychological aspects. | Communication—Psychological aspects.
Classification: LCC BF109.F74 M47 2024 | DDC 150.19/52—dc23/eng/20240424
LC record available at https://lccn.loc.gov/2024015383
DOI 10.3726/b21912

Bibliographic information published by the Deutsche Nationalbibliothek.
The German National Library lists this publication in the German National Bibliography; detailed bibliographic data is available on the Internet at http://dnb.d-nb.de.

Cover design by Peter Lang Group AG

ISSN 1947-6264 (print)
ISBN 9783034349932 (paperback)
ISBN 9781433131202 (hardback)
ISBN 9783034350112 (ebook)
ISBN 9783034350129 (epub)
DOI 10.3726/b21912

Published by Peter Lang Publishing Inc., New York, USA
info@peterlang.com - www.peterlang.com

This publication has been peer reviewed.

CONTENTS

	Preface	vii
Chapter 1	Who Was Sigmund Freud?	1
Chapter 2	What Were Freud's Main Theories?	19
Chapter 3	How Have Freud's Theories Been Used?	57
Chapter 4	What Would a Study Look Like?	99
Chapter 5	Freud in the 21st Century	147
	Appendix 1: Freud Timeline	169
	Appendix 2: Publications of Sigmund Freud	173
	Index	179

PREFACE

> I am in the position of Louis Pasteur telling doctors that their greatest enemy was quite invisible, and quite unrecognized by them.
>
> McLuhan (1964, p. 18)

> Television and television series should be taken seriously as an object of psychoanalytic research.
>
> Poscheschnik (2008, p. 1006)

Sigmund Freud is more typically associated with psychology than he is studies of the media. Yet Freud's ideas, especially those associated with fundamental human drives, the role of humor, repressed sexual urges, and regression, can be utilized as the theoretical basis for studies of advertising, cinema, and other forms of media content. This volume is the first of its kind to examine Freud, his central ideas, and the applicability of his theories to studying media and popular culture. It begins with a brief biography, followed by a discussion of his main theories and methods, examples of how media scholars have applied his ideas, and finally, an example of application of his theory of sex and sexuality to cinema through example in the film *Melancholia* (von Trier, 2011), for studying advertising, and a public relations event.

This book is not intended to be a biography of Freud, a deep analysis of his theories and practice, nor resolution of controversies about his ideas. There are dozens of volumes that take on the finer points of depth, description, and debate. Through wide correspondences, note keeping, and books, Freud's ideas are widely available and accessible. Freud was a good writer and there are many translations.[1] Instead, this book is meant as an overview of the psychoanalytic perspective with a focus on how it can contribute and be applied to studying media. Whether his theories were or are accurate or appropriate

I agree with biographer Peter Gay (2006, p. ix) who writes that we are "duty bound to find his work epochal in its importance, no matter how many details of his work will need amendment." Interestingly, Freud himself often revised his theories, much to the chagrin of some of his critics. Importantly, "He recognized that humans—all humans—must face the dilemma of civilization. For civilization is at once humankind's greatest achievement and its greatest tragedy. It requires individuals to control their impulses, deny their wishes, limit their lusts" (p. ix).

Freud's theories and practices, upon which many psychologists and social psychologists developed their own work, provide fertile ground from which ideas about human motivation, personality, and social order grew. In agreement with de Berg (2003, p. 2), I argue that Freud's psychoanalysis "is first and foremost a *critical theory of society*" (ital. orig.).[2] While he did not take on the media directly, he was of course aware of radio, books, newspapers, and cinema. Terms with very specific clinical meaning have lived on beyond him in popular parlance such as Freudian slip, neurotic, libido, repression, catharsis, and anal (personality) (described in greater detail in Chapter 3).

There are those who criticize taking popular culture seriously. What people use for entertainment, for example, has, in some camps, been disregarded as not worthy of serious attention. And yet, I argue, what could be more valuable than examining an industry worth billions of dollars, with global impact, and that employs hundreds of thousands of people? And among those same people are billions of individuals who get *something* from the experience of consuming media (and ancillary services such as public relations and advertising). What goes into the production and consumption of those products certainly resonates individually and collectively. While Horkheimer and Adorno (2002) famously argued that popular culture and the culture industries "degrade[s] its viewers to mere consumers and condemn[s] them to intellectual stagnation through their manipulatory attempt" (p. 1013), it is my view that the very process of getting inside someone's head is worthy of analysis particularly psychological study. As a media and cultural studies scholar, I, as well as others (Bainbridge, 2014; Barker & Jane, 2016; Yates, 2014), see the mediated environment as rich in meaning construction as well as resistance. Whether active or passive, audiences consume media for reasons that might *only* be understood through a psychoanalytic lens. That meaning is encoded (drawing on Hall, 1973, 1993) by creators of content also offers an opportunity to examine societal and individual motivations when audiences decode that same content. Yet support from the psychoanalytic community for studying media and popular culture is even more significant. This recognition from therapists and scholars is particularly valuable. Examples include the book series *Psychoanalysis and Popular Culture* which began in 2009 (Taylor & Francis), Poscheschnik's 2018 study of *Game of Thrones*, and MacRury and Rustin's (2013) look at *Dr. Who*). Freud's theories and expansion into psychoanalytic theory are perhaps particularly qualified to examine media "by offering a comprehensive theory about the human condition, that is, dealing with the dynamics of mental processes, the intersubjective nature of the e self, and the relation between individual and society" (Poscheschnik, 2018, p. 1014). The ability of a psychoanalytic lens to peer below manifest/surface/connotative levels reveals latent/below surface/denotative meanings which can "enrich the understanding of cultural phenomena in general" (p. 1014).

Much academic research as well as speculation accompany the break between Sigmund Freud and Carl Jung between 1909 and 1913 (Doran, 2017). A discussion of this is beyond the scope of this book. In addition, while I will make mention of controversies around Freud, his treatment of women (Horney, 1993), feminist responses (Horney, 1993; Millett, 1969/2016; Mitchell & Mishra, 2000), and drug use (see Botticelli, 2017; Teive et al., 2019), there is ample literature on all these topics. They will of course be included as appropriate, but the focus here is on how Freud's theories, which were modified over time the more he learned, can be applied to studies of the media and media theory. In the preface to *New Introductory Lectures on Psycho-Analysis* Freud wrote (1932, pp. 6–7):

> No reader of an account of astronomy will feel disappointed and contemptuous of the science if he is shown the fronters at which our knowledge of the universe melts into haziness. Only in psychology is it otherwise. … What people seem to demand of psychology is not progress in knowledge, but satisfaction of some other sort; every unsolved problem, every admitted uncertainty is made into a reproach against it. Whoever cares for the science of mental life must accept these injustices along with it.

Overview of the Book

Chapter 1, "Who Was Sigmund Freud?" is an overview of Freud's life, from his birth in Příbor Moravia in the Czech Republic to his death in London. Particular attention is paid to the historical context within which he was raised, studied, and later practiced. Family dynamics (a very young mother married to Freud's much older father) played an important early role in his eventual theory of psychosexual development. Important details of his personal life, sociopolitical influences of his childhood as well as the historical era in which he practiced influenced his ever-evolving ideas.

Chapter 2 is a multipart overview of Freud's main theories. These include those about dreams, sex, aggression, group behavior, and the unconscious. It includes a discussion of Freud's main theories, emphasizing definitions, brief discussions of concepts, and applications of his ideas. The purpose of this chapter is not only to clarify what he might have intended with these pivotal ideas but also how many of them have lived on while others have been distorted and even misused in contemporary life and popular culture.

Chapter 3, "How have Freud's theories been used in media studies?" summarizes the major literature in film, advertising, news, and public relations where Freud's theories have been used and/or referenced. These studies span multiple disciplines including film studies, psychology, sociology, and art.

Chapter 4, "What Would a Study Look Like?" is an analysis of four examples from media and popular culture wherein Freud's ideas can be applied using psychoanalytic theory.

Finally, Chapter 5 concludes this book with a discussion of how scholars and students might see Freud's ideas as tools to understand contemporary 21st-century experiences. In addition, it includes ideas about how Freud's concepts contributed to the formation of modern psychology and still have relevance for studying media and popular culture in the 21st century.

Notes

1 The most famous and widely used of Freud's works is the *Standard Edition (SE)*, translated by James Strachey.

2 I do not agree with, and feel compelled to point out, de Berg's (2003) sexist usage as written in the preface of his book: "In order to avoid awkward phrases such as *he or she*, *s/he*, and *him or her*, I have used the masculine pronoun to refer to both sexes" (p. viii).

References

Bainbridge, C., Ward, I., & Yates, C. (Eds.). (2014). *Television and psychoanalysis*. London: Routledge.

Barker, C., & Jane, E. (2016). *Cultural studies: Theory and practice*. London: Sage.

Cherry, K. (2018, July 1). Sigmund Freud timeline. Verywellmind. https://www.verywellmind.com/sigmund-freud-timeline-2795846

de Berg, H. (2003). *Freud's theory and its use in literary and cultural studies: An introduction*. Rochester, NY: Camden House.

Gay, P. (2006). *Freud: A life for our time*. London: W. W. Norton.

Hall, S. (1973). *Encoding and decoding in the television discourse*. University of Birmingham.

Hall, S. (1997). *Representation: Cultural representations and signifying practices*. New York: Sage.

Horkheimer, M., & Adorno, T. W. (2002). *Dialectics of enlightenment. Philosophical fragments*. Stanford University Press.

MacRury, I., & Rustin, I. (2013). *The inner world of Doctor Who: Psychoanalytic reflections in time and space*. London: Routledge.

McLuhan, M. (1964). *Understanding media*. New York: McGraw Hill.

Poscheschnik, G. (2018). *Game of Thrones*—A psychoanalytic interpretation including some remarks on the psychosocial function of modern TV series. *International Journal of Psychoanalysis*, 99(4), 1004–1016.

Sigmund Freud chronology. Sigmund Freud Museum Vienna. https://www.freud-museum.at/online/freud/chronolg/chrnlg-e.htm

von Trier, L. (2011). *Melancholia* [Motion Picture]. Zentropa. United States.

Yates, C. (2014). Psychoanalysis and television: Notes toward a psycho-cultural approach. In C. Bainbridge, I. Ward, & C. Yates (Eds.), *Television and psychoanalysis*. London: Routledge.

· 1 ·

WHO WAS SIGMUND FREUD?

To us he is no more a person now but a whole climate of opinion.

W. H. Auden (1939) *In Memory of Sigmund Freud*, copyright 1940 and © renewed 1968 by W. H. Auden; from COLLECTED POEMS by W. H. Auden, edited by Edward Mendelson. Used by permission of Random House, an imprint and division of Penguin Random House LLC. All rights reserved. Reprinted by permission of Curtis Brown, Ltd. All rights reserved

Mention a cigar, a train, a slip of the tongue, jokes, dreams, Oedipus, or anything resembling a penis and Freud's name is almost certain to follow. No other figure in psychology, past or present, is as visible or as controversial as Sigmund Freud. Some consider him a freak, a fake, while others admire his veracity and skills as a writer and his willingness to modify theories as he learned more about himself and his patients. Feminist scholars have wrestled with whether he was inherently misogynistic or in fact gave voice to women at a time when their concerns were largely dismissed as mere "hysterics." While this book is concerned with Freud's potential contribution to media and communication theory, it is also a foray into the controversy surrounding methods and means to consider the influence of Freud's theories on the making and studying of media. I also consider the person behind the ideas. As is discussed later, Freud lived in a particularly volatile and vulnerable time—when, as a Jew living in Europe, he felt the force of Nazi extermination efforts, narrowly escaping with his family to safety in London. Not to consider this when exploring Freud's theories and applying them to case studies would give short shrift to this complex individual. As Winkin and Leeds-Hurwitz (2013, pp. 2–3) state, "To believe there is no direct causal link between life and work is an illusion; to believe life unfolds with no twists and turns is another illusion. But to believe that work is produced outside of any social and historical context—that is yet another illusion." Erich Fromm pronounced that psychoanalysis's "great achievements, as well as its defects, show the imprint of the founder's personality. No doubt, then, the origin of psychoanalysis is to be sought in Freud's personality" (1959/2013, p. 1).

Sigmund Freud, neurologist, physiologist, medical doctor, psychologist, and father of psychoanalysis and depth psychology, was born into a Jewish family as Sigismund Schlomo Freud to Jacob and Amalié Freu in Příbor Moravia in the Czech Republic on May 6, 1856. Příbor is a small market town about 150 miles north of Vienna.[1] The village was mostly Catholic when Freud was a child; the Jewish community was small. Freud's father was a merchant who traded mostly in wool. His mother, to whom he was very close, was said to be idealized by him, yet she could be both domineering and caring. He would later describe the relationship as "the most perfect, the most free from ambivalence of all human relationships. A mother can transfer to her son the ambition she has been obliged to suppress in herself" (1933/1989, p. 165).

Freud's humble beginnings seem in some ways unlikely to foster the kind of critical thinking and enthusiasm he brought to his training, and yet there's much to suggest his keen mind was already aware of the interpersonal dynamics at play in his immediate family. He was cognizant of familial dynamics and tensions between stepparents and half-siblings that polite society didn't discuss and yet of course existed everywhere. What was special about Freud, that others of his generation or upbringing didn't share? According to Fromm, it was his "intellectual endowment and a vitality," possibly his "wish for prominence," and a "passion for truth" (1959/2013, p. 5). At the same time, he was thought not to be a particularly warm person, and whether he perceived that as a strength or shortcoming we'll never know, but "given the cultural climate … the special European, Austrian and Jewish elements[2] in his environment, a boy with his wish for fame and recognition and his lack of joy in life had to turn to the adventure in knowledge if he wanted to fulfill his life's desire" (p. 5). He was also courageous in his pursuit of truth and knowledge.

This chapter provides biographical information about Freud to situate him, his theories of the mind, and his impact on psychology and media studies, within the historical context within which he arose, amid significant social upheaval (World War II). Highly controversial in methods and theories then and now, Freud's qualitative approach to studying human nature remains a powerful tool in diagnosing and treating a variety of psychological problems. His theories, when seen through the lens of depth psychology, apply not only to the individual analysand but also collectively to societies and cultures. As such, his theories have been used to predict behavior related to the media (effects) as well as tools to unpack intentions of film directors and other artists. The goal of this background is to build a foundation upon which discussions of Freud's major ideas are then applied to media theory, as discussed in later chapters.

Origins

Young Sigismund (Sigmund)[3] was the oldest of seven children (five girls and two boys), born to his father's second wife, Amalia. He had two older half-brothers from the first marriage. When he was only 3 ½ years old (due to the collapse of his father's business), the Freud family moved to Leipzig, Germany and then to Vienna when Sigmund was four years old. It would be in Vienna where he would live, marry, and build a private practice. As a young man he studied at the Sperl Gymnasium and then at the University of Vienna (1873–1882), where he became a medical doctor, specializing in pathological medicine and neurology. Just prior to his graduation from medical school, Freud changed his name from the Hebraic (Sigismund Schlomo) to the Germanic "Sigmund," "both as an expression of his wish to avoid, as much as he could, the regnant anti-Semitism of the period, and to pronounce, with Wagnerian bravado, his knightly intentions" (Kahr, 2015, p. 3). He met Martha Bernays in April 1882 and fell hopelessly in love. Two months later, on June 17, 1882, they became engaged (Gay, 1998/2006, p. 37).

Essentially penniless, Freud needed to gain professional experience and while he was passionate about research, he also needed to create the kind of life he and Martha desired. For the four years between engagement and marriage, the couple remained celibate (as was fitting the times). Gay (1998/2006) suggests that this waiting may have influenced his theories about suppression and sexuality. Martha and Sigmund were apart during much of the four years, relying on letters, apparently quite romantic ones, to sustain their relationship until they could wed. In fact, what might be suggestive of future, foundational early theories about sublimation and substitution are apparent as he wrote to her of his passion for cigars, which he justified smoking due to Martha's absence from his daily life. He wrote, "Smoking is indispensable if one has nothing to kiss" (qtd. in Gay, 1998/2006, p. 39). Freud worked as a doctor at the General Hospital in Vienna during these years, learning as much as possible about various medical specialties. To gain what he sought for his personal life, Freud aggressively climbed the hospital professional ladder, beginning as a clinical assistant to training for his eventual private practice as an avenue of interest but also needed income.

Children quickly followed the marriage to Martha, marriage, six in all (Anna, Ernst, Sophie, Oliver, Mathilde, and Martin). Three daughters and three sons. His daughter Sophie died, at age 26, of influenza in 1919. Freud's father died in 1896 at age 65 and his mother died in 1930 at age 95. His sons served in World War I. Anna, the youngest became an important psychologist.

Professional World

Freud primarily considered himself a scientist, postulating and testing theories, revising them, and applying them in clinical settings. "The most striking and probably the strongest emotional force in Freud was *his passion for truth and his uncompromising faith in* reason [ital. in orig.]" (Fromm, 1959/2013, p. 8). It was by way of reason, in Freud's view, where one could "ameliorate the suffering inherent in human life" (p. 2). In 1873 he enrolled in medical school at the University of Vienna. The focus of his initial studies was biology and physiology, studying under renowned German scientist Ernst Brücke, founder of what became known as neurology. Freud eventually turned to a specialization in neurology and graduated in 1881 with a medical degree. Most of the underpinnings of his psychological work took root in Paris during the winter of 1885–1886 when Freud worked under the tutelage of French physician Jean-Martin Charcot (1825–1893) with patients suffering what was then termed "hysteria." He had traveled on stipend to Paris in the spring of 1885, where he became intrigued with mythology, beautiful museum items, and history. With Charcot he learned more about scientific research but more so about the diagnosis of mental illnesses, something relatively new in those times. Charcot "had diagnosed hysteria as a genuine ailment rather than the malingerer's refuge. What is more, he had recognized that it afflicts men—all traditional notions to the contrary—no less than women" (Gay, 1998/2006, p. 49). Freud was also fascinated by hypnosis and saw "Charcot inducing and curing hysterical paralyses by means of direct hypnotic suggestion" (p. 49). This was a controversial technique Freud was to take back to Vienna and use with some success, although he came to believe the effects did not last (and "because [he admitted] he wasn't very good at it"; Lear, 2005, p. 3). He resigned from the General Hospital upon return and began seeing patients privately, established private practice in 1886, married Martha in 1886, and became an affiliated professor at the University of Vienna in 1902 as a docent in neuropathology.

One of Freud's major insights while working with Charcot was that many patients could be helped, and even cured, using hypnosis. Two findings came from this work that were to direct his future trajectory: (1) the use of words and associations to help patients process problems and release unconscious content, which became known as "the talking cure," and (2) diagnoses of illness believed traceable to repressed contents of the mind, typically to a traumatic event during childhood and even infancy. In Freud's view, the associations and trauma were "found invariably to have a sexual character" (Wollheim 1981, p. xii). Freud would go on to work with the physician Josef Breuer (1842–1925), otolaryngologist Wilhelm Fliess (1858–1928), psychologists Carl Jung (1875–1961), Alfred Adler (1870–1937), Karl Abraham (1877–1925), Otto Rank (1884–1939), and Sándor Ferenczi (1873–1933). With Breur in particular Freud learned the technique of getting patients to talk about themselves and how doing so sometimes released traumatic experiences previously hidden. It was Freud's insistence on the sexual origins of neuroses that drove a wedge between him and Breuer (and later Carl Jung). After an extensive period of intense self-analysis (part of psychoanalytic training to this day), Freud published *The Interpretation of Dreams* (1900) in which he introduces his theory of the unconscious.

Freud invented the method and practice he termed psychoanalysis (1896) or, as his patient Fräulein Ann O. (Bertha Pappenheim) called it, "the talking cure," which was, at the time, revolutionary. During this therapeutic process, the analysand would lay on a couch with the analyst out of view, behind him or her, and invited to free-associate, describe dreams, or other memories—all shared in a way that felt free from the influence of the analyst. "There is no appeal to authority here; nothing needs to be accepted on faith. There is no behind-the-curtains mystery; indeed, there are no curtains" (Lear, 2005, p. xv). Freud encouraged his patients to reconstruct their childhood experiences and, through giving them voice, bring to consciousness experiences that might have heretofore been forgotten or hidden and yet that produced very real physical and psychological symptoms. Psychoanalyst Astrid Gessert (2016, 0.33) illustrates the power of the psychoanalytic process through language. By talking about an experience, "language can function like a lift where words can lift other words and other meanings from the level of the unconscious to consciousness." Gessert (2016, 0.40) describes one of Freud's patients who recalled cutting red roses in her garden, emphasizing "red," asked what she felt about red roses, the patient remembered her father's funeral, and how her father's second wife threw a red rose into his grave "as a token of love. At that moment she felt a pang of pain, a pang of jealousy." Through associations with red roses, a memory of a funeral and difficult emotions resulted in feelings of panic and jealousy. Thereafter, funerals and red roses combined to generate complicated emotions later in her life. The findings from verbal therapy were first published with Breuer in *Studies on Hysteria* (1895). In 1901 Freud published *The Psychopathology of Everyday Life* and, in 1905, *Three Essays on the Theory of Sexuality*. Despite the eventual impact of these books, it wasn't until 1908 at the First Psychoanalytical Congress held in Salzburg, that Freud's ideas gained traction.

Freud's work and reputation grew outside Europe but began in his practice and eventually grew to what would be called the Psychoanalytic Movement. The Movement developed out of what was called the Wednesday Evening Meetings, started in the fall of 1902, and were comprised of fellow (male) professionals. This group of psychoanalysts, and occasional others, met at Freud's home (Berggasse 19) to discuss their work and explore new ideas in the field. Freud wrote, in his invitation to Adler:

> A small circle of colleagues and supporters afford me the great pleasure of coming to my house in the evening (8:30 PM after dinner) to discuss interesting topics in psychology and neuropathology. (Davies, 2020)

In 1912 he described the gathering, which included Alfred Adler, Max Kahane, Rudolph Reitler, and Wilhelm Stekel:

> a number of younger physicians gathered around me with the declared intention of learning, practicing, and disseminating psychoanalysis. A colleague who had experienced the beneficial effects of analytic therapy on himself gave the impetus. (Davies, 2020)

Participant Max Graf (1942, pp. 470–471) wrote:

> First, one of the members would present a paper. Then, black coffee and cakes were served; cigars and cigarettes were on the table and were consumed in great quantities. After a social quarter of an hour, the discussion would begin. The last and the decisive word was always spoken by Freud himself. There was an atmosphere of the foundation of a religion in that room. Freud himself was its new prophet who made

> the heretofore prevailing methods of psychological investigation appear superficial. (Davies, 2020)

Over time, group dynamics changed including how one became invited to participate and the nature of the exchanges. Freud dissolved the group in 1908 and established the Vienna Psychoanalytic Society which included Hans Sachs, C. J. Jung, Karl Abraham, Ludwig Binswanger, Max Eitingon, Carl Furtmüller, and Sándor Frenczi. 1908 was also when the first International Psycho-Analytical Congress was held in Salzburg, Germany and, in 1910, the International Psycho-Analytical Association was founded. Freud's one and only visit to America was on September 7, 1909, as an invited lecturer at Clark University in Worchester, Massachusetts. In "Five Lectures on Psychoanalysis," Freud "introduced intellectuals and professionals to his idea that sexuality was a central part of life and identity" (Czuczka, 2000, p. 15). Prior to this event, sex and sexuality were topics not spoken of, at least not publicly, not by "nice" people. Berger notes that hostility toward Freud's theories were misunderstandings because, "in the United States at least" (2017, p. 98) there was "extreme sensitivity to the topic of sexuality. We Americans resist intrusion into this most private and personal aspect of our lives and may even repress—refuse to admit to consciousness—ideas and insights that would explain sexuality in general and our behavior in particular." Because he thought Americans were too conservative to accept his ideas (he referred to them as "the gentle zephyrs of prudery"), Freud almost didn't make the journey. In fact the amount of money offered was so small that the voyage, along with missing a peak month of earnings in private practice (July) were nearly reason enough not to go. And, knowing the suspicions of American therapists about Freud's ideas, he also anticipated their defensiveness, mostly related to money. Prochnik writes

> From the outset, as would be the case for the remainder of his career, Freud's feelings about America were directly tied up with the issues of money. And questions of money were associated with fears of American prudery, which in turn went hand in hand with fears of American whorish trendiness. (2006/2012, p. 52)

In a letter to Jung, he wrote, "once they discover the sexual core of our psychological theories, they will drop us" (McGuire, 1974, p. 92). "They" did not, and doctors Freud, Jung, and Ferenczi, psychoanalytic colleagues at the time, traveled by ship to America. In a letter to Jung before the trip Freud wrote, "we are bringing the plague and they don't even know it."

Dr. Freud's rather shocking ideas were delivered in Worchester in a manner as if to a lay audience, thus were easily understood and, to his surprise, warmly received. In fact, the theories spread like wildfire. American physician and neurologist Henry Morton Prince (2006/2012) wrote, "Freudian psychology … flooded the field like a full rising tide and the rest of us were left submerged like clams buried in the sands at low water" (qtd. in Prochnik). These lectures were to form *Five Lectures on Psycho-Analysis* (1916). It was while speaking in America that Freud met American neurologist James Jackson Putnam (1846–1918), who immediately connected to Freud's ideas about psychoanalysis. The two would become friends (not without tensions) and correspondents. Putnam would go on to lecture, write papers, analyze patients, and debate anti-Freud colleagues. Putnam died in 1918 but his efforts played a large role in launching psychoanalysis in America (Prochnik, 2006/2012).

By the 1920s, Freud was a household name in the United States. His influence was seen and felt not only in the therapeutic setting but also in the arts, particularly among the surrealists (see Chapter 3 for more on this). Freud's tripartite model of the mind, containing id, ego, and superego, was a radical concept for research and treatment of patients. He published this in his 1923 book *The Ego and the Id.* Other major theories such as infantile sexuality, repression, transference, and dream interpretation are discussed in more detail in Chapter 2. For example, in the 1950s, Freud's theories of the unconscious influenced film, such as those directed by Alfred Hitchcock and later Bernardo Bertolucci and Woody Allen. To this day Allen applies Freud's theories liberally, as something of a running joke, throughout his films as his characters deal with existential angst and repression. Even television programs such as *The Sopranos* employed transference as a dramatic element. Artists such as Salvador Dalí incorporated the work of the subconscious into their expressions. Dalí's surreal dream sequence in Hitchcock's 1945 *Spellbound* is a classic use of Freud to illustrate dreams and sexual symbolism. The film opens with the following narration:

> The method by which modern science treats the emotional problems of the sane. The analyst seeks only to induce the patient to talk about his hidden problems, to open the locked doors of his mind. Once the complexes that have been disturbing the patient are uncovered and interpreted, the illness and confusion disappear … and the devils of unreason are driven from the human soul. (Hitchcock, 1945, 0:04:58)

Freud felt that nothing was self-evident and that more could be learned about the inner workings of the mind (versus the brain) by talking with people who would eventually reveal deeper aspects of themselves. As the founder of what would become known as Depth Psychology[4] and a leading contributor to what would become known as psychoanalysis, Freud's work shows us that, as he wrote, "The facts in psychoanalysis have a habit of being rather more complicated than we like. If they were as simple as all that, perhaps it might not have needed psychoanalysis to bring them to light" (1917/1977, p. 372). Thus, to get at the deepest sources of turmoil, troubles, terrors, and temptations required going deep into the psyche, into that which the conscious mind has yet to consider and draw that content out.

Freud took seriously the concerns of men and women, especially physical and psychological symptomology accessed through the four main techniques (interpretation, transference analysis, technical neutrality, and counter transference analysis) (Kernberg, 2016, p. 287) using strategies such as free association and dream analysis. He assisted his patients in finding the answers that ultimately existed within themselves. Freud termed the process psychoanalysis. What *is* psychoanalysis? According to Mitchell and Black, "Movies and cartoons offer images of a patient lying on a couch, speaking endlessly into a vacuum, while a silent, colorless, older gentleman with a beard takes notes" (1996, p. xv). That might be the popular culture rendition, understanding of psychoanalysis, but it is "an intensely emotional, highly charged, deeply personal experience for both participants," (xv) that is both the analysand and the therapist. The goal is to engage with experiences, both present and past, dreaming, and awakened, feeling, thinking, and fantasy.

Desires, longings, urges, and perversions were all, as will be discussed in the next chapter, part of being human. Being a relatively "uncivilized" being at birth who had to learn how to get along in a recently "civilized" world, in Freud's view, required repressing, redirecting, or reforming otherwise natural drives. "He had discovered, he said, primitive sexual and aggressive forces hidden deep inside the minds of all human beings, forces which if not controlled led individuals and societies to chaos and destruction" (*Century of the Self*, 2002). Knowledge of these compulsions, if used by those with interests in controlling mass populations, could also be used for evil ends. Furthermore, Freud (1920/2015, p. 1) believed we are all motivated by what he called "the pleasure principle," i.e., attaining easy emotional and physical rewards, thus turning away from perceived boring or routinized activities. When we are born and throughout infancy we are completely motivated by pleasures, Freud argued. This can get us in to trouble if not controlled or channeled in culturally and socially approved ways. For example, what we eat or who or how we have sexual relations with one another. Freud's realization that, if not taught how to be part of culture, we naturally head in primal, instinctual directions. He called acceptance of civilized ways the "reality principle" (p. 4). Should we not adapt to the demands of living in societies this can result, in the extreme, in neuroses, that is, if we repress the pleasure principle (id).

Personal Practices

From 1886 until he and his family were forced to flee to London on June 4, 1938, Freud practiced in Vienna. In his work he invited readers and patients to think about that which we prefer not to speak, "about [our] appetites and … intellectual powers, about self-knowledge and self-deceit, about [our] profoundest passions and about [our] most intimate or trivial failings, in ways that would have seemed to earlier generations at once scandalous and silly" (Wollheim, 1981, p. x). In his writings on dreams, for example, Freud recognized the traces everyday life leave on what we re-envision in the night world and how they can be reinscribed and expressed through neurotic symptoms. Freud drew on mythology, for example the Oedipus concept, to help us understand eternal questions faced by human beings over time, offering a metaphorical way of discussing them. But at least three areas influenced the formation of Freud-the-man and Freud-the-psychiatrist: early life experiences, historical context, and knowledge of physics.

Early life experiences, discussed earlier, no doubt influenced Freud, not only those excavated during deep self-analysis, but also lived experiences. Having half-brothers and knowing his father had been married more than once, shaped his thinking about relationships. On the occasion of the death of his father, whom Freud simultaneously admired and yet felt shame toward, he had a series of dreams, influenced by deep grief, mixed with feelings of rivalry (his older half-brother was the same age as Freud's mother). Freud's ambivalence, along with feelings at times of wishing his older brother was his father, led later to the Oedipus complex, as a metaphor for these dynamics.

The times Freud lived in also impacted his views. The 19th century was particularly rich in pivotal figures. Charles Darwin was one of the most prominent among them; his *Origin of Species* was published when Freud was four years old. The ideas of Darwin, although today highly controversial, particularly in terms of connection with eugenics (see Yakushko, 2019 for more on this) included the idea that the fittest who survives is the most adaptive to changes in their environment. Not necessarily the largest, the most aggressive, or the most attractive, but the one who sees or senses a changing world and adapts to it, passing on that genetic memory and those experiences, to those who follow. Humans thus became, as animals ourselves, objects of scientific study (and of course, abuses. For more on this see Ferdowsian, 2021).

Freud was also no doubt influenced by theories and discoveries of physics. During his studies at the University Vienna under Brücke (who had published *Lecture Notes on Physiology* [*Vorlesungen über Physiologie*] in 1873–1874), Freud learned of and adopted *dynamic physiology*. The general principle in physics, formulated by Hermann von Helmholzt (1821–1894), was that physical systems always have energy and while the amount might change, it is never destroyed, rather if energy is one part of the system it is not in another and vice versa. While studying with Brücke Freud expanded the physics energy model and applied it to *psychic* energy within the human mind. While the energy changes can be transmitted, converted, modified, or even repressed, they never fully dissipate or disappear. This was to become a crucial aspect of psychoanalysis.

Freud was a prolific and interesting writer, primarily from 1886 to shortly before his death in 1939. What became known as the Standard Edition (translations of his work from German to English), comprises 23 volumes of clinical notes, writing, and letters. His landmark study, *The Interpretation of Dreams*, was published in 1900. Other significant publications include *Studies on Hysteria* (1895, co-written with Breur), *Three Essays on the Theory of Sexuality* (1905), *Jokes and Their Relation to the Unconscious* (1905), *The Psychopathology of Everyday Life* (1905), *The Future of an Illusion* (1927), and *Civilization and Its Discontents* (1929) (see Appendices for a complete list of publications).

Life in London

Freud lived and practiced in Vienna until he was 82 years old. It was a dangerous time to be Jewish in Europe, and some say he waited too long to leave. However, he had lived there most of his life. When, On March 13, 1930, Germany annexed Austria (Anschluss), he realized it was no longer safe for him or his family to remain. Friends had been pleading with him to leave. The family was constantly monitored by the Nazis, their home had a swastika affixed to the door, and Anna was arrested and interrogated (Storr, 1986). Despite consistent urging from family and associates, they were reticent to leave, and almost didn't get out. Freud "changed his mind after his daughter Anna was arrested and interrogated by the Gestapo" (Menand, 2017). While Freud got his immediate family members out, four sisters were left behind and "all of them died in the camps, one of starvation, at Theresiendstadt; the others, probably by gas, at Auschwitz and Treblinka" (Menand, 2017). According to his physician Max Schur, Freud required "legal permission" (Yagoda, 2018). Biographer Ernest Jones[5] played a pivotal role in getting the family out. A message sent between American John Wiley, intended for Freud's friend U.S. Ambassador in France, William C. Bullitt, noted: "Fear Freud, despite age and illness, in danger." Bullitt was a friend to Freud, "his one-time psychoanalyst and co-author on what might be oddest literary project in the Freudian canon" (Yagoda, 2018). Called "a disastrously bad book," by NY Books reviewer Erik H. Erikson (1967), in part because of the way in which Woodrow Wilson "is, with obsessive frequency … referred to as 'little Tommy," the book reflects both Bullitt and Freud's intense dislike of Wilson but also their sense of him as dangerous to American democracy. Bullitt had for some time welcomed Freud to immigrate to the United States were things to become too difficult in Vienna. Nazis burned and destroyed his books in 1933, and he was allowed to leave in 1938. On June 4, 1938, it was to Paris, however, the family first embarked, met at the train station at the Gare del l'Est by his friend Marie Bonaparte and Ambassador Bullitt. In a curious collaboration built of shared animosity toward President Woodrow Wilson, Bullitt, and Freud would author *Thomas Woodrow Wilson: A Psychological Study* (1967). The family then settled in Hampstead, in London, where Freud was visited by H. G. Wells, Salvador Dalí, and others who came to support him. Virginia and Leonard Woolf visited as well, since they had published Freud's works since 1924, founding and owning Hogarth Press (Menand, 2017). Virginia Woolf (1986) wrote of him: "Dr. Freud gave me a narcissus. Sitting in a great library with little statues at a large scrupulously tidy shiny table. A screwed up shrunk very old man: with a monkey's light eyes, paralyzed spasmodic movements, inarticulate: but alert" (p. 202). Woolf's husband, Leonard (1973) wrote, "Nearly all famous men are disappointing or bores or both. Freud was neither; he had an aura not of fame but of greatness. The terrible cancer of the mouth … had already attacked him. Freud was extraordinarily courteous in a formal old-fashioned way."

For that brief year in London, Freud set up shop. His home, an unpretentious brick residence,[6] contains his many art objects, collections of pottery (Greek), bronzes, and antique furniture. Freud was passionate about collecting antiquities and intrigued by mythology. His famous couch is there along with beautiful rugs and his extensive library. Photographer Edmund Engleman (1976; see also Werner, 2017) took photographs of Freud's office before the family left Vienna. Engelman (1976, p. 131) wrote of his journey to do so: "I was both excited and afraid as I walked through the empty streets toward Bergasse 19 that wet May morning in 1938 …. I was convinced that anyone who saw me would instantly know that I was on my way to the offices of Dr. Sigmund Freud—on a mission that would hardly have pleased the Nazis." This was ten days before the Freuds were to depart for London. The "shoot" took Engelman two days, of which he wrote:

> I entered and had my first glance of the famous couch; it was relatively small. Antiquities filled every available spot in the room. I was overwhelmed by the masses of figurines which overflowed every surface … the couch itself was covered with an Oriental rug and pillows piled on it, so that it seemed a patient lying on it would almost have to sit up. The walls were covered with pictures, pieces of art, mementos, and awards … wherever one looked, there was a glimpse into the past. (pp. 96–97)

It is said that where once his beloved objects were cramped in their Vienna apartment, in London he could display them quite liberally. His extensive library (despite having to leave more than 800 books behind, now in a collection in New York) contained literature, history, and art, in many languages. His office opens on to a garden where he spent a good bit of time, particularly as his health declined.

A growth was discovered on Freud's palate in 1917, what was eventually to become identified as cancer. Around Freud's 76th birthday, a lump was discovered in his mouth that proved to be malignant. In surgery, Freud's entire upper jaw and palate on the right side were removed and he wore a prosthesis for the rest of his life. He was to endure at least 30 more surgeries and was in constant chronic pain for the remaining 16 years of his life. Still he did not stop smoking. In fact he adamantly refused to give it up:

> For Freud, smoking would represent the choice, the exertion of will on unpromising circumstances. Part of his smoking was a resistance, a rebellion, a declaration of himself. He wrote, 'annoyed that the discomfort will not give way, I am again sinning more' (Roiphe, 2016, p. 6).

Freud's nonstop, sunrise to sunset smoking of cigars has become part and parcel of representations of him.[7] If you see an image of Freud, you will see a cigar. As in real life, the good doctor is never seen without one. Cigar smoking has not been uncommon in powerful figures (Mark Twain, Winston Churchill, John F. Kennedy). Although he knew they were killing him, Freud often resorted to rather childish explanations to rationalize continued smoking—in fact saying it was *not* smoking, during those rare moments, that was responsible for his ill health. Elkin (1994/1995) wrote, "When it came to cigars, Freud's capacity for self-knowledge broke down."[8] While the ill effects of smoking are something we now know a great deal about it would seem that Freud's representations with the ever-present cigar are true to who he was as well as function as sign of him. His last completed book, *Moses and Monotheism* (1939) was as usual controversial. In it he argued that Moses was in fact Egyptian. Freud died on September 23, 1939, at age 83, "asking his physician for a lethal dose of morphine. Freud did not believe in personal immortality, but his work lives on" (Gay, 1964, p. xxii). He refused painkillers (Roiphe, 2016, p. 107) and continued to work throughout his decline, even seeing four patients. Just days prior to his death, he completed reading Balzac's (1831) *La Peau de Chagrin* (*The Wild Ass's Skin*) and asked his daughter Anna, to assist him in dying. No longer working, done reading, he was done. At first, she refused, then assented, she wrote, in a letter to a friend, "His bodily pain grew more and more but his spirit never changed in spite of everything" (in Roiphe, p. 109). Freud had written, "the organism wishes to die only in its own fashion," and yet he chose when and where. Anna declared her father was "himself to the last minute." Anna, who became a psychoanalyst, lived in the London house, which is now a museum, until her death in 1982 (see Appendices for Chronology of Freud's life).

In the next chapter, I summarize Freud's main theories to provide context for studies using these theories to examine perspectives and/or inform points of view in media and popular culture.

Notes

1 One can visit the home in which Freud was born in the town of Příbor, at *17 Zámečnická Street in Freiberg, Moravia* (now Příbor, Czech Republic). It is now a museum. See: https://www.visitczechrepublic.com/en-US/2a4429f2-7f74-438a-bbd5-1e92c95f4389/place/c-pribor-sigmund-freud-museum and https://www.freud.org.uk/2019/07/09/exploring-freuds-czech-birthplace/
In Příbor there is also a Society of Sigmund Freud, founded in 1990, a monument and bust of Freud by sculptors František Navrátil and Zdeněk Makovský, and a square named for him.

2 Fromm (2013, p. 2) notes "the Jewish tradition itself was one of reason and intellectual discipline, and besides that, a somewhat despised minority had a strong emotional interest to defeat the powers of darkness, of irrationality, of superstition, which blocked the road to its own emancipation and progress."
3 Freud officially changed his first name in 1878 (Kahr, 2015, p. 3).
4 "The term 'depth psychology' was coined at the turn of the twentieth century by Eugen Bleuler, a professor of psychiatry at the University of Zürich and director (1898–1927) of the Burghölzli Asylum in Zürich, where C. G. Jung began his career as a psychiatrist. It has become used by Freudians and Jungians to indicate those psychologies that orient themselves around the idea of the "unconscious." For more on this see https://www.pacifica.edu/about-pacifica/what-is-depth-psychology/.
5 Ernest Jones established the American Psychoanalytic and the British Psychoanalytic Associations. Jones played a crucial role in assisting the Freud's escape to London and wrote a three-volume biography of Freud. For more on Jones see: https://psychoanalysis.org.uk/our-authors-and-theorists/ernest-jones.
6 The Freud's home in London (20 Maresfield Gardens) is now a museum. https://www.freud.org.uk/.
7 Freud called smoking his "first addiction," and the hazards of smoking were less known then than now. "His 'sweet habit' of smoking was a pleasure he took seriously, relishing his cigars with quiet concentration, as an epicure does his food" (Shortland, 1993, p. 4).
8 For more on this topic, see "Freud and his cigars" at https://www.freud.org.uk/2020/04/22/freud-and-his-cigars/.

References

Auden, W. H. (1939/1991). In memory of Sigmund Freud. In E. Mendelson (Ed.). *W. H. Auden: Collected poems* (pp. 273–276). New York: Vintage.

Balzac, H. de (1831). *La peau de chagrin* (E. Marriage, Trans.).Philadelphia: Gebbie.

Berger, A. A. (2017). *Media analysis techniques*. New York: Sage.

Botticelli, S. (2017). My Freudian cocaine fantasia. Altering consciousness, theorizing desire *Studies in Gender and Sexuality*, *18*(3), 212–222.

Century of the Self. (2002). Part 1: "Happiness Machines." A. Curtis & L. Kelsall (Prod). London: RDF Television and BBC.

Czuczka, D. (2000). The twentieth century: An American sexual history. *SIECUS Report*, *28*(2), 15–18.

Davies, B. (2020, May 14). *Freud at home: The Wednesday Psychological Society*. Freud Museum London. https://www.freud.org.uk/2020/05/14/freud-at-home-the-wednesday-psychological-society/#_ftn1

Doran, C. (2017). Rage and anxiety in the split between Freud and Jung. *Humanities*, 6(3), 1–13.

Elkin, E. J. (1994/1995). More than a cigar. *Cigar Aficionado*. https://www.cigaraficionado.com/article/more-than-a-cigar-6051

Engelman, E. (1976). Sigmund Freud's home and office, Vienna 1938 [Photography]. New York: Basic Books.

Erikson, E. H. (1967, February 9). The strange case of Freud, Bullitt, and Woodrow Wilson. *New York Review of Books*. https://www.nybooks.com/articles/1967/02/09/the-strange-case-of-freud-bullitt-and-woodrow-wils/

Ferdowsian, H. (2021). Stop torturing animals in the name of science. *Scientific American*. https://www.scientificamerican.com/article/stop-torturing-animals-in-the-name-of-science/

Freud, S. (1917/1977). *Introductory lectures on psychoanalysis* (J. Strachey, Trans.). New York: Norton.

Freud, S. (1920/2015). *Beyond the pleasure principle*. New York: Dover Thrift Editions.

Freud, S. (1932/1933). Preface. *New introductory lectures on psychoanalysis* (J. Strachey, Trans., pp. 5–7). New York: Norton.

Freud, S. (1933/1989). *New introductory lectures on psychoanalysis* (J. Strachey, Trans.). New York: Norton.

Freud, S., & Bullitt, W. C. (1967). *Woodrow Wilson: A psychological study*. New York: Houghton Mifflin.

Fromm, E. (2013). *Sigmund Freud's mission: An analysis of his personality and influence*. New York: Open Road.

Gay, P. (1964). Sigmund Freud: A brief life. In J. Strachey (Ed.), *Sigmund Freud: New introductory lectures on psycho-analysis*. New York. W. W. Norton.

Gay, P. (1998/2006). *Freud: A life for our time*. New York: W. W. Norton.

Gessert, A. (2016, June 10). *A talking cure*. Freud Museum London. https://www.youtube.com/watch?v=8RYKGrwiXfg

Graf, M. (1942). Reminiscences of Professor Sigmund Freud. *The Psychoanalytic Quarterly, 11*(4), 465–476.

Hitchcock, A. (Director). (1945). *Spellbound* [Film]. United Artists.

Horney, K. (1993). *Feminine psychology*. New York: W. W. Norton.

Kahr, B. (2015). *Freud: Great thinkers in modern life*. New York: Pegasus Books.

Kernberg, O. F. (2016). The four basic components of psychoanalytic technique and derived psychoanalytic psychotherapies. *World Psychiatry, 15*(3), 287–288.

Lear, J. (2005). *Freud* (2nd ed.). New York: Taylor & Francis.

McGuire, W. (1974). *The Freud/Jung letters: The correspondence between Sigmund Freud and C. G. Jung* (R. Manheim & R. F. C. Hull, Trans.). Princeton, NJ: Princeton University Press.

Menand, L. (2017, August 21). Why Freud survives. *The New Yorker*. https://www.newyorker.com/magazine/2017/08/28/why-freud-survives

Millett, K. (1969/2016). *Sexual politics*. New York: Columbia University.

Mitchell, J., & Mishra, S. K. (2000). *Psychoanalysis and feminism: A radical reassessment of Freudian psychoanalysis*. New York: Basic Books.

Mitchell, S. A., & Black, M. J. (1996). *Freud and beyond: A history of modern psychoanalytic thought*. New York: Perseus.

Prochnik, G. (2006/2012). *Putnam camp: Sigmund Freud, James Jackson Putnam, and the purpose of American psychology*. New York: Other Press.

Prince, H. M. (2006/2012). In G. Prochnik (Ed.), *Putnam camp: Sigmund Freud, James Jackson Putnam, and the purpose of American psychology*. New York: Other Press.

Roiphe, K. (2016). *The violet hour: Great writers at the End.* New York: Dial Press.

Shortland, M. (1993). Powers of recall: Sigmund Freud's partiality for the prehistoric. *Australasian Historical Archaeology, 11*, 3–20.

Storr, A. (1986, August 10). Visiting Freud's home in London. *New York Times*. https://www.nytimes.com/1986/08/10/travel/visiting-freud-s-home-in-london.html

Teive, H. A. G., Marques, P. T., Oliveria, L. P., Germinani, F. M. B., Paola, L., Camargo, C. H. F. (2019). Overcoming bashfulness: How cocaine aided Freud to summon the courage to meet Charcot. *Neuoro-Psiquiatria, 77*(1). https://www.scielo.br/j/anp/a/5PCk7Gn6Z46tRXSrThgVrDk/?lang=en

Yagoda, B. (2018, September). *What drove Sigmund Freud to write a scandalous biography of Woodrow Wilson?* Smithsonian.com. https://www.smithsonianmag.com/history/what-drove-sigmund-freud-write-scandalous-biography-woodrow-wilson-180970042/

Yakushko, O. (2019). Eugenics and its evolution in the history of western psychology: A critical archival review. *Psychotherapy and Politics International, 17*(2), e1495.

Werner, A. (2017). Edmund Engelman: Photographer of Sigmund Freud's home and offices. *International Journal of Psychoanalysis*, 83(2), 445–451.

Winkin, Y, & Leeds-Hurwitz, W. (2013). *Erving Goffman: A critical introduction to media and communication theory*. New York: Peter Lang.

Wollheim, R. (1981). *Sigmund Freud.* New York: Cambridge University Press.

Woolf, L. (1973). *The journey not the arrival matters: Autobiography of the years 1939–1969.* London: Hogarth Press.

Woolf, V. (1986). *The diary of Virginia Woolf. Vol. 5: 1936–1941* (A. O. Bell, Ed.). Fort Washington, PA: Harvest Books.

· 2 ·

WHAT WERE FREUD'S MAIN THEORIES?

> ... a man like me cannot live without a hobby-horse, a consuming passion—in Schiller's words, a tyrant. I have found my tyrant, and in his service I know no limits. My tyrant is psychology.
>
> Sigmund Freud (1895) in *A Letter to Wilhelm Fleiss*

To understand how Freud's theories can be and have been used in the study and production of media and popular culture it is important to review what they are. This chapter is not intended to be all inclusive, but rather illustrate and define major theories and terms so that they can function as tools for media and cultural studies scholars in applying psychoanalytic perspectives.

As discussed in Chapter 1, it was Freud who defined and declared his approach to assisting patients and analyzing culture as psychoanalysis (sometimes written as psychoanalysis).

Psychoanalysis is many things: a theory, a method, and a practice. It was used in the past, as is discussed below, as part of a radically new approach to helping patients who presented with psychological, and sometimes physical, symptoms such as depression, panic, or bodily behaviors. It "began as a would-be science of enigma" (Haughton, 2003, p. 1). and can be used as to creating and analyzing media content. Freud referred to psychoanalysis as depth psychology (*Tiefenpsychologie*) as it explores aspects of psychological life that are withdrawn from consciousness.[1] Psychoanalysis is also a widely misunderstood concept. In terms of the therapeutic setting, "many people who are unfamiliar with psychoanalysis fear it as a coward's way out, an admission of defeat, a ceding of control and authority to a stranger" (Mitchell & Black,

1995, p. xv). Whereas other psychological theories such as behaviorism look at surface-level symptoms/behaviors that are responses to stimuli or cognitive psychology's conceptualization of the human mind as "an extraordinary machine, processing, storing, and combining information" (Billig, 1999, p. 12), psychoanalysis/depth psychology argues there is a deep, hidden life in the mind, that harbors secrets, and wishes, sometimes expressed in behaviors, slips of the tongue or pen, jokes, or physiological symptoms that, through the therapeutic encounter, can be brought to light and engaged with. "The element of depth in the Freudian vision comes from the notion that we have secrets, which we keep from ourselves" (Billig, 1983, p. 12).

Central to the "vision of psychoanalysis" is "exploration and development of our humanity on two fronts" or levels: (1) Theory, emphasizing "the inner subjective life … the life of our preoccupations" and (2) Practice, as recovery and restoration of our agency, our inner lives, and making the unconscious conscious to restore our subjectivity (Gipps & Lacewing, 2019, p. 5). The unconscious is one of the most consistent and persistent of Freud's theories; "one can think of it as Freud's answer to the question of human agency: are we self-determined, do we know what we are doing, or are we never fully self-present in our actions, however rational they appear to us?" (Elsaesser, 2009, p. 100). There are many unconscious activities that many of us are unaware of. Freud (190/1963, pp. 235–236) wrote:

> It was a triumph for the interpretative art of psychoanalysis when it succeeded in demonstrating that certain mental acts of normal people, for which no one had hitherto attempted to put forward a psychological explanation, were to be regarded in the same light as the symptoms of neurotics: that is to say that had a meaning, which was unknown to the subject but which could easily be discovered by analytic means … A class of material was brought to light which is calculated better than any other to stimulate a belief in the existence of unconscious mental acts even in people to whom the hypothesis of something at once mental and unconscious seems strange and even absurd.

Furthermore, according to de Berg (2003, p. 2), "psychoanalysis is first and foremost *a critical theory of society*" (ital. orig). It is both "a clinical encounter" that describes an interpersonal interaction between therapist and patient (analysand), a vision of society, and an experience: "psychoanalysis makes sense of experience through identifying some patterns among others that may justly be found in the occurrent psychological phenomena, past and present" (Lacewing, 2019, p. 420). According to Tummala-Narra (qtd. in Novotney, 2017, p. 40), "When psychoanalysis came to the United States in the early

1900s, it developed into a form of treatment that seemed to only be accessible to the middle and upper-middle classes, which was never Freud's intention. He viewed psychodynamic therapy as a universal treatment for all people." Through self-analysis and work with patients, Freud sought explanations and insights into what might underly psychological suffering. He was fascinated with and concerned about how human psychological life develops, is influenced, manifests in physiological symptoms, and thus is expressed in a variety of behaviors.

Freud himself went through many changes, keeping track of them as a research subject himself. Gay (1988/2006, p. 98) writes:

> The method Freud employed for his self-analysis was that of free association, and the material he mainly relied was provided by his dreams. To be sure, he did not confine himself to dreams; he also collected his memories, his slips of tongue or pen, his forgetting of lines of poetry or patients' first names and allowed these clues to lead him from one idea to the other, through the 'usual roundabouts' of free association.

The Therapeutic Setting

In Freud's 1913 paper "On Beginning Treatment," he details the recommended process by which an analyst should engage with a patient. This paper was not issued as a rigid order but rather as suggestions that could be modified as the analyst deemed to be helpful. Freud was clear about certain things, however, such as discrimination in accepting patients, recommending the patient and therapist not know each other before or outside of therapy, and that initial sessions should be used to determine if the patient needed therapy. Freud recommended, particularly during the early sessions, that the therapist remain as quiet as possible to learn as much as possible about the patient. This led in part to the use of a settee or sofa, probably drawn from Freud's experiences using hypnosis.

Lear notes that Freud had a "fundamental rule" for psychoanalysis: "an analysand is asked to say whatever it is that comes into his or her mind, without censorship or inhibition" (2005, p. xiii). The point of *free* association is to do just that, speak freely, without concern for how one might sound. Easier said than done? Indeed. And Freud recognized that. There is a necessary humility, sense of culpability, and moral responsibility that comes with acceptance of the unconscious. In 1913, Freud wrote of the process.

> What you tell me must differ in one respect from an ordinary conversation. Ordinarily you rightly try to keep a connecting thread running through your remarks and you exclude any intrusive ideas that may occur to you and any side-issues, so as not to wander too far from the point. But in this case, you must proceed differently. You will notice that as you relate things various thoughts will occur to you which you would like to put aside on the ground of certain criticisms and objections. You will be tempted to say to yourself that this or that is irrelevant here, or is quite unimportant, or nonsensical, so that there is no need to say it. You must never give in to these criticisms, but say it in spite of them—indeed, you must do so precisely because you feel an aversion to doing so. … Act as though, for instance, you were a traveler sitting next to the window of a railway carriage and describing to someone inside the carriage the changing view which you see outside. Finally, never forget that you have promised to be absolutely honest, and never leave anything out because, for some reason or other, it is unpleasant to tell it. (pp. 134–135)

Defined as "a strategic device … to help the analyst discerns the patient's secrets, the unconscious wishes *while* the defenses remain active and can be addressed" (Mitchell & Black, 1995, p. 6). Free association is designed therefore to "bypass the normal selection process that screens out conflictual content" (p. 6). The patient is completely awake, present, and demonstrates how they might be suppressing or avoiding particular thoughts. Once a person begins to interrogate the contents, a flood of emotions typically ensues. Resistances to association and responses to this process allow, according to Freud, the analyst to "gain access to both sides of the pathogenic conflicts: (1) the secret feelings and memories, and (2) the defenses—the thoughts and feelings rejecting those secret feelings and memories" (p. 7).

Freud's grounding of ethical responsibility in what they refer to as "the promise of ancient Greek ethics: namely the development of a robust moral psychology" (Lear, 2005, p. xv). The virtuous person, drawing on Aristotle and Plato, "must have an integrated, harmoniously functioning psyche" (p. xv). This development, what Jung would go on to call "individuation," is the result of a process of becoming. The kind of self-awareness, the transparency of one's central being, is the potential outcome of psychoanalysis. What makes up this inner self (psyche), the levels of personality both revealed and concealed?

One of the hallmarks of psychoanalysis is the "talking cure" (Breuer & Freud, 1895/2001, p. 30). This therapeutic practice relies on the analysand facing away from the therapist (to remove any self-consciousness or editing in response to perceived reactions from the therapist). While this approach is language-focused, without the opportunity for the therapist to observe nonverbal forms of communication, it was considered a radically new approach for accessing thoughts, feelings, and memories. Models of the talking cure include: (1) catharsis (Breuer & Freud, 1895/2001), (2) symbolization (Freud, 1915/1957), (3) narrative (Schafer, 1992), (4) metaphor (Buchholz, 2007), and (5) neurocognitive inhibition (Marx, Benecke, & Gumz, 2017).

Each of these is briefly discussed as a component of Freud's theories of accessing the deeper, inner workings of the mind, wherein

> the doctor uncovers the resistances which are unknown to the patient; when these have been got the better of, the patient often relates the forgotten situations and connections without any difficulty. The aim of these different techniques has, of course, remained the same. Descriptively speaking it is to fill in the gaps in memory; dynamically speaking, it is to overcome resistances due to repression. (Freud, 1914b, pp. 147–148).

Freud's time working with Charcot in Paris yielded two primary findings[2] that directed the trajectory of his work: (1) the use of words and associations to help patients work through problems and release unconscious content, which became known as "the talking cure," and (2) diagnoses of illness were traceable to repressed contents of the mind, typically to a traumatic event during childhood and even infancy. In Freud's view, the associations and trauma were "found invariably to have a sexual character" (Wollheim, 1971, p. xii).[3]

The case that launched Freud into this focus was that of Bertha Pappenheim (pseudonym Anna O). Not originally his patient, she had been treated by Josef Breuer. Together they published her case history (among others) in *Studies über Hysterie* (*Studies on Hysteria*, 1895). She presented with what was called "hysteria," a word that was used to account for a number of symptoms such as twitches and inability to move a limb, but with no concurrent medical explanation possible. Mostly women were considered hysterics and frequently dismissed as people simply seeking attention. Rather than accept that, Freud and Breur looked for psychological, rather than physical, explanations. This is not to say they say physical and psychological issues were separate, but rather mental processes were given fair footing when treating a patient and viewed as intertwined. In the case of Anna O., she was unable to drink, existing on the liquids in fruit. Why? They were able to trace her repulsion of drinking from a glass to her witnessing her lady companion's little dog drinking from his mistress's glass. She didn't care for her companion and to see the dog drink from the glass repulsed her, but she said nothing out of politeness. That traumatic event and associated bodily responses stayed with her. Until she articulated that event it remained buried, but active, below the surface. After talking it through, it was resolved. This was one of the early cases of noting that indeed psychological issues can result in physical problems. Freud and Breuer realized that if an emotion is not released, if it remains suppressed (see also repression), the energy it contains will find another avenue to be expressed. They termed this hysterical conversion.

In addition to hysterical conversion, Freud described other key theories in the sections that follow, with a focus on what might have contributed to a maladaptive behavior's formation, and an understanding of how Freud believed they manifested not only at the individual but also at the collective level. In his work he invited readers and patients to think about that which we prefer not to speak, "about [our] appetites and … intellectual powers, about self-knowledge and self-deceit, about [our] profoundest passions and about [our] most intimate or trivial failings, in ways that would have seemed to earlier generations at once scandalous and silly" (Wollheim, 1971, p. x). In his writings on dreams, for example, he recognized the traces everyday life left on what we re-envision in the night world and how they can be reinscribed and expressed through neurotic symptoms. He drew heavily on mythology, as in the development of the Oedipus concept, to help us understand eternal questions faced by human beings over time, offering a metaphorical way of discussing them.

The Couch

According to the Freud Museum in London, "undoubtedly, the most famous piece of furniture in the collection is Freud's psychoanalytic couch on which all of his patients reclined." Furthermore, "those innumerable cartoons depicting that analyst in his chair, notebook on his lap or by his side, have perpetuated a misconception that Freud explicitly addressed in [his] early papers; he cautioned analysts against taking notes during the session since doing so would only distract their attention" (Gay, 1988/2006, p. 296). A holdover from his days as a hypnotist, Freud also had personal reasons for this furniture arrangement: "I cannot stand being stared at eight hours a day (or longer) by others."

The couch served as tool by which this separation could occur— "the patient lies on the couch with the analyst behind him, out of sight, listening intently" (Gay, 1988/2006, p. 296). Despite popular culture portrayals, which are discussed later, Freud recommended against the therapist taking notes, rather that he or she should rely on memory. In addition, he felt that the therapist's facial expressions might distract or influence the patient; thus, facing away would allow the patient full access to their emotions and memories, leaving them "free … from the constraints that ordinary social intercourse imposes" (p. 296). Topics such as sex and desire were so private and even shameful in 19th-century England that doing so face-to-face might have been too uncomfortable for many patients and kept them from seeking treatment. Freud said of the men and women who came to him that they "treat matters of money as they do matters of sex, with the same inconsistency, prudishness, and hypocrisy" (p. 297). The analyst's attention as well won't be diverted by trying to maintain social conventions or be distracted while trying to absorb and process what the patient is saying:

> The hypnagogic state of the supine analysand and its resonance with the empathic reverie of the unseen analyst discussions of what constitutes analysis, what the interaction ought to be. When people lie down, they look at their world differently … nice supine, they begin focusing less on their perceptions of material objects in their surround, whose sensory impressions they register and organize from a distance, and more on the images that emanate from their stream of consciousness. In one fell swoop, Freud had brought the dream … to life, approximating in the waking but altered state of the analysand that of the dreamer. (Ross, 1999, p. 93)

The couch is such a significant part of Freudian lore and legend that, in 2006, the Freud Museum in London (located in Freud's home) was the site for an exhibit titled "On the Couch: Psychoanalysis in Cartoons, Art from *The New Yorker*." The description reads: "This all-important piece of furniture becomes the setting of countless comic situations involving who lies on it or under it, accompanied by the analyst or alone, overexcited, or asleep, etc." ("Because psychoanalysis," 2006, para. 14). "Like a desert island with the lonely palm tree," says *New Yorker* cartoonist Paul Peter Purges, "the Freudian couch has become a cliché: Both are visually funny and show absurd situations" ("On the couch," 2006, para. 7). Even though this arrangement for therapy is rare today, the couch semiotically stands in for therapy in the quick communication needs of a film, cartoon, or advertisement. In addition, many of the items in the museum's store are representations related to Freud's famous sofa. There are coasters in the shape of little carpets like the one that covered his couch as well as a mouse pad of the same design. There is Freud finger puppet w/tiny red finger puppet sofa as well as a greeting card set that features a photograph of Freud and another his therapeutic sofa.

The Cigar

Sigmund Freud was "fatally addicted" to cigars (Gay, 1988/2006, p. 169). He allowed himself few pleasures, had some favorites, and was generally indiscriminate with food, but had great fondness for cigars. The ill effects of smoking were not a part of the thinking of the time as they are today; in fact, historically tobacco was sometimes prescribed as a health aid (Charlton, 2004). Freud began smoking cigarettes at age 24 and graduated later to cigars, which he felt helped him concentrate. His favorite brand? Don Pedro (Aziz, 2000, p. 320). In a letter he wrote, "I believe I owe to the cigar a great intensification of my capacity to work and a facilitation of my self-control. My model in this was my father, who was a heavy smoker and remained one till his 81st year" (Schur, 1972, p. 62). It is reported Freud smoked upwards of 20 per day (Heller, 2005, p. 40).

Smoking cigars was also rather fashionable during Freud's time, particularly among Jews living in Vienna (Freidenreich, 2002). Since cigars were expensive, they became a symbol of status (Gilman, 1993, p. 178) and power. While he acknowledged cigar smoking as a substitute for other oral needs or perhaps as an alternative to masturbation in the everyday person, Freud denied this applied to him. It is said the air in the Wednesday evening meetings in his home was thick with smoke. Furthermore, Freud apparently was so committed to smoking that when his nephew Harry refused his offer of a cigarette, Freud said, "My boy, smoking is one of the greatest and cheapest enjoyments in life, and if you decide in advance not to smoke, I can only feel sorry for you" (Gay, 1988/2006, p. 170). Did Freud ever say, "A cigar is just a cigar"? No one seems able to document this quotation, although he is reputed to have said something like that to a reporter.[4] According to The Freud Museum such a comment might not be beyond Freud's dry sense of humor but there's no evidence of him saying or writing it ("10 Quotes," 2019). The very idea of his recognizing that we can't or perhaps shouldn't always make something into a marker of a psychological condition speaks as well to there being a lighter side to Dr. Freud. Despite the highly symbolic nature of cigars and smoking (called everything from "nipple substitutes" to phallic symbols), "once having entered the Freudian universe it becomes extremely difficult to take things at face value once again: a cigar can never be just a cigar" (Josephs, 1989, p. 498).

The Revisions

In the tradition of scientific inquiry and rigor, Freud modified and revised his theories, sometimes resulting in criticisms by colleagues and peers. As both a practitioner and scholar, Freud was always learning about himself and his patients, and when new information came along he was not afraid to write about what he learned. "Freud had witnessed many things that his Viennese medical colleagues found unrespectable, indeed largely incredible: the mysterious effects of hypnotism, the amorous advances of patients, the talking away of hysterical symptoms, the hidden work of sexuality" (Gay, 1988/2006, p. 91).

Major Theories

Between 1896 and 1901 Freud isolated himself from colleagues, working on the foundations of his psychoanalytic theories. These appeared in *The Interpretation of Dreams* (1899), *The Psychopathology of Everyday Life* (1901), and *Three Essays on the Theory of Sexuality* (1905/1949). The following sections draw upon these works, briefly describing the central ideas and key terms reflecting areas of psychological research and practice that were of interest to Freud, organized according to three primary areas: (1) Spirit (dreams), (2) Mind (the tripartite model), and (3) Body (psychosexual stages).

SPIRIT: Dreams and the Uncanny

> Sweet dreams are made of this
> Who am I to disagree
> I travel the world and the seven seas
> Everybody's looking for something.
>
> Lennox (1983)

Freud believed *The Interpretation of Dreams* (1899) to be his major and most important contribution to psychoanalysis (Lansky, 1992). While not a how-to textbook on dream interpretation, the book, "a basic psychoanalytic manifesto," was based on Freud's analysis of his own dreams, of systematically documenting and tracing associations and material. By way of the "associative method," the book "reveals a truly convincing connection between the instigation in the events of the dream day and the infantile conflict discovered in the latent dream thoughts" (p. 4). Freud would revisit his dream theories in 1933 adding material he gained from increased knowledge of trauma. That traumas are sometimes repeated in dreams came to expand his theories after 1920. "He argued that the purpose of the replay, so to speak, was to allow the ego to prepare itself with anticipatory anxiety so that then the situation could be mastered" (p. 25; see also Jones, 1931; Lidz, 1946).

Freud argued that there are two primary ways psychologists can gain access to the patient's unconscious: dream analysis and the interpretations of "slips." The interpretation of dreams, he wrote (1900, p. 608), is "the royal road to a knowledge of the unconscious activity of the mind." Yet getting there is rarely without bumps. Can we ever really know what our dreams mean? What some*thing* or some*one* means in them? Probably not, the process of interpretation is rich with possibilities that can be discussed between therapist and patient, or the layperson can journal and consider. Dreams can also operate like steam vents, reassure valves, that relieve tensions and anxieties that have carried over from the conscious to the unconscious world.

It is within our dreams that our deepest longings and desires take form, but "in a civilized disguise" (de Berg, 2004, p. 23). They take symbolic shapes, are dramatized, the content displaced, and condensed to make them more palatable. The information takes story form, narratives, then are transformed "in the manner which the poet maliciously ascribes to philosophers; it fills up the gaps in the dream-structure with shreds and patches." This secondary revision removes the story even further from any literal sense.

Sigmund Freud's theory of dreams evolved, as did his others, over time. He drew not only upon patient reports but also observations of his own dreams. He saw dreams as containing traces of waking life that appear in dreams, often representing desires, repressed contents (particularly from drives of aggression and sex) wish fulfillment, and other motivations. In *The Interpretation of Dreams*, Freud writes: "[W]hen an author makes the characters constructed his imagination dream, he follows the everyday experience that people's thoughts and feelings are continued in sleep, and he aims at nothing else than to depict his heroes' state of mind by their dreams" (1900, p. 8). Thus, sometimes dreams have clear connections to the awakened life, and other times appear abstract. Scientists have varying opinions, but they do agree that everyone dreams, for about two hours per night, whether they remember the dream. And many of us can relate to waking, remembering briefly what we dreamed, then promptly forgetting them.

Dreams can be both pleasurable or terrifying, literal, or abstract. Freud said that dreams contain both manifest (what we remember when we awaken) and latent (hidden message) content, the latter being an unconscious wish. Sometimes wishes are repressed and pushed out of consciousness "because there is a clash between the individual's wishes and [their] social conscious" (de Berg, 2003, p. 19). In dreams our unconscious wishes become distorted, appearing in a more acceptable form, offering us the opportunity to process the material. "To put it simply, they get censored" … "Instead of dreaming what we really want (say, bashing the boss's head in), we dream about something less immoral (having a heated argument with him or insulting him)" (p. 19). In Freud's own succinct formulation, "a dream is a (disguised) fulfillment of a (suppressed or repressed) wish." How does this happen? Freud called the analysis of dreams dream work (*Traumarkbeit*), which contains five mechanisms:

Symbolization (*Symbolisierung*)

Where people, places, things, animals, become symbols, they stand-in-for something else. Of course the overused example is pointed, or sharp objects being said to symbolize a penis, i.e. male power and rounded objects with holes symbolizing a vagina. Advertising uses this association/interpretation (Chapter 3). But it is important not to regard a symbol as sufficient unto itself. Any object or symbol in a dream must be viewed in the context of the entire dream.

Dramatization (*Dramatisierung*)

This second mechanism is the translation of mental content, such as wishes, into images. Freud saw this as articulating in symbolic form, the wish. Thus latent dream thoughts take the form of visual images. A series of actions and words take the felt or sensed into concrete meanings. "Clearly what has to be accomplished by the dream work is the transformation of the latent thoughts as expressed in words, into perceptual images" (Freud, 1922, p. 152).

Displacement (*Verschiebung*)

This is movement, or displacement, of one thought or idea about one person on to another. De Berg (2003, p. 21) uses a scene from the 1974 film *The Front Page*, directed by Billy Wilder,[5] to illustrate this concept. A psychoanalyst (Dr. Eggelhofer, "bow-tie, spectacles, heavy German accent) questions someone accused of murdering a policeman" (pp. 21–22)

DR. EGGELHOFER: Tell me about your father.

EARL WILLIAMS: My father was a train conductor.

DR. EGGELHOFER: Ah! So your father wore a uniform, just like ze policeman. Zat is very significant. Now tell me about your youth.

EARL WILLIAMS: I had a perfectly ordinary youth.

DR. EGGELHOER: So you wanted to kill your father and sleep with your mother?

EARLY WILLIAMS: (Turning to the sheriff) If he starts talking filth, I'm out of here!

What the doctor is implying in this scene is that Williams wanted to kill his father but displaced this wish onto the policeman, whom he did kill.

Displacement also occurs in waking life. When we take out our frustrations on our partners, redirect a characteristic in someone we don't like to that person, blame someone for something we don't like in ourselves on them, we are displacing. This "shifting of accent" (Roth, 2019), is one where some ideas are pushed aside, replaced, or minor ones become major. "Displacement is the principle means used in the *dream-distortion* to which the dream-thoughts must submit under influence of the censorship" (ital. orig.). Thus, whatever the motive for the dream finds its way through.

Condensation (*Verdichtung*)

This is when different ideas are combined or blended, even contradictory ones. One element of manifest content might be condensed, fused, with latent elements. Thoughts that might be objectionable are concealed by being mixing up, breaking into new elements, or forming composite persons to represent those ideas.

Secondary Revision (*Bearbeitung*)

At this stage, information from symbols from stage one are made meaningful by sense making, giving palatable sense of material in a dream but that revises it as such that conceals true significance. Thus the displaced, condensed, and symbolic parts become consistent with waking logic. What is below consciousness thus remains and true meaning veiled. Jones (1910, p. 297) noted, "Secondary elaboration is closely related to rationalization." Dreamers are encouraged to keep a journal or notepad near their bed and upon waking write everything down they can remember before this revising/elaborating takes over.

"What lies beneath" is an apt description of the repressed contents of the conscious mind. As discussed earlier, sometimes this material is from childhood, an experience that might have been too complex or too painful for a little person to process. Or there is a behavior, thought, act that an adult hasn't had the resources (on their own or with assistance of a therapist) to deal with. "The unsayable and the unspeakable are dangerous and destructive only as long as they remain unthought, unsaid, or unconscious .... speaking the unspeakable about the self in the context of the 'talking cure' can produce a liberating or therapeutic awareness of thoughts and memories that would otherwise become pathogenic" (they would fester)" (Jonte-Pace, 2001, p. 13). Dreams can facilitate, in Freud's view, processing, but do so in ways that might not be obvious, requiring interpretation. He also recognized not everything in a dream can be interpreted, writing that there is a "spot in every dream at which it is unplumbable, a navel as it were, that is its point of contact with the unknown" (SE, 4: 111, n. 1).

The Uncanny (*Das Unheimlich*)

An important concept from dreamwork found in media analyses (particular cinematic) is the uncanny. "The Uncanny" (Das *Unheimlich*) was written mid-career for Freud. It is one that will be revisited and applied in Chapters 3 and 4. The theory is "rooted in everyday experience and the aesthetics of popular culture, related to what is frightening, repulsive, and distressing" (Ruers, n.d., para. 1). The term in some languages is very close to the word "familiarity." What is uncanny can be when the familiar becomes unfamiliar. The feeling is one of ambivalence, of being unsettled, and unnerved. The essay was written in two parts. The first is an exploration of the terms "*Heimlich*" and "*unheimlich*," translated as "homely" and "unhomely" or "familiar" and "belonging to the home" (*heimlich*). It's about what becomes uncanny if something seems just a little bit off. These aren't opposites, there's just something that's familiar yet unfamiliar, more than mysterious, truly creepy, even taboo. "Unheimlich is in some way or other a sub-species of Heimlich" (Freud, 1919, p. 226). According to psychiatrist Chris Heath (2016, qtd. in Goodhill), "Things are creepy when they invoke memories of a time when believed this thing to be true, for instance, magic or the undead." Think Easter Bunny, Tooth Fairy, Santa Claus, or clowns. When we are children, rather than thinking of some of these images/enactments as simply makeup and costumes, they seem real. Freud believed these experiences stick with us, and the felt sense of unease, even fear, becomes embodied, remaining within us throughout life. This response is a result of our primitive, instinctual fight/flight/freeze response. In the presence of the uncanny, we might do a double-take as everything seems ok, but then something catches our eye (or ear). fMRI studies show the response at a very primal, lower brain level function that is experienced before the higher brain can sort it out (Cheetham, Suter, & Jäncke, 2011). It is a visceral response, not a rational reaction, and is driven by the unconscious. Stephen King's book *The Shining* as well as director Stanley Kubrick's cinematic adaptation is an example, particularly in the case where mirrors are used. When Jack talks with the bartender or Lloyd does so with Mr. Gray in the bathroom mirrors, they reflect what is and what isn't real. Group photos of hotel workers of the past who are identical to the movie's present are example of uncanny doubling. Twin sisters who "appear" in the hallways, dressed in white then drenched in blood, and blood pouring from elevators are simultaneously real and unreal to the characters,

In the second part of the essay, Freud applies the uncanny concept to examples of experiences, expressions, and individuals. As noted, when we are children there are ideas, stories, and representations that frighten us. Some we mature out of, and some never leave us. A common example is Coulrophobia, fear of clowns. This is the experience of "extreme, irrational reactions when [a person sees] clowns in person or view pictures or videos of clowns. … They may go out of their way to avoid any exposure to clowns" ("Coulrophobia"). Media portrayals can build on or contribute to this fear. In books, art, or movies. The term became known starting in the late 1990s, "Recent movies featuring creepy-looking clowns, like *It* [1986] and *Joker* [2019] made people more aware of this phobia" (Coulrophobia). Triggers include costumes (birthday parties, Halloween), fast food restaurants that use clown figures as mascots (McDonald's), fairs, festivals, and circuses. According to the Cleveland Clinic, this fear has been documented as young as age 3. Hospitals are another place where individuals in clown costumes often appear. However, according to the journal *Nature*, "Some children's wards are reverting to having plain walls after researchers found that most kids find pictures of clowns scary, rather than amusing" ("Fear of clowns")

E. T. A. Hoffman's short story "The Sandman" is another example of stories that invoke fear as technique to keep children at bed at night ("the story goes that the child must be asleep for the Sandman to put sand in the child's eyes—if they are not asleep, the Sandman will take out their eyes" (Ruers, n.d., para. 5). The fear of losing one's sight is also present in the Oedipus tale.

Another uncanny figure is the dopplegänger, the body double, the twin, even an imaginary companion. Otto Rank (1884–1939) first explored this figure (1914/1971) and Freud (1919) expanded on this topic as a kind of second ego, at odds with the first, containing repressions, suppressions, and drives. They are confused selves. He wrote that the dopplegänger is found in

> Mirrors, shadows, guardian spirits, with the belief in the soul and the fear of death. The idea of the eternal soul allows us an energetic denial of the power of death. This was the first double of the body. From having been an assurance of immortality, it becomes the uncanny harbinger of death.

The double, doubling, twinning offers both recognition of one's own mortality but also the concept of eternal life. Freud writes:

> We can understand why linguistic usage has extended das Heimliche into its opposite, das Unheimliche; for this uncanny is in reality nothing new or alien, but something which is familiar and old-established in the mind and which has become alienated from it only through the process of repression. (p. 241, SE XVII)

Several books, films, and television programs have used the dopplegänger as a storytelling device. Alfred Hitchock's *Vertigo* (1958), *The Double Life of Véronique* (1991), *The Prestige* (2006), *The Man Who Haunted Himself* (1970), *Femme Fatale* (2002), *Dead Ringers* (1988), *Black Swan* (2010), and *Possession* (1981) are cinematic examples. Of course in novels, novellas, and short stories the dopplegänger presence is found in Robert Louis Stevenson's *Dr. Jekyll and Mr. Hyde* (1886), Dostoevsky's *The Double* (1846), and Henry James *The Jolly Corner* (1908) are other examples.

Slips and Humor

Another way that the unconscious sometimes sneaks through is by way of what's commonly referred to as Freudian slips. Freud called them parapraxes (faulty actions *Fehlleistungun*); these "slips" of memory or mistakes are revelatory of suppressed, perhaps secret thoughts and feelings. These can be spoken or written, such as "pubic" when one means "public." Just a typo? Maybe, maybe not. According to Freud, who describes them in humorous detail in *The Psychopathology of Everyday Life* (1901). While the most widely read of Freud's books (Gay, 1988/2006, p. 127), it is quite unlikely many who use the term "Freudian slip" have read it. However, the term is so commonplace that it stands in for all kinds of verbal accidents. The Web site Urban Dictionary provides these examples of slips:

> For seven and a half years, I've worked alongside President Reagan. We've had triumphs. Made some mistakes. We've had some sex … uh … setbacks. President George H.W. Bush
> Episode of M*A*S*H
> Frank Burns loses his temper and snaps at Father Mulcahy:
> Hot Lips: Frank!
> Frank: Oh, sorry, Father. Sorry, Mother … Margaret.
> In Buffy the Vampire Slayer, Xander's first words to Buffy were a Freudian Slip:
> Xander: Can I have you? I mean, can I *help* you?

Freud saw these parapraxes not as accidents, but rather unconscious thoughts rising to the surface, repressed material finding a way out. In *Sigmund Freud* Richard Wollheim (1971) notes Freud's use of common sense when interpreting the presentation of symptoms and situations. In his work with patients Freud (1914b) contextualized their stories and his interpretations of them, recognizing who and what we are arises out of set of circumstances. The parapraxes draw on everyday experiences to explain deeper psychological phenomenon. For example, "he entrusted his money to a savings crank" (p. 72). These "speech blunders" (p. 75) in recalling names, or other disturbances, the origin comes through the disturbance made by the mistake. The Freud Museum includes many items related to slips. For example, there are, quite literally Freudian slippers—fuzzy footwear with the face of Dr. Freud into which a person slides his or her feet. A coffee mug has a cartoonish drawing of Freud and examples of famous slips, such as the one about one's mother.

Another example of the unconscious interrupting or toying with our conscious is forgetting. While sometimes things just happen, we get busy, and distracted, Freud viewed much forgetting as examples of not wanting to deal with someone or something. Thus we "forget" the key to our mother-in-law's house because we don't like our mother-in-law and didn't want to visit her. Freud (1898, p. 33) uses the example of forgetting someone's name:

> In the middle of carrying on a conversation we find ourselves obliged to confess to the person we are talking to that we cannot hit on a name we wanted to mention at that moment, and we are forced to ask for help—usually ineffectual—help. "What's is his name? I know it so well. It's on the tip of my tongue. Just this minute it escaped me."

This is that feeling that the name/word is there, floating, so closely we can almost taste it. The harder we concentrate, the less it comes to us. We might use the first letter that feels right but might not even be close. Then, later that day, in the shower, mowing the lawn, or thinking about something else, we remember! Other examples are mixing up the order of words ("the Milo of Venus instead of the Venus of Milo"), what Freud (1901) called "anticipations" ("the shoes made her sore feet … the shoes made her feet sore"), and "substitutions" ("he entrusted his money to a 'savings crank,' instead of 'a savings bank'") (1914b, p. 845). He argued that this apparent mix-up is in fact that which wants to rise to consciousness, be it what one really thinks or cares about, wants to avoid thinking about, or might in fact be thinking about (calling out the name of a former lover when kissing a current one).

Despite his contemporary image as a curmudgeonly, stern, and severe man (which he may have well been) humor was not unfamiliar territory to Dr. Freud.[6] He considered humor, like dreams, a fundamental part of human psychology, and an opportunity for unconscious material to become conscious. Whether he found the slips of the tongue he wrote about funny or not, who knows? Yet he clearly was familiar with plenty of examples and jokes. In the book *Jokes and Their Relation to the Unconscious* (1905) and an essay, "Humour" (1927), Freud identified three types of humor: jokes, comics (fixed images), and humor. He argued all three serve as ways of releasing the pressure of libidinal repression, of condensing this energy and expressing it in discrete forms to release tension. Ultimately, Freud saw humor as a defense mechanism—a way of simplifying scary things, reducing uncertainty, or making playful that which is serious. If someone is sad or frightened, for example, he or she can find release through laughter. Freud's drive theory of sex (reproduction) and aggression (self-preservation) are rich fodder for jokes. Would he find humor in the plethora of popular culture representations of his ideas? Impossible to know, but, according to a curatorial assistant at the Freud Museum in London, where they sell everything from Freud head lollypops to after-therapy mints, tea towels, and Freudian slippers, it is quite likely:

> The lollipops are particularly unusual, aren't they? Personally, since we sell all types of Freud paraphernalia in our museum shop I don't think they diminish Freud's ideas and theories as a whole—it is more like appropriating the image of Freud we usually see, as a stern and serious Professor, and making it light-hearted. Almost all of the images and products I have seen which involve Freud in this way are light-hearted and fun, and particularly when they use aspects of his work (such as 'sometimes a lollipop is just a lollipop' taken from his famous saying 'sometimes a cigar is just a cigar') it is amusing on many levels. There are similar ones like the Freudian sticky notes, which are printed with 'When you say one thing but you mean your mother.' And given that Freud wrote *The Joke and Its Relation to The Unconscious* I'm sure he would be quite interested to see all these strange things. (Personal communication, 2012).

Mind

Early in Freud's career he identified aspects of the mind, the conscious and unconscious. This is not the same as "the brain," which, as a medical student, he also was familiar with. Rather the mind is comprised of those thoughts that we are aware of, that are present to us, that includes

> terms such as awareness, reflective awareness, phenomenal awareness, and phenomenal awareness [that] have all been used to refer to the same thing. Awareness has been used to refer to what we mean when are at the moment conscious of something but also refers to the latent knowledge of something. (De Sousa, 2011, p. 213)

The unconscious contains compressed, previously conscious ideas that become repressed, or those which have yet to rise to the level of consciousness. But the unconscious is made up of more than repressed material, it also contains primal fantasies and an individual's phylogenetic heritage (Freud, 1938).[7]

Freud originally viewed the unconscious as "a hidden and repressed realm of wishes pressing for gratification" (Lear, 2005, p. 5). Eventually he came to see this as too simplistic, in fact the unconscious must be understood "as a peculiar *form of thinking* [ital. orig.] … Ideas and images are associated loosely … linked" because they have similar sounds, thoughts, or associated images. These thoughts, desires, and drives are forced from consciousness by the process of repression. They aren't disorganized but live in-relationship with consciousness. Repression involves several issues:

1. "There is an issue which must be cleared up" (Billig, 1999, p. 21). What is buried must be exposed.

2. Repression is not to be abolished; it serves a purpose. Freud wrote of the "ego accepting, after a fresh examination, an instinctual demand which has hitherto directed" (from outline of psychoanalysis, PFL, 15, p. 413).
3. Several ideas can be held simultaneously, even contradictory ones, through the process of condensation. Or, they can be shifted to another, associated thought through displacement. Condensation and displacement are what Freud called primary processes (conscious thought is secondary process) that lead to several expressions including dreams (described below), physical symptoms, and slips of the tongue (or pen). These wishful impulses, saying what we really mean, but by mistake, say something else are ways they assert themselves, whether we want them to or not, sometimes in rather embarrassing ways.

Furthermore, as noted by De Sousa (2011), consciousness relies on consistency, "a special kind of unity, on account of which it does not tolerate gaps of any kind" (p. 212). Gaps in "the data of consciousness" exist where there might be a moment where, for example, one forgets something they ordinarily remember or know. The conscious and unconscious aren't at odds with each other; they are connected, both being "a set of states" in which we move in and out of (p. 212). The mind is "not a place, but a process, always active, always in motion, always exerting its influence" (de Berg, 2003, p. 5).

Events during our childhood, Freud believed, tremendously influence who we are as adults, how we relate to ourselves, and to others (see section "Body" for more on this). He wrote "that germs of sexual impulses are already present in the new-born child and that these continue to develop for a time but are then overtaken by a progressive process of suppression; this in turn is itself interrupted by periodical advances in sexual development or may be held up by individual peculiarities" (p. 176).

According to this theory, the deepest, darkest traumas are often suppressed, hidden from consciousness, until such time as they reveal themselves in physical and/or psychological problems when we are adults. When asked to explain our behaviors to ourselves or to others, we then tend not to speak honestly about our motivations, not because we are consciously lying, but rather, this deception, as it were, is part of not confronting the past. Freud's work focused on assisting patients in accessing these deepest truths that hide our true personalities.

The idea of there being buried psychic content we are unaware of had been known for thousands of years before. First coined by philosopher Friedrich Schelling (1775–1854) in *System of Transcendental Idealism* (1800), English poet Samuel Taylor Coleridge translated it to English. Their poem "Kubla Kahn" (1816) is, among other things, a journey into the depths of symbols and images in the unconscious. Psychologist William James wrote about it in *The Principles of* Psychology (1890), but it was Freud who popularized and ran with the concept (as did C. G. Jung but in a slightly different direction).

To illustrate this theory of the unconscious, Freud developed a topographical model of the mind, "dividing it into three different realms: an *unconscious*, containing unacceptable ideas and feelings; a *preconscious*, containing acceptable ideas and feelings that are capable of becoming conscious; and the *conscious*, containing those ideas and feelings in awareness at any particular time" (ital. in orig.) (p. 6). An iceberg is often used as an analogy to explain Freud's tripartite model of the psyche. Above the surface of the water, little is visible (the conscious mind which consists of thoughts and perceptions). Below the surface is where the largest part of the iceberg is found. Applying this metaphor, immediately below the surface is the subconscious which contains things we could bring to the level of consciousness easily, if we wanted to. Deeper down is the unconscious which contains material (memories, stored knowledge) that we are not yet aware. Freud believed that some memories and thoughts are simply too painful to exist at the conscious level, but when a person is mature enough, prepared enough, they can bring this repressed information to the surface and deal with it. The goal of psychoanalysis then is to make the unconscious conscious, helping the patient process and understand why they suppressed and then to release these pent-up energies.

Crucial to understanding the nature of personality and the mind is Freud's (1923) tripartite structural model comprised of the Psyche comprised of id (unconscious), ego (conscious), and superego ("the psychic apparatus").

The id (unconscious) is the most fundamental component of personality that develops when a person is still a baby. The id contains two instincts: Eros (sexual) and Thanatos (aggression). These are not parts of the brain such as the prefrontal cortex or amygdala, but rather are functions of the mind. The Id is focused on life-affirming (Eros) motivations known as "the pleasure principle" (1920/2015) (*Lustprinzip*). This drive is instinctive, leans away from pain and displeasure toward gratification through the satisfaction of basic physical and psychological instincts such as eating, breathing, and sex is a driving force, clearly evident in the behavior of children, but with us throughout our lives. It demands gratification. Freud (1920, p. 3) came to modifying this theory in terms of how dominant the principle is, noting that "there exists in the mind a strong *tendency* toward the pleasure principle, but that that tendency is opposed by certain other forces or circumstances, so that the final outcome cannot always be in harmony with the tendency towards pleasure." Freud (1933, p. 93) wrote, "The id … knows no judgements of value; no good and evil, no morality" rather it is linked to instincts. The id is what helps one survive, directs activities, but also contains darker psychic energy, in the form of self-destructive impulses, "the death instinct" (Thanatos), expressed as aggression. Freud believed that Eros is stronger, in most people, than Thanatos which is why, as a species, we have survived so far.

Ego is a frequently misused term. This component develops from the id during infancy and serves a mediating role between the primal demands of the id but modifies impulses for a person to have what it takes to survive in modern civilization. Thus the ego straddles both the conscious and unconscious mind catching id motives before they can be expressed in socially unacceptable ways. The repression of many of our urges and desires is deemed necessary to live, as we do, in social groups, or as Freud termed it "civilization." How difficult this might be was illustrated in the play *The Talking Cure* (Hampton, 2003, pp. 38–39) and movie *A Dangerous Method* (2011) conversation between psychologist Carl Jung and his patient, Otto Gross:

JUNG: And you don't find it necessary or desirable to exercise some restraint, as a contribution, say, to the smooth functioning of civilization?

GROSS: What, and make myself ill?

JUNG: I should have thought that some form of sexual repression would have to be exercised in any rational society.

GROSS: No wonder the hospitals are bulging at the seams.

The superego is that aspect of the Self that develops when children identity with their same-sex parent, learning from them, operating on morality principles that teach and direct them to behave in socially acceptable ways by modeling on that same-sex parent.[8] It also includes experiences of tension and jealousy. This universal tension exists in humans, between what we crave, what we want, what our inner child demands in terms of satiating urges and controlling and redirecting necessary to successfully live with others. It creates inner turmoil and conflict at times. Guilt, for example, can happen if a person senses rules aren't being followed, or when the id wants satisfaction, or the ego is frustrated, trying to referee. To calm this inner storm, the ego can draw upon several tools to restore balance, one of which is deploying defense mechanisms (Freud, 1894, 1896). Defense mechanisms serve as buffers to prevent us from becoming overwhelmed. There are at least 11 of them (Berger, 2019):[9]

1. *Ambivalence*. Simultaneously feeling love and hate toward a person.
2. *Avoidance*. Refusing to pay attention to psychological material that is disturbing or upsetting
3. *Denial*. Unwillingness "to accept the reality of something by blocking it from consciousness." (p. 543)
4. *Fixation*. "An obsessive preoccupation with or attachment to something or someone." (p. 543)
5. *Projection*. A denial of negative and hostile feelings in oneself by attributing them to someone else.
6. *Rationalization*. A means of excusing one's behavior by offering reasons or excuses.
7. *Reaction formation*. A situation that occurs when ambivalent feelings create problems and which are dealt with by suppressing one element and overemphasizing the other, usually its opposite.
8. *Regression*. An individual's return to an earlier stage in psychological development when confronted with stressful or anxiety-provoking situations.
9. *Repression*. A barring of wishes, memories, and desires from consciousness that are derived from the unconscious.
10. *Sublimation*. A transferring of sexual impulses and other desires and impulses into other kinds of behavior, such as writing, painting, and other kinds of creative arts.
11. *Suppression*. A voluntary attempt to put out of mind and consciousness something we find upsetting and distasteful. Suppression is voluntary, unlike repression which works at the unconscious level.

Two of these defense mechanisms need elaboration: repression and suppression. Repression, the most basic defense mechanism, is "the idea of self-deceit, or willed forgetting" (Billig, 1999, p. 13). And, even more so, "if we have secrets from ourselves, then not only must we forget the secrets, but we must also forget that we have forgotten them" (p. 13). Freud used the case of Elisabeth von R. to illustrate repression. This case, along with four others, appeared in *Studies on Hysteria* (Freud & Breuer, 1895). Freud (1914a, p. 6) declared that "the theory of repression is the corner-stone on which the whole structure of psychoanalysis rests." Freud used the term *verdrängung*, meaning to push or thrust away, to describe this phenomenon. While consciousness and unconscious are central to the development of these theories, Freud was not the first to declare the existence of these mental processes. To repress, however, was a more significant part of his theoretical orientation as "he knew that it was insufficient to say that a thought was being kept secret just because it was unconscious. Something other than merely being unconscious was necessary to turn thoughts into shameful secrets" (Billig, 1999, p. 15). The second most important defense mechanism is suppression.

Body: Psychosexual Development

Freud took a decisive step that Breuer did not: positing that repressed materials are related to sexuality. He saw various impulses/needs as shared between humans and animals, that there are fundamental to all beings such as sex, but include others such as satisfying hunger, thirst, and connection with conspecifics. Sexual wishes and affect originate in sexual wishes. The word Freud used to describe sexual wishes was *Triebe*, which has been translated to "instincts," or perhaps more accurately, as "drives." Instincts are present, but mostly on an as-needed basis, such fight/flight/freeze. Other examples include birds sensing it is time to migrate, bears to hibernate, or that prickly feeling we get on the backs of our necks (*frisson*) when we sense an impending threat. Drives are always active. They influence us, push us, move us through a process of being and doing. They can be suppressed, redirected, or morph into their opposites. For example, the opposite of love? Hate. Longing? Abhorrence. While sexual drives are present in adulthood they are formed during childhood. Freud argued that these drives are present from birth onward. Certainly puberty (ages 10–16) is the most obvious time to witness the development. In his view, we enter the world with urges. Our entire lives become "an interplay of unconsciousness and consciousness," but it is "childhood that sets the stage for what we become" (de Berg, 2003, pp. 7–8). Then, throughout development and life, various traumatic experiences occur, the effects of which can be consciously processed and dealt with or are stored away until we are either capable of dealing with them or expressing ourselves in other ways. Freud wrote (1910/1916) of a kind of amnesia "which veils from most people (not from all!) the first years of their childhood, usually the first six or eight years" during which time we experience many things including feelings of abandonment, jealousy, pleasure, and pain (p. 38). Yet, as we grow, we can recall little of these experiences. Where do they go? Are the completely forgotten memories? In some cases yet, but in others:

> … we know nothing of all this when we become older. Why does our memory lag behind all our other psychic activities? We really have reason to believe that at no time in life are we more capable of impressions and reproductions than during the years of childhood. And yet, the very impressions which we have forgotten have nevertheless left the deepest traces in our psychic life and acted as determinants for our whole future development. (Freud, 2016. p. 1588)

This amnesia exists either to shield us from painful memories or for those that await a call of some kind to the surface.

That children are sexual beings is among the most controversial of Freud's ideas, controversial in terms of public response but also professional rivalries for the idea. Sauerteig (2012) argues that Freud was not the first to suggest that sexuality was a normal part of a child's development. Rather this is a "composite of many ideas about human development" including "sexual education, sexual feelings in children, masturbation, or intercourse; and sexual relations could involve another child or an adult, even a parent" (Kern, 1973, p. 118). Around 1900, interest in the sexuality of children began to change. From viewing acts such as masturbation as pathological, several pediatricians, psychologists, psychiatrists, educational experts, and physicians began seeing sexuality as a normal and natural part of infancy. Whereas Freud's theories became the best known and most influential, others such as Albert Moll (1862–1939), Carl Gustav Jung (1875–1961), William Stern (1871–1938), and Charlotte Bühler (1893–1974) had discussions about this. In *Drei Abhandlungen zur Sexualtheorie (Three Essays on the Theory of Sexuality)*, Freud (1905, p. 173) indicated that explorations and activities of babies and children were not pathological but normal.

> One feature of the popular view of the sexual instinct is that it is absent in childhood and only awakens in the period of life described as puberty. This, however, is not merely a simple error but one that has had grave consequences, for it is mainly to this idea that we owe our present ignorance of the fundamental conditions of sexual life. A thorough study of the sexual manifestations of childhood would probably reveal the essential characters of the sexual instinct and would show us the course of its development and the way in which it is put together from the various sources. … It is true that in the literature on the subject one occasionally comes across remarks upon precocious sexual activity in small children—upon erections, masturbation, and even activities resembling coitus. But these are always quoted as exceptional.

This was consistent with the intellectual climate of the time and while it ran contrary to previous attitudes, prior to the 18th century, that children were somehow impure, corrupt/able, and even evil, a growing number of European individuals began to see them differently. American psychologist Earl Barnes noted, in 1892 (cited by Langfeldt from Kern, 1973), that most studies of sex focused on the pathological and "none of them make any attempt to trace the normal development of sex feeling and ideas in children, nor to examine the sex conditions actually existing in children's lives." Children don't necessarily see their impulses as sexual per se. This was also part of seeing childhood as a distinctly different time in life than adulthood. This shift is captured by Jean-Jacques Rousseau (1763), who wrote that children are unaware of shame and that they are innocents: "A sense of shame proceeds only from the knowledge of evil; and how can children who neither have, nor ought to have this knowledge, shew its effects?" (p. 12). It was at puberty then that children began becoming aware but should be protected prior to this time. Freud noted that when he spoke of baby and child bodily exploration or expressions that these were about pleasure, in touch and being touched, in learning and were not, as often alleged, about sexuality. In *Five Lectures on Psycho-Analysis*, lecture 4, Freud explained his stance concerning sexuality:

> I have been using the word [sexuality] in a far wider sense than that in which you have been accustomed to understand it. ... But the question arises whether it is not you who have been using the word in far too narrow a sense by restricting it to the sphere of reproduction" It means that you are sacrificing an understand of the perversions and the connections between the perversions, the neuroses and normal sexual life; and you are making it impossible for you to recognize in its true significance the easily observable beginnings of the somatic and mental erotic life of children. (1910/1961, p. 50)

Freud was speaking of pleasure such as that a baby experiences when breast-feeding, sucking their thumb, or being given a bottle. While the sucking impulse is "biologically determined," it "is modified by social attitudes toward nursing as well as the particular psychological disposition of the mother" (Kern, 1973, p. 118). Breast versus bottle feeding has gone through cycles of support or concern. During the time when Freud was developing his theory on this topic, "Every manual on childcare devoted a long section to the nourishment of new-born children, and they all recommended breast feeding" (pp. 123–124). Brücke, who directed the physiology lab where Freud worked (1876–1882), published a manual (1892) wherein he "recommended breast feeding for both nutrition and hygiene" (Kern, 1973, p. 124). Sudden weaning, he warned, prior to ten months, was discouraged, which was "practiced among the upper classes" (p. 124). Some mothers feared breast-feeding would ruin their figures, but "the real obstacles were psychological: disgust at their corporeality and anxiety about the sensual pleasures aroused by nursing" (p. 124). Other theorists of the time emphasized the bonding that takes place at this crucial time in a child's development.

Even the release of urine and feces can bring relief to a child and an adult. But given the amount of sexual repression including discussing sex or elimination publicly, it is no wonder that Freud's theories were viewed as outrageous. He described babies and small children as polymorphously perverse, meaning they are focused on deriving pleasure about all else from whatever they engage (id-based). This is not the same as being perverted. As they grow and develop, children begin to care about the feelings and interests of others but not until a certain age when the ego develops. Until then, they do not experience any of the shame or guilt that is taught later, but rather are fully present with pleasures and seek them out.

Psychosexual energy, aka libido, is, in Freud's view, the driving force behind behavior. It's important to remember that Freud's training was first medical. He had studied as a physician, who then went on to connect the dots between mind and body, not seeing them as distinct, but as closely interrelated. This led him to be notably straightforward, almost clinical, in his descriptions of anatomy and activities. Many of these activities, such as babies exploring their own bodies, not yet having been taught shame and other cultural taboos, are very open in their sense of pleasure and self-interests. Concepts of not touching oneself, not releasing gas, and other social rules are taught. Freud focused on the essential drives, instincts, that motivate these behaviors, prior to socialization. Personality, he argued, was essentially formed by the age of five, but earlier experiences such as scolding, denial, and withholding were internalized by the young child and would impact their development in the years to follow. Freud argued that, as part of personality development, children go through five stages: Oral, anal, phallic, latent, and genital, described below.

Oral (Birth—1 Year). Erogenous Zone: Mouth

According to Freud, erotogenic zones are those parts of the body that can become sexually excited. He described how, "in conformity with the way in which an infant in arms is nourished, the erotogenic zone of the mouth dominates what may be called the sexual activity of that period of life" (1933/1989, p. 123).

What characterizes this first phase is the child having no self-consciousness related to the mother's breast, or, for that matter, any breast. This Freud called "cannibalistic pregenital sexual organization." Mouth-to-breast contact is an infant's first and primary form of interaction with another person. This early form of connection and identification is not only functional (nourishment) but also gives the baby a sense of power and autonomy. That this desire is at times interrupted or regressed to is exemplified by thumb-sucking as a breast replacement. Weaning, for example, can mean conflict, perhaps the first friction the baby experiences. If the separation is traumatic, oral fixation can result in problems later in life such as nail-biting, smoking, drinking, or overeating. "Here the sexual activity became separated from the nourishment activity and the strange object was given up in favor of one from his own body" (Freud, 1910/1916, p. 59). This fundamental first connection can also be related to trust issues. Once breast-feeding and contact are no longer available, and connection is detached from nourishment, some children simply move on. Others express frustration, feelings of ambivalence, or even anger with the mother for causing this.

Anal (1–3 Years). Erogenous Zone: Bowel & Bladder Control

Freud believed that the focus for the anal stage was elimination control (bladder and bowel). The primary opportunity for frustration at this point occurs during toilet training, what might be seen as controlling one's needs perhaps for the first time. Learning to do so can lead to confidence and independence. Not going to the bathroom in the toilet, as per parental dictates, holding back elimination, is also an opportunity for a child to have autonomy. This can become painful, or can be linked to pleasure once release happens. How parents (or adults involved in toilet training) approach this teaching can determine a child's success. If the child is encouraged, praised, and rewarded for appropriately using the toilet, they will feel capable and successful. If, however, the child is punished, ridiculed, or shamed for mistakes, the opposite can happen. Even if parents are too relaxed in their approach, Freud averred that an anal-expulsive personality can result in which the adult person is messy, wasteful, or destructive. If they are too strict or try to train the child too early an anal-retentive personality could result which is expressed by overly strict, rigid, emphasis on order. Kern describes how the "image of the overprotective mother, anxiety-ridden about a child's toilet training, has become a part of a humorous stereotype of mid-twentieth century life. The reasoning behind this peculiarity of our culture is that this first social experience greatly includes the child's personality" (1973, p. 129). The expression "anal retentive" originally related to the psychological process of some neurotics of having precise, even ceremonial, and secret practices of elimination. Freud (1905, fn. p. 67) drew on Andreas-Salomé (1916), who wrote:

> [H]ow the history of the first prohibition which a child comes across—the prohibition against getting pleasure from anal activity and its products—has a decisive effect on his whole development. This must be the first occasion on which the infant has a glimpse of an environment hostile to his instinctual impulses, on which he carries out the **first 'repression' of his possibilities for pleasure. From that time on, what is 'anal' remains the symbol of everything that is to be repudiated and excluded from life.**

Freud described those who are anal-retentive as frequently displaying three characteristics, known as "the anal triad": "orderliness, stinginess, and stubbornness" (1908, qtd. in Gay, 1989, p. 297). Orderliness can function as a defense mechanism, a reaction against perceived disorder and criticism. Stinginess, as a form of greed, is related to controlling what's pleasurable, and stubbornness is an unwillingness to vary from one's sense of order and rightness. Popular use of the idea of "anal retentive personality, peaked in the mid-1950s, and reappeared in the late 1980s. Has it disappeared? No, according to Haslam (2017):

> Reports of its death are greatly exaggerated, as anal traits have reappeared in several new guises in more recent personality psychology. Active research programs explore the complexities of perfectionism, orderliness, disgust proneness and detail focus. However, the best preserved expression of this very undead idea is obsessive-compulsive personality disorder (OCPD).

Phallic (3–6 Years). Erogenous Zone: Genitals

"It seems," wrote Freud, "that the sexual life of the child mostly manifests itself in the third or fourth year in some form accessible to observation" (1910/1916, p. 40). The child's primary focus during the phallic stage is on their genitals. Children of this age begin to notice differences between themselves and other children and male versus female body parts. Once again, how parents and caregivers' respond to a child's bodily exploration can shape development. "These psychic forces are loathing, shame, and moral and esthetic ideal demands" (p. 40). During this time children are also separating somewhat from the mother (primary identification) and will often see the father, in that type of household, as a threat to their relationship with mom (secondary identification). A desire by a boy child to keep mother's undivided attention can be described as the Oedipus complex was meant metaphorically. At the same time, fearing potential punishment by the father can result in castration anxiety, a fear of being rejected, punished, shamed by the father. Girls might experience competition for dad's attention, wanting to identify so closely with mom they want the attention dad is giving her to go to them. This was termed "penis envy." In *Three Essays on the Theory of Sexuality*, Freud (1905/2000, p. 59) noted the phallic phase was less about the organ and more about an "instinct to mastery," as in gaining the object, and not in a sexual way. Thus the connection that we might see today as not literal longing to change one's anatomy (unless) but rather the penis signifying maleness. In patriarchal societies, that equates to having power, something women of Freud's time did not have.

Freud (1910/1916) describes this dynamic using another myth and metaphor: The Riddle of the Sphinx (see Side Box). Wanting to keep mom to himself, a boy will typically develop a conflict with his dad. The mother might also begin paying less attention to the child as he is growing up urging independence as she spends more time with the father, hence competitiveness and even jealousy. Girls are shocked sometimes by the realization they do not have a penis, which is symbolic of maleness. The girl then also, feeling competitive with mom for dad's attention, might take on some of the mother's affect when in dad's presence.

Ages three to five of the phallic stage is also a time not only "when the sexual life of a child reaches its first bloom" but also "evinces the beginning of that activity which is ascribed to the impulse for knowledge and investigation" (Freud, 1910/1916, p. 55). Masturbation attempts are sometimes suppressed by parents during this time, even to the point of shaming. If the child witnesses a parent doing so, this can bring about moral and physical confusion at the contradiction.

Latent (6-Puberty). Erogenous Zone: Libido

As a child grows, id energies are suppressed. Freud (1923) saw this as necessary if a child, who is basically at the whim of their instincts unless taught otherwise, is to become part of a so-called civilized society. The latency period is when "mental forces" are "built up … which later … impede the course of the sexual instinct and, like dams, restrict its flow—disgust, feelings of shame and the claims of aesthetic and moral ideals" (1953, p. 177). Love is present, but it is beginning to change. That which was pure love between mother and child, from the mother's perspective, is when the child is learning *to* love and part of this process is imposed separations where the child learns to be apart from the parent(s) and form other attachments. A particularly vulnerable time, Freud (1905/1949, p. 101) warned: "[H]ere are ways more direct than inheritance by which neurotic parents can hand their disorder on to their children." Sexual and gender identity become clearer to the child at this point as well. In Freud's time, that was clearly a binary: male or female. There is a shift in the object of attachment from parent to other in the world. Separation from parental authority is key and at this stage, as Freud (1905/1949) saw it, crucial for becoming a civilized person: "at every stage in the course of development through will all human beings outby right to pass, a certain number are held back; so there are some who have never got over their parents' authority and have withdrawn their affection from their either very incompletely or not at all" (p. 277). Girls sometimes continue in a kind of girly, childish behavior that lasts beyond puberty. This can explain the idea of one "marrying his mother" or "marrying her father."

Even a person who has been fortunate enough to avoid an incestuous fixation of libido does not entirely escape its influence. A man, especially, looks for someone who can represent his idea of his mother, in terms of qualities, as they have dominated his mind from his earliest childhood; and accordingly, if his mother is still alive, she may well resent this new version of herself and meet it with hostility. In view of the importance of a child's relations to his parents in determining his later choice of a sexual object, it can easily be understood that any disturbance of those relations will produce the gravest effects upon his adult sexual life. Jealousy in a lover is never without an infantile root or at least an infantile reinforcement. According to this view, if there are quarrels between the parents or if their marriage is unhappy, the ground will be prepared in their children for the severest predisposition to a disturbance of sexual development or to a neurotic illness. A child's affection for his parents is no doubt the most important infantile trace which, after being revived at puberty, points the way to his choice of an object.

At this point, the superego is developing. Social skills and manners are taught, and relationships increasingly develop with individuals outside the family such as peer-aged friends, older children, and adults besides parents and grandparents or primary caregivers. The ego continues to develop during this time, doing the mediating work between primal desires (id) and functional superego. This is when a child typically enters school, develops interests, and engages in activities and outings where parents might not be present, and peers become more important. Sexual energies remain but they are repressed or dormant, suppressed with the development of intellectual interests as well as individual and social communication skills. Some children can become stuck in this phase, fixating on bodily interests that make it challenging to form mature adult relationships later.

Genital (Puberty-Death). Mature Sexual Interests

The libido becomes active during this, the final stage of psychosexual development. Prior to this time, "the sexual impulse has been preponderantly autoerotic; it now finds the sexual object" (Freud, 1910/1916, p. 68). Sexual interest in others arises and where before the child's interest was self-focused, now caring about and for others becomes stronger, as well as propagation interests. This includes warmth, caring, and empathy. Whereas younger children, particularly babies, are ruled by the id, Freud believed at this point the ego and superego are fully in place. Healthy individuals can balance appetites and urges. While much writing and concern in the early 20th century was focused on heterosexuality as normal, Freud was not entirely convinced. He did not, like many others, believe homosexuality to be pathological and believed attempts to change a person's sexual makeup could be harmful to them. In response to a 1935 letter written by a mother concerned for her homosexual son, Freud (1935/1960) replied: "[I]t cannot be classified as an illness; we consider it to be a variation of the sexual function, produced by a certain arrest of sexual development" (p. 423). While the latter half of that sentence is problematic, at least Freud did not classify homosexuality as an illness or a biological "mistake." He posited there at being least three ways in which a child grows into adult sexuality.

Normal Sexual Development

At the time of Freud's writings (not one of Freud's beliefs) is that normal meant heterosexual and with the goal of producing offspring. To reach this level of "civilized" relating, many urges and desires/drives must be repressed. For example, defecating or urinating freely, whether into a diaper or without concealment, including toilet training. Suppression of voyeurism is another example. Some drives are so strong or forbidden by law that they are redirected through fantasies sometimes found in cultural pursuits such as films, reading, and writing. Freud's term sublimation is the diversion of sexual energy elsewhere (see Chapter 3 for more on this).

Abnormal Sexuality and Perversion

Freud's classification system is, like many of his ideas, controversial. Two important takeaways are important: (1) unconscious influences can impact human behavior, and (2) early childhood development experiences can have lasting influences. In the introduction to Freud's (1905) *Three Contributions to the Theory of Sex*, Putnam (1910, pp. v–vi) describes how

> the instincts with which every child is born furnish desires or cravings which must be dealt with in some fashion. They may be refined ('sublimated'), so far is necessary and desirable, into energies of other sorts—as happens readily with the play-instinct—or they may remain as the source of perversions and inversion, and of cravings of new sorts substituted for those of the more primitive kind under the pressure of conventional civilization.

The idea that humans, as a species, crave, have impulses, and socially construct what is accepted desire, appropriate touching, or other bodily related yearnings and behaviors, was something "proper society" during Freud's time did not accept. There remains to this day a great deal of resistance to this idea. Studies of sex and sexuality, even with medical and psychological communities, have been and to extent remain if not suspect, at least curious. Havelock Ellis' (1897) *Studies in the Psychology of Sex*, for example, was not permitted publication in England.[10]

However, this collective repression does not eliminate the interests or needs individuals express and wrestle with.

> All the thoughts and emotions and desires and motives which appear in the man or woman of adult years were once crudely represented in the obscure instincts of the infant, and among these instincts, those which were concerned directly or indirectly with the sexual emotions, in a wide sense, are certain to be found in every case to have been the most important for the end-result (Putnam, 1910, p. viii).

Contemporary psychologists such as Pratyusha Tummala-Narra, continue to employ psychoanalysis techniques to help her clients access "thoughts and feelings that may lie outside awareness affect their social, cultural and political experiences" (Novotney 2017, p. 40).

In summary, Freud's theories are vast and deep, each having been modified over his career as he learned more about himself and from his patients. The primary theoretical areas in this chapter were organized around the concepts of Mind (Unconscious/conscious and the tripartite model), Body (psycho-sexual stages of child development), and Spirit (dreams). Those sections and contain important terms for researchers to use as beginning points, context, for developing analysis of media content, creators, and consumers. Defining psychoanalysis in terms of theory and method, Freud's concept of the talking cure, as well as elaboration on two particularly powerful symbols of psycho-analysis (the couch and the cigar) were included.

The next chapter is a discussion of how Freud's ideas have been used to study media and popular culture, have influenced the creation of media and popular culture content (including ancillary services such as advertising and public relations), and examines a few popular, but inaccurate or incomplete ideas about Freud and his theories.

Notes

1 Freud did not invent the term depth psychology. It was introduced by Bleuler. However, Freud, along with Jung, Hillman and others situate their study of psychology within the field of depth psychology, referring to the exploration of the depths of the conscious and unconscious mind. For more on this see Ellenberger, H. (1970). *The Discovery of the Unconscious*. New York: Basic Books.

2 Freud eventually abandoned hypnosis as treatment.

3 There is a body of criticism that says Freud modified his "seduction theory," from literal sexual memories to being fantasies. This has brought criticism. See Masson, J. M. (1984/2003). *The Assault on Truth* for more on this.

4 An interesting Web site called Quote Investigator includes references to this: http://quoteinvestigator.com/2011/08/12/just-a-cigar/.

5 Prior to becoming a film director, Billy Wilder was a journalist, writer of crosswords, theater reviews and the like for *Die Bühne* and *Die Stunde*. In December 1925, at age 19, Wilder was sent to interview Sigmund Freud at the Freud's home and office in Vienna at Berggasse 19. "Sigmund Freud appeared, with a napkin around his neck; Billy Wilder had the bad taste to interrupt his lunch. Freud ignored his proffered business card and curtly told him to be on his way" (Bradshaw, 2021).

6 Mark Edmundson describes Freud, in middle age, as "a robust, full-faced man with a burgher's well insulated body and a dense regal beard, streaked with gray. His usual facial expression somehow conveyed both contentment and ambition. He had a hawk nose and bright, all-consuming eyes. Freud was not tall, only about five foot seven inches, but his presence was formidable: he seemed to be more than a match for life" (5).

7 Phylogenetics are the natural, evolutionary relationships acquired during development.

8 Freud's work, of its time, was heteronormative in orientation.
9 For an example of how a media analyst could apply knowledge of defense mechanism is contained in A. A. Berger's (2019) Media Analysis Techniques, p. 20. Another example is Martin Grotjahn's (1971) study of horror films.
10 Ellis was, however a proponent of eugenics (Crozier, 2008).

References

"10 quotes wrongly attributed to Sigmund Freud." (2019, April 30). https://www.freud.org.uk/2019/04/30/10-quotes-wrongly-attributed-to-sigmund-freud/

Andreas-Salomé, L. (1916). "Anal" und "Sexual." *Imago*, 4, 249–273.

Aziz, S. R. (2000). Sigmund Freud: Psychoanalysis, cigars, and oral cancer. *Journal of Oral and Maxillofacial Surgery*, 58(3), 320–323.

"Because psychoanalysis is a serious business, it has become a classic target of cartoonists." (2006, November 29–December 14). https://www.freud.org.uk/exhibitions/on-the-couch/

Berger, A. A. (2013). Psychoanalytic theory. In *Encyclopedia of media and communication*. Toronto: University of Toronto Press.

Berger, A. A. (2019). *Media analysis techniques: Psychoanalytic criticism*. Thousand Oaks, CA: Sage.

Billig, M. (1999). *Freudian repression: Conversation creating the unconscious*. Cambridge University Press.

Blum, H. (1976). The changing use of dreams in psychoanalytic practice. *International Journal of Psychoanalysis*, 57, 315–324.

Bradshaw, P. (2021, May 28). *Billy Wilder's escape from the nightmare of Europe*. Critical Mass. https://newrepublic.com/article/162543/billy-wilders-escape-nightmare-europe-director-hollywood-review

Breur, J., & Freud, S. (1895/2001). *Studies on hysteria*. London: Vintage.

Charlton, A. (2004). Medicinal uses of tobacco in history. *Journal of the Royal Society of Medicine*, 97(6), 292–296.

Cheetham, M., Suter, P., & Jäncke, L. (2011, November 24). The human likeness dimension of the "uncanny valley hypothesis": Behavioral and functional MRI findings. *Frontiers in Human Neuroscience*, 5. https://doi.org/10.3389/fnhum.2011.00126

Coleridge, S. T. (1816). *Kubla Kahn*. https://www.poetryfoundation.org/poems/43991/kubla-khan

"Coulrophobia." *Cleveland Clinic*. https://my.clevelandclinic.org/health/diseases/21835-coulrophobia-fear-of-clowns

Crozier, I. (2008). Havelock Ellis, eugenicist. *Studies in History and Philosophy of Biological and Biomedical Sciences*, 39(2), 187–194.

Curatorial assistant. Personal email. Freud Museum London. November 6, 2012.

De Berg, H. (2003). *Freud's theory and its use in literary and culture studies: An introduction*. Rochester, NY: Camden House.

De Sousa, A. (2011). Freudian theory and consciousness: A conceptual analysis. In A. R. Singh & S. A. Singh (Eds.), *Brain, mind, and consciousness: An international interdisciplinary perspective* (pp. 210–217). Mens Sana Research Foundation.
Ellenberger, H. (1970). *The discovery of the unconscious*. New York: Basic Books.
Elsaesser, T. (2009). Freud as media theorist: Mystic writing-pads and the matter of memory. *Screen*, 50(1), 100–113.
"Fearofclowns."(2008,January24).*Nature*,451(7177),385.*GaleAcademicOneFile*.link.gale.com/apps/doc/A189796859/AONE?u=euge94201&sid=bookmark-AONE&xid=9b7b4235
Freidenreich, H. P. (2002). *Female, Jewish, and educated: The lives of Central European University Women*. Bloomington: Indiana University Press.
Freud Museum, London, UK. https://www.freud.org.uk/
Freud, S. (1897). In J. M. Masson (Ed.), *The complete letters of Sigmund Freud to Wilhelm Fliess*. Cambridge, MA: Harvard University Press.
Freud, S. (1898/2013). *The psychical mechanism of forgetfulness*. British Library. Kindle Edition.
Freud, S. (1901/1965). *The interpretation of dreams*. New York: Avon.
Freud, S. (1901/2016). *The collected works of Sigmund Freud: Psychoanalytic studies, theoretical essays & articles* (A. A. Brill, M. D. Eder, S. Hall, & H. W. Chase, Trans.). e-artnow.
Freud, S. (1901/2019). *The psychopathology of everyday life* (J. Strachey, Trans.). Indirapuram, Ghaziabad, UP: Samaira Book Publishers.
Freud, S. (1905/1949). *Three essays on the theory of sexuality* (J. Strachey, Trans.). Germany: Imago Publishing.
Freud, S. (1905/2022). *The joke and its relation to the unconscious*. London: Penguin.
Freud, S. (1905/2000). *Three essays on the theory of sexuality* (J. Strachey, Trans. & Ed.). New York: Basic Books.
Freud, S. (1910/1961). *Five lectures on psycho-analysis* (J. Strachey, Trans. & Ed.). New York: W. W. Norton.
Freud, S. (1910/1916). *Three contributions to the theory of sex* (2nd ed., A. A. Brill, Trans.). Lancaster, PA: New Era Printing.
Freud, S. (1913). *On beginning treatment (Further recommendations on the technique of psychoanalysis)* (J. Strachey, Trans.). London: Hogarth Press.
Freud, S. (1914a). *On the history of the psychoanalytic movement*. London: Hogarth.
Freud, S. (1914b/1958). Papers on Technique (1911–1915). In *The standard edition of the complete psychological works of Sigmund Freud, Vol. XII* (J. Strachey, Ed.). London: Hogarth Press.
Freud, S. (1915). *The psychopathology of everyday life* (A. A. Brill, Trans.). New York: Macmillan.
Freud, S. (1919). *The uncanny (Das Unheimliche)*. London: Hogarth Press.
Freud, S. (1920/2015). *Beyond the pleasure principle* (J. Strachey, Trans.). New York: Dover.
Freud, S. (1922). *Introductory lectures on psychoanalysis* (J. Riviere, Trans.). London: George Allen & Unwin.
Freud, S. (1927/2018). *The ego and the id*. London: Hogarth Press.
Freud, S. (1933/1989). *New introductory lectures on psychoanalysis* (J. Strachey, Trans.). New York: Norton.
Freud, S. (1935/1960). Anonymous (Letter to an American mother). In *The letters of Sigmund Freud* (pp. 423–444). New York: Basic Books.

Freud, S. (2016). *The collected works of Sigmund Freud: Psychoanalytic studies, theoretical essays & articles* (A. A. Brill, M. D. Eder, S. Hall, & H. W. Chase, Trans.).

Gay, P. (1988/2006). *Freud: A life for our time*. New York: Norton.

Gay, P. (Ed.). (1989). *The Freud reader*. New York: W. W. Norton.

Gilman, S. L. (1993). *Freud, race, and gender*. Princeton, NJ: Princeton University Press.

Gipps, R. (2019). *The Oxford handbook of philosophy and psychoanalysis*. New York: Oxford.

Gipps, R., & Lacewing, M. (2019). Intellectual prehistory: Introduction. In R. Gipps (Ed.), *The Oxford handbook of philosophy and psychoanalysis*. New York: Oxford University Press.

Goodhill, O. (2016, October 8). A Freudian theory, now backed up by neuroscience, explains why so many fear clowns. *Quartz*. https://www.frontiersin.org/articles/10.3389/fnhum.2011.00126/full

Hampton, C. (2003). *The talking cure*. New York: Faber & Faber.

Haslam, N. (2017, February 27). *Leaving the past behind: What became of the anal personality?* The Conversation. https://theconversation.com/leaving-the-past-behind-what-became-of-the-anal-personality-73716

Haughton, H. (2003). Introduction. In S. Freud (1899). *The Uncanny*. New York: Penguin.

Heath, C. (2016, October 8). Qtd. in O. Goodhill. A Freudian theory, now backed up by neuroscience, explains why so many fear clowns. *Quartz*. https://www.frontiersin.org/articles/10.3389/fnhum.2011.00126/full

Heller, S. (2005). *Freud A to Z*. New York: John Wiley & Sons.

James, W. (1890). *The principles of psychology*. New York: Henry Holt & Company.

Jones, E. (1910). Freud's theory of dreams. *The American Journal of Psychology*, *21*(2), 283–308.

Jones, E. (1931). *On the nightmare*. London: Hogarth.

Jonte-Pace, D. (2001). *Speaking the unspeakable: Religion, misogyny, and the uncanny mother in Freud's cultural texts*. Berkeley: University of California Press.

Josephs, L. (1989). The world of the concrete: A comparative approach. *Contemporary Psychoanalysis*, *25*, 477–500.

Kern, S. (1973). Freud and childhood sexuality. *History of Childhood Quarterly*, *1*(1), 117–141.

Lacewing, M. (2019). How should we understand the psychoanalytic unconscious? In R. Gipps (Ed.), *The Oxford handbook of philosophy and psychoanalysis* (pp. 407–431). New York: Oxford.

Lansky, M. R. (1992). The legacy of *The Interpretation of Dreams*. In M. Lansky (Ed.), *Essential papers on dreams* (pp. 3–31). New York: NYU Press.

Lear, J. (2005). *Freud* (2nd ed.). New York: Taylor & Francis.

Lennox, A. (1983). *Sweet dreams are made of this*. The Eurythmics. *Universal* Music Publishing Mgb. Ltd. https://genius.com/Eurythmics-sweet-dreams-are-made-of-this-lyrics

Lidz, T. (1946). Nightmares and the combat neurosis. *Psychiatry*, *9*, 37–49.

Marx, C., Benecke, C., & Gumz, A. (2017). Talking cure models: A framework of analysis. *Frontiers in Psychology*, 8, 1589. https://doi.org/10.3389/fpsyg.2017.01589

Masson, J. M. (1984/2003). *The assault on truth: Freud's suppression of the seduction theory*. New York: Ballantine.

Mitchell, S. A., & Black, M. J. (1995). *Beyond Freud: A history of modern psychoanalytic thought*. New York: Basic Books.

Novotney, A. (2017). Not your great-grandfather's psychoanalysis. *APA Monitor*, *48*(11), p. 40.

On the couch: Psychoanalysis in cartoons, art from The New Yorker. Freud Museum. https://www.freud.org.uk/exhibitions/on-the-couch/

Purges, P. (2016). In "On the couch: Psychoanalysis in cartoons, art from *The New Yorker*." Freud Museum. https://www.freud.org.uk/exhibitions/on-the-couch/

Putnam, J. J. (1910/1916). Introduction to translation. In S. Freud (/1916). *Three contributions to the theory of sex* (2nd ed., pp. v–viii; A. A. Brill, Trans.). Lancaster, PA: New Era Printing.

Rank, O. (1914/1971). *The double: A psychoanalytic study*. Chapel Hill, NC: University of North Carolina.

Reurs, J. (n.d.). *The uncanny*. London: Freud Museum. https://www.freud.org.uk/2019/09/18/the-uncanny/

Ross, J. M. (1999). Once more onto the couch: Consciousness and preconscious defenses in psychoanalysis. *Journal of the American Psychological Association*, *47*(1), 91–111.

Roth, M. S. (2019). Technique of dream interpretation and the dreamwork. *Psycho-analysis as history: Negation and freedom in Freud* (pp. 33–51). Ithaca, NY: Cornell University Press.

Rousseau, J.-J. (1763). *Émilius; or A treatise of education* (Vol. 2). Edinburgh: A. Donaldson and J. Reid.

Ruers, J. (n.d.). *The uncanny*. https://www.freud.org.uk/2019/09/18/the-uncanny/

Schelling, F. (1800). *System of transcendental idealism*.

Schur, M. (1972). *Freud, living and dying*. New York: International Universities Press.

Spellbound. (1945). Dir. Alfred Hitchcock. Selznick International Pictures.

Tummala-Narra, P. (2017). In A. Novotney. Not your great-grandfather's psychoanalysis. *APA Monitor*, *48*(11), 40.

Wollheim, R. (1971). *Sigmund Freud*. New York: Cambridge University Press.

· 3 ·

HOW HAVE FREUD'S THEORIES BEEN USED?

Know thyself. Inscription at Temple of Delphi

The road whose goal it is to observe the precept γνῶθι σεαυτόν [gnothi seauton: know thyself] runs via the study of one's own apparently accidental actions and omissions.

Freud (1901, p. 210)

The guiding principle of psychoanalysis is that knowing oneself requires knowing also one's unconscious and dealing with it, so that its unrecognized pressures will not lead one to act in a way detrimental to oneself and others.

Bettelheim (1982, p. 23)

The whole field of twentieth-century culture—from the shocking disconnections of surrealism to the DIY self-healing manifestoes of pop psychology—exhibits the fundamental insights of Sigmund Freud (1865–1939) and his followers.

Mansfield (2000, p. 25)

Although he studied medicine and had a firm understanding of the physical aspects of being human, Sigmund Freud was fascinated by cultural expressions. Culture is how humans, who are essentially wired for a more primitive existence given our relatively short time in the modern world, cope with the requirements of living in societies (what he called "civilization") and how we repress or express these urges and desires. It was not Freud's intention in analysis to make people feel better, rather "in a sense, he tries to make them feel worse. He shows people what they are by confronting them with what they do not want to know. Cutting through the layers of self-deception with which society papers over the cracks in its foundation, he questions even our deepest certainties" (de Berg, 2003, p. 2).

While nature versus nurture is highly debated within this scholarship, as was discussed in detail in the previous chapter, Freud wrote extensively about the power of early childhood experiences to influence our adult lives. Some experiences are entirely natural and naive explorations of the body, for example, and foundational in the formation of a healthy self. Early traumas in particular fascinated Freud and he focused in particular on how these experiences often remain buried in the unconscious. The unconscious, in psychoanalytic terms, "refers to the existence of ideas which are not just being thought about (hence not just 'not in consciousness') but which are also radically *unavailable* to thought-they cannot be brought to awareness even if the person tries really hard, or at least it is more of a struggle than one person can manage on her or his own. These hidden ideas, however, have a profound influence on psychological life" (Frosh, 2013, pp. 12–13) including those who make and consume media and popular culture. I argue that these ideas may not be, in some cases, hidden to media creators who wish to use the very notion of the power of the unconscious to tell their stories, or, in the cases of advertising and public relations, discussed below, to manipulate unsuspecting audiences into thinking, believing, and/or acting in ways that bypass critical thinking.

While the therapeutic use of psychoanalysis is widely disputed, the "tools," that is, the theories "are not only valid but illuminating in the study of literature, biography, and history" (Brooks, 2000, p. 2). Psychoanalytic theory, as a hermeneutical tool for reading media texts and their construction, is also referred to as "psychoanalytic media research" (Krüger & Johanssen, 2016, p. 8). As a theory it predicts that the many goings-on of the mind and body will be experienced by those creating content, through the products they generate and in the experiences of audiences who receive those products. Freud (1908/1989) used the "untranslatable" German word *Dichter* "which embraces storytellers, novelists, poets, and playwrights" (Gay, 1989, p. 436). He wrote:

> We laymen have always been intensely curious to know … from what sources that strange being, the creative writer, draws his material, and how he manages to make such an impression on us with it and to arouse in us emotions of which, perhaps, we had not even thought ourselves capable. (1989, p. 436)

What is considered media today (television, film, internet, radio in particular) was not the same array available in Freud's time. Johanssen (2016, p. 689) writes: "Sigmund Freud's *oeuvre* is peppered with references to an example of media and their content in the broadest sense. He used plays, literature, poetry, and ancient archaeological examples to illustrate his clinical and theoretical ideas" (see also Bainbridge & Yates, 2014). His essays, such as "Creative Writers and Daydreaming" (*Der Dichter und das Phantasieren*, 1908/1989), "The Moses of Michelangelo" (1914/1989), "Leonardo da Vinci and a Dream of his Childhood" (1910/1990), and "Dostoevsky and Parricide" (1928), were his viewings of these artists and their works through a psychoanalytic lens. Books of course had been available for decades but were not as widely available in price or numbers as today's relatively inexpensive newspapers, books, and magazines. Cinema was developing and becoming popular around the time of Freud (see also Elsasser, 2009), and the encoding and decoding of meanings that we see today were gaining footing then. It was in Europe, France specifically, where cinema is claimed to have started with the 50-second-long Lumière film *The Arrival of a Train at La Ciotat Station* in 1895.[1] Freud (1929/2017, p. 16) identified stimulations, pleasures, and sensations (*jouissance*) evoked by certain experiences and memories, as well as intoxicants used as means to keep suffering at bay, which he termed "media," as in the physiological responses and yet, this quotation from *Civilization and Its Discontents* could in fact be talking about communication media, especially binging on media content, today:

> The service rendered by intoxicating media in the struggle for happiness and in keeping misery at a distance is so highly prized as a benefit that individuals and people alike have given them an established place in the economics of their libido. We owe to such media not merely the immediate yield of pleasure, but also a greatly desired degree of independence from the external world. For one knows that, with the help of this 'drowner of cares' one can at any time withdraw from the pressure of reality and fine refuge in a world of one's own with better conditions of sensibility. (1929/1995, in Gay, p. 730)

While the material Freud considered came from literary analyses, the same lens can be used to consider the creative process of visual artists, filmmakers, and others who create that something-special that resonates with audiences, often in ways hard to find words to describe. He appreciated how creative individuals, "who were free from the shackles of 'scientific seriousness,'" could, "like children … play with ideas and thus attain valuable insights that scientists could achieve only after years of experimentation and doubt" (Braga & Logan, 2013, p. 166). Freud wrote:

> Creative writers are valuable allies, and their evidence is to be prized highly, for the are apt to know a whole host of things between heaven and earth which our philosophy has not yet let us dream. In their knowledge of the mind they are far in advance of us everyday people, for they draw upon sources we have not yet opened up for science. (1908/1995, p. 438)

Freud (1908/1989) compared the creative process to that of childhood, when children create complex phantasy worlds. "The creative writer does the same as the child at play (see Winnicott for later development on this). He creates a world of phantasy which he takes very seriously, that is, which he invests with large amounts of emotion—while separating is sharply from reality" (p. 437). Eventually the child leaves this activity behind, but adults who create may have given up the literal physical objects of play but replaces the pleasure with fantasies and daydreams. Many adults hide their phantasies. Freud (1908/1989) saw this applying to gender roles: "The well-brought up young woman is only allowed a minimum of erotic desire, and the young man has to learn to suppress the excess of self-regard which he brings with him from the spoilt days of his childhood" (p. 439). This of course fits the times when Freud wrote and the stereotypes that persist to modern times, but there is some truth to the observation, despite the realities of desires among girls and women. He noted that "the relation of a phantasy to time is in general very important," three moments as it were, linking the three (p. 442). One moment is an earlier childhood experience in which a play, wish, or phantasy was satisfied (particularly during the infantile stage). The second moment is when memories of this feeling, satisfaction harken back to a time when the wish was fulfilled. In the third moment, traces of these sensations carry forth into adult life. Some are reexperienced, some repressed or denied, and others enacted, in the case of the arts, through expression. Freud emphasized that daydreams, waking-like phantasies, are not the same as night dreams and dreaming. Through interpretation we can sometimes get at the meaning of what might be suggested by a dream. The meaning might be clear, then we might feel shame and conceal from ourselves and others or express in an abstract form. But both night dreams and daydreams are wish fulfillments. The "imaginative writer" or any creating individual thus, could be "the dreamer in broad daylight" (p. 440). Freud made explicit he was talking about writers who generate their own materials versus retelling tales written by others including those who are widely popular thereby not focusing only on the so-called classic authors, "we will choose not the writers most highly esteemed by the critics, but the less pretentious authors of novels, romances, and short stories, who nevertheless have the widest and most eager circle of readers of both sexes" (p. 440). He identified the common trope of the hero,[2] the sense of invulnerability embodied and emboldened by this egocentric character. In addition, the love conquers all theme, good overcoming evil, as common storylines. It is common, noted Freud, that these works take the perspective of the main character, whose psychological goings-ons are described from inside the mind of that individual.

In terms of the creation of this figure and the creative process, Freud (1907) notes that the insight, the idea of the character, often comes from "a strong experience in the present [that] awakens in the creative writer a memory of an earlier experience (usually belonging to his childhood) from which there now proceeds a wish which finds its fulfillment in the creative work. The work itself exhibits elements of the recent provoking occasion as well as the old memory" (p. 139). Whereas an everyday person might feel shame were they to disclose the content of daydreams and phantasies, the creative person is able to translate individual-level desires: "[T]he writer softens the character of his egoistic day-dreams by altering and disguising it, and he bribes us by the purely formal—that is, aesthetic—yield of pleasure which he offers us in the presentation of his phantasies" (p. 153).

Bainbridge (2011, p. 31) posits that representations of psychotherapy in media, particularly U.S. media, have cultivated and supported a "culture of feeling" and "matters of emotion that appears to dominate media images on the contemporary Western cultural scene." This "mediatization" thus "impact[s] notions of selfhood and subjectivity" because of its foundation in psychoanalysis. Dreams and "the varieties of spiritual experience" (Spector, 2001, p. 479, paraphrasing William James) are the subjects of psychological interpretation. The experience of consuming some forms of media, particularly television and film, is dream-like in creation and consumption. Many 20th-century artists, such as Klee, Miro, Dalí, and others, explored in their work the tension of the opposites, of space between order and chaos (for more on this, see Spector, 2001).

Psychoanalysis and the Arts

It is no wonder then that artists, writers, filmmakers, and other creators have drawn upon psychoanalysis and symptomology to create images, tell stories, and re-present Freudian ideas. "Psychoanalysis … emerges from the cracks: from the pauses, intrusive thoughts, changes of subject, bodily complaints, feelings of inhibition, all of which disrupt the free flow of self-conscious thought" (Lear, 2005, p. xv). Psychoanalytic theory can be utilized both as "theory and method" (Johanssen, 2016, p. 688) by which to apply applying Freud's ideas such as ambivalence, denial, fixation, projection, regression, and repression, to media and popular culture content, creators, and audiences. Not surprisingly those who create content also work through some of their own issues in characters and plot lines. Repression and defense mechanisms thus serve as narrative tools creators use to tell stories about characters wrestling with many of these psychological states. That media creators and consumers are subjective beings bumps up against some conceptions of media professionals as well as audiences. Johanssen (2016, p. 689) argues "that psychoanalysis may offer us the tools and vocabulary to *acknowledge* subjectivity and modes of experience beyond rationality—and these always include foci on ourselves as media researchers and how we are invested in a particular topic." Both audiences and content creators maybe not always be aware of why they create what they do or, for example, "how they have come to like a specific television programme" (Johanssen, 2016, p. 690), or film, novel, advertisement, or photograph.

Here exists a natural theoretical connection to media and cultural studies theories and psychoanalytic interpretations. Stuart Hall (1973, 1980) identified a similar process in which the creator of a message encodes that meaning and the audience member decodes it. During Freud's time, physics was "elevated to the rank of ideal science" (The Magistretti & Ansermet, 2018, p. 1861). His interest in the discipline resulted in his positing a connection between neurosciences and psychoanalysis. In *Project for a Scientific Psychology* (1895), Freud saw this exchange as a form of energy in his concept of ideational mimetics, "a relationship of exchanges of energy (physical and mental) between the viewer and the work of art, in some respects similar to empathy" (Hoffeld, 1973, p. 414). Thought itself is therefore a kind of energy. While he mostly avoided any discussion of the aesthetics of creative production, his analysis of the creative process sometimes appeared to be precisely that, sometimes to the chagrin of the artists. This was particularly so as it concerned visual media and the artist, evident in Freud's observations on such subjects as the representation of conversation (in medieval art), and the pictorial devices for indicating time and the episodes of narrative (in the Renaissance), provide analogies to the dreamwork, and they are most definitely concerned with problems of form and structure. Taken together, these speculations, undoubtedly based on a close reading of paintings and sculpture, enable us to determine how the psychoanalytic material of a work, its images and their symbolism, are conveyed by a carefully structured visual vehicle (Hoffeld, 1973, p. 414).

Psychoanalytic criticism "is a form of applied psychoanalysis, a science concerned with the interaction between conscious and unconscious processes and the laws of mental functioning" (Berger, 2019, p. 95). Psychoanalytic criticism is interdisciplinary, with examples in political science, anthropology, sociology, and media studies. When used as both theory and method, it provides a tool for thinking about "contradictions, incoherences, ambivalent and non-sensical subjective experiences that also find expression in cultural products such as media texts and in responses towards them" (Johanssen, 2016, p. 690). The prevalence of media in everyday lives is, as Silverstone notes (1994, p. 1), a "constant media mastication of everyday culture." Whatever is presented to the public ear and eye is repeated, reinforced, and recirculated. This "reflects the role of the media in relation to the social, cultural, political, and economic dimensions of our lives," and "highlights the need for media scholars to engage with notions of *experience*" (ital. orig., p. 5). The experience then also includes the audience. Silverstone (1994, p. 11) notes: "If we are to study the media, then we have to confront the role of the unconscious in the constitution as well as the challenging of experience, and likewise, if we are to answer the question why study the media, then part of our answer must be because it offers a route, if not a royal route, into hidden territories of mind and meaning." According to Hoffeld (1973, p. 414),

> Freud's work legitimized the material images — drawn from dreams, the unconscious, sexual fantasies and neuroses—but in addition to this by now familiar rehearsal of the Freudian's stock-in-trade, we should also note Freud's contribution to the devices—the technical metaphors—made in such paintings as Magritte's.

Johanssen (2016) gives as an example of method, interview-based research and Freud's free-association technique. One can think of marketing research, focus groups, and other verbal feedback techniques in which participants might be asked for the first thing that comes to mind, such as a word or image. A psychoanalytic response "allow unconscious moments to come to the surface" (p. 691). Not subject to censorship that might occur in written responses, for example, "repressed, forgotten, or negated fragments could thus come to the surface" (p. 691). Even silences, or the inability to come up with an association is full of information.

As mentioned in Chapter 2, Freud engaged in self-analysis, which is consistent with a philosophy of, first and foremost, knowing thyself, because self-knowledge serves in understanding others. He called psychoanalysis an interpretive art, one that appeared in a variety of communications, whether speech, writing, or other representations (Freud, 1923). This endeavor is also one found in some forms of literature and films of, for example, the surrealists. The full "inventory of the documents of self-analysis" includes "dreams, screen memories, slips, instances of forgetting, and parapraxes" (Anzieu, 1975/1986). Heroism, masochism, castration anxiety, and other ways of being are captured in case studies in the clinical setting, but also provided and continues to provide fertile fodder for the arts. Elliott (2004, p. 2) suggests that "one of the foremost achievements of Freud's uncovering of the unconscious imagination was his innovative application of clinical concepts to the spheres of culture, literature, politics, and art, that which he termed 'applied psychoanalysis.'" Examples of this came early in literature, which makes sense given Freud's interests. In 1958 Frederick Crews wrote his dissertation at Princeton on E. M. Forster. ("The dissertation explained what Forster thought by looking at what Forster wrote" (Menand, 2017, para. 11). Crews then studied Nietzsche at Yale, which led him to Freud. In 1966 he published *The Sins of the Fathers*, "a psychoanalytic study of Nathaniel Hawthorne" (para. 11). In 1966 Norman Hollan's *Psychoanalysis and Shakespeare* was published, "one of the pioneering works in psychoanalytic literary criticism" (para. 11).

In the introduction to his (1919) essay "The Uncanny," Freud speaks of the psychologist's reticence to write about or deal with art. Freud determined that "only rarely does the psychoanalyst feel impelled to engage in aesthetic investigations" (p. 1). It is curious, given his appreciation of historic objects, theories, and appreciation of mythology, that he would in many ways avoid aesthetics. "Freud has had a huge impact on subsequent art and writing about art" (Haughton, 2003, p. 1). In *Civilization and Its Discontents* (1929/2017, p. 13), Freud wrote that art was one of the two highest achievements of human beings, the other being science. He was an avid collector of objects, antiquities, and his study famously displayed these items to which he often returned to gaze upon, consider, examine, and contextualize within his studies. That humans create to speak without words, but rather in images testifies to the power of the mind to generate expressions of values, ideals, mythologies, and symptoms that one can thus read psychologically.

Freud's colleague, friend, and biographer Ernest Jones (1957, p. 408) noted how Austrian psychologist Ernst Kris, as well as Freud's artist son Ernst

L. Freud,[3] advised Jones not to write a chapter in the three-volume biography about art, "since Freud had little aesthetic appreciation." However, as Jones and others have pointed out, this is not quite true, noting "two definite statements about Freud's attitude to art":

1. He had a consistently … high and unstinted admiration for 'artists' of whatever king; this was occasionally tinged with a trace of envy for their superior gifts" (p. 408)
2. "His enjoyment and appreciation (whether strictly aesthetic or not) of the arts were in this descending order: poetry first, then sculpture and architecture, then paining, and music hardly at all (with a very few exceptions" (p. 408).

In "The Moses of Michelangelo," Freud (1914, p. 211) wrote how he is "no connoisseur in art, but simply a layman," and yet he read voraciously of art, of history, of literature. He noted that mostly it was literature and sculpture that most "exercise[ed] a powerful effect" on him, less so painting. He noted a "paradoxical fact" that could perhaps be applied to visual media as well:

> Some of the grandest and most overwhelming creations of art are still unsolved rid dles to our understanding. We admire them, we feel overawed by them, but we are unable to say what they represent to us. … I do not mean that connoisseurs and lovers of art find no words with which to praise such objects to us. They are eloquent enough it seems to me. But usually in the presence of a great work of art each says something different from the other, and none of them says anything that solves the problem for the unpretending admirer. In my opinion, what grips us so powerfully can only be artist's *intention*, in so far as he has succeeded in expressing it his work and in getting us to understand it completely. (pp. 211–212)

If Freud was so committed *not* to write about art, "what is it that tempts him to stray from the straight and narrow path of psychology to walk the primrose path of aesthetic dalliance?" (Haughton, 2003, p. 1). Freud (1928, qtd. in Jones, 1953, p. 414) was curious about the process of creating, and while many artists did not appreciate what he wrote about them, his critiques were not about technique but rather about what was symbolized and about the process of creating. In his piece on Dostoevsky, Freud (1928, p 177) wrote, "unfortunately analysis has to lay down its arms before the problem of the creative writer."

Potentially riffing on Hamlet ("there are more things in heaven and earth, Horatio, / Than are dreamt of in your philosophy"; 1.5.175–176; in Bevington,

2008, p. 152), Freud (1907, p. 8), with typical wit, wrote: "Creative writers are valuable allies, and their evidence is to be prized highly, for they are apt to know a whole host of things between heaven and earth of which our philosophy has not yet let us dream." Reflecting on concepts in dream analysis, Freud wrote: "[T]he unconscious mechanisms familiar to us in the 'dream-work' are … also operative in the processes of imaginative writing." Hence, artists can thus be "allies of psycho-analysis …" which might indeed provide "some small insight into the nature of creative writing." Dreams are thus riddles waiting to be interpreted, investigated, as part of the "imaginative life and memory of the dreamer."

Media and Psychoanalytics

Several media products, perhaps most obviously advertising and film, deal with tensions between the unconscious and conscious worlds of characters, "the representational dream-work of the self" that illustrates how one might be "at odds with one's conscious ideals" (Elliott, 2004, p. 7). These visual forms of re-presentation, including photography, are viewed as additional encapsulations, more public allies, of what was also contained in language and words, spoken and written. Fashion is another creative realm that can be viewed through a psychoanalytic lens (Bancroft, 2012; Hollander, 1993). Of course reading, critiquing, and analyzing representations, particularly visual representation, brings up the tension of interpretation; the "translation of images into words … as interpretating a painting [or film, advertisement] "is necessarily an incomplete rendition of the image's 'muteness' into speech, and the explanation will always be partial at best pointing to that 'something more' which is latent within the object and cannot be fully communicated through a verbal paraphrase" (Brooks, 2000, pp. 67–68). Brooks (2000) notes that "the art critic must 'listen' to the work of art in the same way as a psychoanalyst should listen to a patient: the gap between a verbal paraphrase and the surplus of meaning within the image itself parallels the gap between the decoding of 'free association' and the full meaning of unconscious desire" (p. 68).

Sublimation (*sublimierung*) is Freud's term for transforming forbidden, antisocial, illegal impulses in which "cultural conversion, the transformation of wishful impulses into 'symptoms' of culture such as literature and art" (de Berg, 2003, p. 11) take place. As it concerns art (widely defined) and literature, sublimation can be a mild redirection" or more graphically in "pornography … [as] a form of sublimation" when "looking at the models in *Playboy*" (p. 12). This alone is not the origin of this. Freud stressed that most psychological phenomena are *überdeterminiert* (overdetermined), resulting from many interrelated influences. Some are contradictory, and some are not. But how to represent, or drawing on Stuart Hall *re-present*, mental concepts in images? Whether those of the creator of the image or in the experience of the receiver? "*Civilization and its Discontents* thus confronts the problem of representing the temporal processes of the mind spatially" (Cavell, 2002, p. 46).

The following sections discuss applications of many of Freud's theories either explicitly inspired or evidentially inspired as interpreted through critical analysis, to media and popular culture, as well as to ancillary services (advertising and public relations). These discussions are intended to provide background on the area of communication and connections to psychoanalytic theory. The guiding question for what follows is: How have Freud's theories influenced and been used to study fashion, film, television, advertising, news, and public relations?

Fashion[4]

Fashion is more than clothing. Of course it includes clothes, but also ways of doing things, ways of appearing, of designing, of being. According to the editor of the journal *Fashion Theory*, fashion is "the cultural construction of an embodied identity" (Steele, 2022). But it is more than identity, argues Bancroft (2012, para. 2); more than trends, business, marketing, and branding, it is "primarily concerned with innovation in the surface decoration of the body, and the wider social and cultural responses to this innovation." An item of fashion does not exist independently from the context within which it is created, worn, or presented. It includes high fashion, street styles, costumes, and trendy styles. Fashion can reflect (or resist) politics, economics, cultural and ethnic identities, and resistance against all those categories. The fetishization of fashion, objects, and gender is fertile ground for Freudian analysis (see Steele, 1997). Steele, who has been called "The Freud of Fashion" (Menkes, 2020), views fashion through an intellectual versus marketing lens and has curated shows on darker aspects of fashion such as gothic, the queer history of fashion, corsets and confinement, and the language of fashion. In an interview, Menkes (2020) asked Steele about fashion differences in different countries, such as the United States and Great Britain, and if people might express their tensions through clothes. Steele responded that she believes that people in all countries use clothing and fashion "to express unconscious desires, conflicts, and fears," although in some places, such as the UK, "there's a much clearer sense of being eccentric or provocative," whereas in the United States, there's a much stronger sense of wearing the "right" clothes to specific occasions, to being conformist. However, among younger people, globally, you see more expression, particularly when exploring identity. In *Fashion and Eroticism*, Steele (1985) writes about the history of fashion, and notes how, today, gender-fluid clothing is more important, rather than binary coding of "men's" and "women's" clothes, that is, what is masculine and feminine (see Chapter 4 and Gucci campaign). Changes are evident in the marketing of clothing. In early 2022, for example, the fitness and active life clothing brand Prana, expanded what so-called Influencers could access, going from gender-restrictive options of Men's or Women's to a more inclusive option to access the entire site.

The history of fashion fills volumes (see Cumming, 2021; Cumming, Cunnington, & Cunnington, 2010; Steele, 2000), and there are many books on psychoanalysis and fashion (see Bergler, 1953; Flügel, 1930). In industrialized nations in particular fashion is connected to the social construction of identity. While all cultures have specific clothing/dress/adornment norms, I am only experienced with the norms in the United States and Europe. The socially constructed binary categories of femininity and masculinity have long related to conformity to cultural rules around dress. Transgressions are either celebrated or punished—showing too much skin (women), notions of power through color (red ties for men), length of skirts, and so forth all work not only to support narrow definitions of gender but also support a massive industry (see Reilly & Barry, 2020; Ford, 2022). As success for women has traditionally been measured by appearance (Germov & Williams, 1999, p. 120; Etcoff, 2000). For men the emphasis is placed more fully upon economic success (Germov & Williams, 1999; Masi de Casanova, 2015). Clothing choices play an important role in identity construction, mood reflection, and social class expression (see Crane, 2012). For women, cosmetics are also part of the equation. The restricted women's body is thus one that has been corseted and contoured to fit an aesthetic ideal. Freud (1909, pp. 155–156) in a lecture rather infamously but interestingly said:

> In the world of everyday experience, we can observe that half of humanity must be classes among the clothes fetishists. All women, that is, are clothes fetishists. Dress plays a puzzling role in them. It is a question again of the repression of the same drive, this time, however, in the passive form of allowing oneself to be seen,

> which is repressed by clothes, and on account of which, clothes are raised to a fetish. Only now we understand why even the most intelligent women behave defenselessly against the demands of fashion. For them, clothes take the place of parts of the body, and to wear the same clothes means only to be able to show what the others can show, means only that one can find in her everything that one expects from women.

He might have been thinking less about gender as a compulsion to buy clothing and more a prompt too our considering how consumer capitalism pressures women to focus time and resources on appearance within a limited range of options, including gender identities, modes of expression, and bodily taboos. This is increasingly happening as well to men, who, in the last 20 years, have had the attention (and advertising) directed toward them. That there is an erotics of fashion has remained largely undisputed. Many analyses of fashion and psychoanalysis focus on sexuality, gender, and projection. Fashion "is concerned with both the body and the mind, and is, arguable, complicit in the psychic process of identification, desire and language … that are central to human subjectivity" (Bancroft, 2012, p. 15). From Freud we learn that the way one looks at (the gaze) an object will shape subjectivity. Meaning is both encoded by the wearer and decoded by observers.

Objects are also fashioned and/or fashionable such as cars, furniture, houses, and even landscapes. They are color-coded with meanings (such as pink for girls and blue for boys). Given that clothing "has … an intimate relationship with the physical body and, by extension, the personal identity of the individual" (Steele, 2022). Thus, it isn't surprising that one could view designers of fashions as well as the fashions themselves as illustrations of several psychological concepts. High fashion events such as runway shows by designers such as Elsa Schiaparelli, John Galliano, Mary Quant, Alexander McQueen, Viktor Horsting and Rolf Snoeren, Marc Jacobs, and Donatella Versace are theatric opportunities for designer statements. Some fashions go on wider public display at spectacles such as the annual Met Gala, Oscars, and music industry awards shows. Events such as Great Britain's Royal Ascot is an opportunity to flaunt one's personal vision, particularly through hats. Visual media, spectacle, and fashion join when fashion designers and film costumes merge. Examples include Hubert de Givenchy's iconic black dress worn by Audrey Hepburn in *Breakfast at Tiffany's* (1961), Paco Rabanne's outfits for Jane Fonda in *Barbarella* (1968), Jean Paul Gaultier in *The Fifth Element* (1997), and Miuccia Prada for *The Great Gatsby* (2013).

Erotics in fashion and fashion advertising (discussed in Chapter 4) is an obvious expression reflecting the intimate association of fashion and the body.

Through this artform one can play with different identities, sexual deviance, S&M, aggression, suppression, and expression. In addition, the *feel* of certain fabrics against the skin can be understood in psychoanalytic terms (Hamlyn, 2003). Hamyln (2003, p. 9) writes that the

> sensory connection that we all (both male and female) have to cloth cannot be adequately expressed in language. This, it is argued in psychoanalytic terms, is because the unique 'language' of fabric straddles the pre-linguistic or Imaginary and the social/linguistic codes that make up the Symbolic order. Fabric is, further, shown to complicate assumptions about sexual difference because it is inevitably caught up in the persistent undecidability of the fetishistic fantasy.

Sexual fetishism is often associated with clothing, in particular shoes, as "objects are not randomly chosen" (Steele, 1997, p. 17). Freud (1909) saw displacement onto objects as substitutes (he often mentioned them as phallic substitutes) with the fetish arising when a child sees female genitals. Simultaneously, if male, he would fear castration (we might see this more on a symbolic level of a male child separating from the mother or mother figure). A male patient who used clothes as "all interest in women [was] displaced onto clothes" and displayed this preoccupation by "conspicuous[ly] adjust[ing of] the creases of his trousers." Despite several attempts at intercourse with women, the man was "physically impotent … and had never successfully completed coitus." Freud (1909, p. 154) described how, on one occasion,

> he awaited a rendezvous with the lady who was his sweetheart: but his feelings of love immediately vanished when she appeared in poor clothes which had been thrown on hurriedly. It also turned out that his sudden fallings-out during later love affairs always originated in the fact that he objected to a piece of her clothing.

Thus, clothing can both attract and repeal as can attention to one's appearance. Clothing thus reveals and conceals. Freud (1927, p. 198) felt that a fetish can operate in a cathartic sense, calming what might be viewed as aberrant desires: "[Fetishists] are usually quite satisfied with [their fetish], or even praise the way it eases their erotic life." But many aspects of psychoanalysis are less obvious perhaps but have a tremendous influence on culture and communications. For example, those stories are told in books.

Novel Ideas

Freud was known to read Balzac. In fact, the last book Freud read before he died was *La Cousine Bette* (*Cousin Bette*) (1846) in which Balzac tells the story of a bitter angry woman who plots to kill her family. It is a warning about how resentments can fester and how family squabbles can get completely out of hand. The short stories of Daphne Du Mauier, for example, clearly invoke many of Freud's concepts of repression, suppression, and the uncanny. "The Birds" (1952/2008), for example, became Alfred Hitchcock's film of the same name, although quite different in the telling. McGrath (2008, p. ix) describes how,

> Of all the short stories du Maurier wrote, 'The Birds' is the masterpiece. Hitchcock shifted the action from rugged, windswept British cliffs to placid Sonoma County, and invented a sophisticated plot involving a couple from San Francisco caught in a bizarre Oedipal struggle with a dreadful controlling mother. Du Maurier's original tale was far bleaker, far more naturalistic, and as a result, far more powerful.

Another story, "Don't Look Now" (1971) was adapted to film (1973) by Nicholas Roeg who stayed true to the original story. Set in Venice it is a story of a couple, the death of a child, in a "horror story driven by coincidence, mistaken identity, clairvoyance, and murder. It contains a gloriously uncanny scene in which the husband glimpses his wife in a vaporetto on the Grand Canal, at the very moment when she is supposed to be on a plane on her way back to England" (McGrath, 2008, p. xii). Other examples of Freudian theories evident in books and plays include Shakespeare's (1599–1601) *Hamlet* (murderous fantasies, repression, Oedipus myth, rivalry); William Faulker's (1929) *The Sound and the Fury* (depth of inner psychological life, memories, perceptions, sibling dynamics, family trauma); and Philip Roth's (1969) *Portnoy's Complaint* (perversity, sexual strivings, masturbation). No doubt dozens of other books come to mind when we consider plots and characters in this way.

Freud has appeared in books, either as a character or by implication. For example, "if you've ever read the book *Lord of the Flies* by William Golding, then you have enjoyed the allegory of Freud's mind as personified by Jack as the Id, Piggy as the ego, and Ralph as the superego" (Ackerman, 2018, para. 19). In *An Introduction to Psychoanalysis or Freud is Fixated*, media scholar Arthur Asa Berger creates a Holmes and Watson mystery novel interweaving ideas of Freud, as well as other late 19th and early 20th-century psychologists and psychoanalyst. The book uses the mystery genre as a way to teach Freud's main theories. Other writers have used fiction to explore Freud's ideas. For example, Brenda Webster (author of *Vienna Triangle*) says that "For me, fiction was a way of answering questions, for gaining imaginative insight" about Freud (qtd. in LaForce, 2010). The book is about "the bizarre and twisted relationship between Freud and his brilliant disciple Viktor Tausk (who later committed suicide" (LaForce, 2010, p. 3). "Freud was one of the great minds of the twentieth century, and we are all fascinated not only by what he taught but also by who he was." Another book, *The Truth About Lou*, is about Lou Andreas-Salomé, one of Freud's contemporaries, as they were to Nietzsche and Rilke. Selden Edwards' *The Little Book*, also uses an encounter with Freud as part of the narrative, a story about an American baseball player to travels back in time and meets Freud in 19th-century Vienna.

Novelist Lisa Gornick (2019) identified five works of fiction in which Freud is present:

1. *The White Hotel* by D. M. Thomas (1981), which "powerfully plumbs Freudian theories of hysteria, the role of narrative in psychoanalysis, and the foreshadowing of the Nazi horror in secular European society" by presenting an opera singer in treatment with Freud (para. 1).
2. In the murder mystery *The Fig Eater* (Shields, 2000), Freud's analysis of Ida Bauer/a.k.a. Dora, whose father is involved in an affair, sanctioned by him, but is then found strangled.
3. *Dreaming for Freud* (Kohler, 2014) is also based on the Dora case, using the name Ida Bauer. This book casts suspicions on the good doctor's motives.
4. In *Playthings* (Pheby, 2015), steps into Daniel Paul Schreber (a judge and patient of Freud's) and his final years in an asylum.
5. *Regeneration* (Barker, 1991) doesn't present Freud but rather his treatment method, focusing on shell-shocked officers during World War I, through the lens of William Rivers, who says "one of the paradoxes of war—one of the many—was that this most brutal of conflicts should set up a relationship between officers and men that was … domestic. Caring … maternal." It's an interpretation Freud himself might have made" (para. 5).

Celluloid Dreams

Dozens of films have drawn upon Freud's theories as inspiration for characters and plots (see Appendix X), and this medium has been lavished with psychoanalytic attention. Psychoanalytic film theory often concerns how the consciousness of a film's director might be revealed in their work, characters, and productions. It also draws our attention to the psychological factors at work in the audience, as well as helping us to consider how the style of the film impels the film to connect with the audience in a particular manner. Macaulay (2005, p. 11) writes that "the inverted Freudian pyramid of motivation has been a Hollywood staple since the 1920s when psychoanalysis became popular." Furthermore,

> Happily for Hollywood, no matter how discredit Freud and psychoanalysis becomes [sic], it will sustain very little lasting damage. As a rule, American cinema has had no qualms in lumping psychiatrists, psychologists, and psychoanalyst as one discipline, and Freud's elaborate theories of development, which provided rich pickings for directors such as Nicholas Ray (*East of Eden*, *Johnny Guitar)* and Alfred Hitchcock (*Vertigo*, *Marnie*) in the fifties, have now been reduced to providing explanations for killing sprees in slasher movies Jason in the *Friday the 13th* series, Michael Myers in *Halloween*). (Andwar, 1994: T6)

Early silent films that explored split personalities include *Deluxe Annie* and *The Case of Becky*. The German expressionist film *The Cabinet of Dr. Caligari* (1920) used hypnotism as a method to commit murder. Other examples of this include Hitchcock's *Rear Window* (1954) (based on the 1942 Cornell Woolrich short story "It had to be Murder"). Other classic examples include *Spellbound* (1945) and *Betrayal* (1983) (based on Harold Pinter's 1978 play).

One of the most famous applications of Freudian thought is the theory in film is the gaze. Mulvey argued that many if not most films are created in ways that appeal to male, heterosexual scopophilia (sexual pleasure from watching). Visual media, that are mostly made by men, are thus created to mostly appeal to them. Women will attend the same media in this view, if for no other reason to learn what appeals to men. This sexual objectification is a controlling gaze. John Berger (1972, p. 43) noted that an image "orchestrates a gaze and its pleasurable transgression. The woman's beauty, her very desirability, becomes a function of certain practices of imagining—framing, lighting, camera movement, angle."

Mulvey's (1973) foundational article emphasized how patriarchy influences the production of visual communications. Mulvey's theory of "visual pleasure and narrative cinema" incorporated film studies, feminism, and psychoanalysis into this work offering a way of adapting/adopting psychoanalytic thought and applying it to media analysis while modifying what to some, particularly feminist scholars, was a shortcoming of Freud's ideas. The article begins situating the concept within dominant/hegemonic views. The section head "A political use of psychoanalysis," establishes that "psychoanalytic theory is thus appropriate here as a political weapon, demonstrating the way the unconscious patriarchal society has structure film form" (p. 803). Phallocentrism thus relies on subservient objectification of women, "it is her lack that produces the phallus as a symbolic presence" (p. 803). The article is a reaction to the lack of consideration of portrayals of women in visual culture as problematic (and would thus set the stage and foundation for decades of scholarship to follow) and that Freud's theories can assist in revealing why this common mode of presentation often bypass critical consideration, perhaps because they are in fact so common and appeal to fundamental drives that are consistent with the social structure. Mulvey (1973, p. 811–812) argues that there are two primary modes ("avenues") of looking:

1. Voyeuristic. This is the controlling gaze that asserts power of one being (usually male) over another (usually female).
2. Fetishistic. The substitution of an object, being, or reproduction of that object or being for the pleasure of someone else, thus transforming them into a fetish.

Freud's (1913) *Totem and Taboo* noted the anthropological origins of fetishes refer to "items, icons, or objects imbued with, most often religions significance" (Merskin, 2014, p. 156). A fetish as referred to in media and cultural studies "simultaneously refers to commodities, to the repression and domination of nature, to alienation, and to the desire for authority that connects all of these" (Brown, 2012, para. 1).

Three of Freud's theories that figure prominently in Mulvey's (1973) work are scopophilia ("taking sexual pleasure in looking" (Merskin, 2014, p. 157), phallocentrism (castrated woman, woman's lack), and ideal ego (self-recognition). Thus, during childhood, when one becomes self-aware there is a felt contradiction, that of self-preservation, sexual curiosity and energy (libido), and the mediating ego. It is natural that humans get pleasure from looking at bodies, per Mulvey's (1973) "scopophilic instinct," that is, "pleasure in looking at another person as an erotic object" (p. 815). It is controlling that gaze, channeling it in ways that are consistent with a heteronormative patriarchal dominating view that is the issue. "The cinema satisfies a primordial wish for pleasurable looking, but it also goes further, developing scopophilia in its narcissistic aspect" (p. 807). The theater experience itself, according to Mulvey and others, is womb-like, it is dark, intimate, shared with others yet private. Audiences gaze at the screen in a directed way by filmmakers but bring their own issues and energizes with them. One Mulvey's most famous passages concerns the place of gender in the gaze:

> In a world ordered by sexual imbalance, pleasure in looking has been split between active/male and passive/female. The determining male gaze projects its phantasy on to the female figure which is styled accordingly. In their traditional exhibitionist role women are simultaneously looked at and displayed with their appearance coded for strong visual and erotic impact so that they can be said to connote *to-be-looked-at-ness*. Women displayed as sexual object is the leit-motiff of erotic spectacle: from pin-ups to strip-tease, from Ziegfeld to Busby Berkeley, she holds the look, plays to and signifies male desire. (ital. in orig., pp. 808–809).

A contemporary example of masculine scopophilia still present in cinema is in the *Transformers* franchise in which the director, Michael Bay's "directorial note to the actress Megan Fox was to 'look hot,' and thus, we see the actress in booty shorts and crop tops to look pleasing to the viewer" (Tilakartine, 2022). Another example is Sharon Stone's character in *Basic Instinct* (1992).

Mulvey (1973) extended the concept of scopophilia to a "fetishistic scopophilia" in which the women-as-object whose purpose is to be looked at, "builds up the physical beautify of the object, transforming it into something satisfying in itself" (p. 811). Whereas voyeurism "has associations with sadism" (p. 811) and guilt "fetishistic scopophilia … is focussed [stet] on the look alone" (p. 812). Mulvey uses Hitchcock's *Rear Window*, *Vertigo*, and *Marnie* to illustrate how the male hero sees what the audience sees, as spectator. In 2007, Roberta Sassatelli interviewed Laura Mulvey about their theory, modifications, and reflection on its present-day use. In 1995 Mulvey wrote that cinema "materialise[s] both fantasy and the fantastic," it is "phantasmagoria, illusion, and a symptom of the social unconscious" (p. xiv). What is there in films reflects latent meanings, is rich in reflective possibilities, not only for the individual but also for society. As Mulvey noted of the seminal 1975 essay, "woman is represented as 'other,' as an object rather than a subject, materializing" a male "unconscious" (Sassatelli, p. 124). While both (if we dichotomize sexes) are invited to participate in the gaze, it is decidedly male, according to this original articulation. Over the years, other scholars pushed back against fixed gender identities in the essay, saying it misses the diversity of spectatorship (see Creed, 1993; Gamman & Makinen, 1994; Mizeroeff, 1999). Yet along with other scholars mentioned in this and other chapters (Berger, 1972; Goffman, 1976; Jhally, 1990; Williamson, 1978), it was foundational, as reflected in the Sassatelli/Mulvey interview:

> SASSATELLI: This is one of the things that seems to emerge from that particular essay, that the male gaze is also the female gaze—namely, that women look at themselves through the male gaze.
>
> MULVEY: Yes, yes exactly, that is the absolutely crucial point. (p. 127).
>
> SASSATELLI: So you can't escape the male gaze as it is 'the gaze': there is no other position from which to look at those films. This is a very strong political statement that has been both applauded and contested.
>
> MULVEY: People could and did watch a Hollywood film against, the grain, to quote the term used at the time, but to a certain extent to take up that position would always involve a shift away from the magic and fascination of the look, the subject position that was established by the aesthetic of the film itself, into a position which could be one of pleasure but would also suggest an alternative and self-conscious spectatorship. (p. 128).

In terms of making Mulvey's psychoanalytically inspired theory relevant today, in theory and production of films since the 1970s, one option is a "gendered scopic regime" extending the male gaze theory to be inclusive of varying subject positions, fluid, and reflexive gendered identities (p. 130). Many of the films that Mulvey referenced were made in the mid-1950s. Special digital effects, a variety of gazes in production and consumption have changed cinema, as has the rise and success of independent films made by a wider range of directors.

Fetishism is amplified in Hamlyn's (2003) analysis of *The Age of Innocence* (1993), seen through the lens of director Marin Scorsese, drawing upon Edith Wharton's novel. The film sets are thick with décor, deep sofas, plush pillows, and scenes of opulence. The glove and exposed wrist become eroticized in the following scene:

> Escaping from heavy snowfall on a busy city street the couple step into a covered carriage. He wears a caped overcoat, and she is bustled and corseted in a fur-trimmed overdress. The interior of the carriage has walls of thick padded silk that force the pair into unaccustomed proximity. For a moment they sit awkwardly. After a pause he pronounces uncertainly, "Each time I see you you happen to me all over again." She smiles, abashed but gratified. "Yes, I know, for me too," she places her gloved hand affectionately on top of his. He contemplates her hand momentarily and then,

> removing his own larger and coarser leather glove, turns it upwards to reveal the several bright pearl buttons that join the soft suede at the wrist. He slowly unfastens them to expose her pale skin. Prying apart the two halves of the opening he lifts the underside of her wrist to his lips. She watches him intently and then, overwhelmed, embraces him. The horses whinny as the carriage jerks forward and pulls away. (Hamlyn, 2003, p. 13)

In film, the audience gets to witness this intimacy, thus if the appeal is there, they become voyeurs and fetishists. Hamlyn (2003, p. 13) clarifies the play of desire in this scene by describing how "it is therefore not the desired object that he lifts to his lips but something else, something like it, something that stands in close contact with it, something nearly but, crucially, not quite it but that is no less an object of extraordinary power and reverence. We see, here, how the fetish treads a tightrope as the focus of desire for it encloses, but at the same discloses the presence of the real object of curiosity and desire."

Other scholars have extended Freud's theories as did Lacan regarding the physiological responses generated by film viewing (*jouissance*, suture), in order "to explain how Hollywood films hid the sociopolitical context of production" (Saper, 1991, p. 33). These analyses explored concepts such as the gaze (incorporating audience studies, same-sex gaze), as well as fetishism and scopophilia. Mulvey's and other works, however, did something many studies at the time did not: consider audience reception. Specifically, they wanted to understand how the filmmaker's (and by extension the culture's) view of the world became confused with, or displaced by, the spectator's view; that is, they asked, how does "their view" become "your view" without provoking any protests?

As such, it is a way to unpack and reveal how dominant, hegemonic perspectives are "taught" to a culture, at times slipping past critical thinking skills since it is all 'just entertainment.' This includes heteronormative, racially and sexually biased views that support the dominant culture. Classically, it was women's "to-be-seenness" that was the topic of gaze construction. This includes how women view themselves through a male lens. Women are taught to see the world, in this view, through an idealized male perspective, focusing primarily on appearance and availability. As such, "psychoanalysis offers a theory of hiding, displacing, and identification" that is helpful in viewing the production and consumption of media products, whether they are cinematic or not (Saper, 1991, p. 57). Saper (1991, p. 56) notes that "cinema … represents a perfect example of how a culture naturalizes ideology: it makes social constructions into natural facts." This is true of all mainstream media, particularly those forms that appeal to commonly held interests, generically defined ideals, and stereotypical race, gender, sexuality, and other stereotypes. Apparatus theorists extend and deepen Mulvey's by interrogating where they gaze originates, in confrontational terms (for more, see Saper, 1991).

The assumption of a heteronormative gaze of media producers, such as film directors and cinematographers, is for the intended primary audience of heterosexual men. This theory has been adapted and challenged over the years, although the reality of Hollywood is that this remains the primary gaze in terms of which films get made and who directs them.

Saper (1991, p. 32) posits that the "gaze is in trouble. After enjoying many years as one of the most influential concepts in film theory, it now seems to suffer repeated efforts to extend, reverse, or simply debunk its scope of explanation." What the original theorizations did not include is how or if this gaze is also present when men look at men, women look at women, and how women look at men. de Lauretis (1984, pp. 113–114) noted that "film theorists try to tell me that the gaze is male, the camera eye is masculine, and so my look is also not a woman's. But I don't believe them anymore because now I think I know what it is to look at a film as a woman … because certain films … have somehow managed to inscribe in the film my woman's look." Furthermore, as more films are made by women who focus on stories about women or at least aren't objectifying in the traditional way "women [are] inside the rectangle [of the screen and of ideology] …. women can be outside … the female subject of feminism is in both places at once" (p. 114). Thus the pleasures cinema can deliver is constructed, but can be deconstructed, by consciousness of the gaze, thus a female gaze "crosses through and writes on vision" (Saper, 1991, p. 41). Mulvey's adaptations of Freud's ideas have themselves proven to be adaptable to a wind range of cinematic content and response. At the same time critiques and revisions have led to a more expansive interpretation of Freud's theories as well as extensions of Mulvey's to be more inclusive of a variety of identities and sexualities.

The small screen

Television is a particularly powerful mode of emotional engagement. It is not simply a medium that "extends our reach and security in a world of information" (Silverstone, 1994, p. 19); rather, "it also serves as a psychological object" (Bainbridge, 2019, p. 291). Our consumption of content is ritualized, time is shifted, binging offers an escape, and ever since the COVID-19 pandemic, the consumption of film has via streaming services has increased. The viewing experience is a place where one can suspend disbelief, disrupt everyday routines, content can be shared or consumed alone. "The media come to function as key objects in the management of ideas about selfhood and interpersonal relationships, enabling a creative engagement with the world around us" and also provide an escape from it (p. 35). Freud (1930/1989, p. 732) urged caution:

> People who are receptive to the influence of art cannot set too high a value on it as a source of pleasure and consolation of life. Nevertheless the mild narcosis induced in us by art can do no more than bring about a transient withdrawal from the pressure of vital needs, and it is not strong enough to make us forget real misery.

Drawing on Winnicott (1953), Bainbridge (2011) argues that "television work[s] as a kind of transitional object." For some the engagement is "the first experience of symbol-making and therefore linked to our capacity for playfulness, thought, and creativity" (p. 51). Television can be used as a distraction, a babysitter, a time killer, or an escape. Both our inner worlds and the world outside are brought together in an experience that also extends to other spheres of life such as discussing the program with friends, in chat groups, at work, and on social media. According to Silverstone (1994), watching TV helps us focus our anxiety, dispel fears, and engage in the creative process. While films are excellent forms for analysis, the repetition of series television programs "can become a ritual occupation in everyday life" (Poscheschnik, 2018, p. 1006). In their analysis of *Game of Thrones*, for example, Poscheschnik (2018) notes that even heavily hyped mega-series resonate with us because they draw upon real "societal, cultural, and political fantasies" (p. 1006).

As with other media, television helps shape "the emotionalization of everyday discourses of being" (Bainbridge, 2011, p. 51). Particularly since the 2020 pandemic, the worlds of cinema and television have combined with many previously streaming services creating content (Netflix, Hulu, Amazon). However, there are television programs created before this time that incorporated psychotherapy practice into their storylines. One of the more famous was the HBO hit *The Sopranos* (1999–2007):

> In fact, *The Sopranos* appears to have escalated the rehabilitation of analysis in the cultural imagination. Tony Soprano's encounters with Dr. Melfi in the consulting room cue all kinds of articles including those which scrutinize them such as contemporary tropes of masculinity, the fascination with the criminal mind, how to recognise panic attacks, and the increased take-up of psychotherapy by men in the US as a result of watching the show. (Bainbridge, 2011, p. 45; see also Gabbard, 2002)

Actor Lorraine Bracco, who played Jennifer Melfi, received an award from the American Psychological Association in 2010 for authentically representing therapy (Observer, 2010, p. 6).

The idea that therapy should fix everything all the time is part of the theme of Tony's visits to Dr. Melfi. He complains about how much sessions cost—"fa what!" "He blames her almost every time he has a panic attack; in his eyes, the fact that they keep happening means that whatever she's doing, it isn't working" (Schwartz, 2020, para. 1). Is Tony fixated on his mother and his childhood as Melfi senses? According to psychiatrist Glenn O. Gabbard, Tony would be incredibly difficult to diagnose (in Schwartz, 2020). Melfi diagnoses him with antisocial personality disorder (APD), also called sociopathy. What is APD? This is someone who "consistently shows no regard for right and wrong … ignores the rights and feelings of others …" and demonstrates "no guilt or remorse" for what they do (Mayo Clinic. Para. 3).

The relationship between Tony Soprano and Dr. Melfi also represents the patient/doctor relationship with its inherent tensions. Melfi is legally obligated to report anything she hears that could put others in danger, but can she? At what risk to her own safety? What if she says the wrong thing to a mobster? There's also a type of attraction between the two, but Melfi does not give in to that. This is an illustration of an aspect of transference, a concept developed by Freud and Breuer (1895). This is the act of a client transferring past emotions, attractions, desires, and fantasies onto another in any type of relationship, but particularly so during therapy when we might be especially vulnerable and open. Countertransference is the therapist's reaction to those projections. Often, they can become entangled.

Melfi does help Tony with his panic attacks, dig into his many difficult relationships, and help manage his anger. According to Gabbard (qtd. in Schwarts, 2020, para. 10):

> He had a place in her office where he could actually look at emotions without changing the subject, turning away—he had to focus on the feelings he had about things that had happened in his life. She helped him grow in self-understanding. He had a better sense of who he was and what he was trying to accomplish in life, instead of just being a very shallow guy who never had any deep thoughts, but only tried to get by and make money and do what he had to do. So she created a more humanistic version of him.

Selling Sex

> Whoever understands the human mind knows that hardly anything is harder for a man than to give up a pleasure which he as once experienced. Actually we can never give anything up; we only exchange one thing for another. What appears to be a renunciation is really the formation of a substitute or a surrogate.
>
> Freud (1908)

Research suggests that consumers are exposed to between 4,000–10,000 digital selling messages per day (Simpson, 2017) and another few thousand in print and more traditional forms. Advertising is about selling things, ideas, services, and candidates, and importantly, about selling things about ourselves to ourselves. But, as Jhally (1990, p. 1) reminds us, "we should not let its enormous presence in a wide variety of realms obscure what it is *really* about." The relationship is a deep one, between people, objects, and ideas about objects and ourselves. The strategies professional communicators use to accomplish these associations are deeply psychological. Forest (2016, p. 339) argues that "attention is a perfect path to the unconscious mind" and that "the advertisement is all the more effective because it does so unbeknownst to the subject." I am not arguing on behalf of the subliminal power of advertising; that has been disproven many times over.[5] However, there is plenty of evidence that some forms of advertising are created in ways that are designed to bypass our more critical (ego-based) thought processes and target deeper, more primitive perhaps, id-based desires. There was a moment, in the early 20th century, when advertising in the United States turned from mostly promoting positive aspects of products, that were largely functional based on reason-why appeals, to strategically persuasive speech, that is, propaganda (see Ewen, 1976).[6] Competition increased with more products on the market and there were those in the category of desires versus needs and this required a new type of selling, one that could access deeper recesses of the human mind. "Advertising integrated the consumer within a rich and complex web of social status and symbolic meaning" (Jhally, 1990, p. 3).

A psychoanalytic approach to understanding advertising is a profound way of unpacking the strategies and tactics used by advertisers and the potential impact on consumers. Dream-like in their fictional story-telling (except perhaps in testimonials), ads "are structured like dreams" (Forest, 2016, p. 339). That most ads are designed to reach a wide variety of people targeting them based on demographics (quantifiable information such as age, race, sex, and education) and psychographics (psychological profiles such as attitudes, beliefs, interests, opinions, and activities), they also reflect a *collective* unconscious. The collective unconscious was a concept expanded on by Carl Jung, but Freud also envisioned individual psychological concepts such as repression as they applied to entire cultures and societies.

Denotative meanings (Barthes, 1964/1977, p. 12) are the surface level of the advertisement, that which everyone in a particular demographic or psychographic target audience would recognize. From there, the connotative, feeling-level work begins. This is the domain of deeper-level associations that come to seem like common sense, even though the emotion or behavior might have nothing to do with the product. Take the example of a fragrance. There is nothing to say that a particular perfume or aftershave will make one more attractive or appealing, but through connotative techniques, such as showing someone as beguiling, sexy, or attracting others, the association comes to be fixed between the product and its sexy connotations. Budweiser uses horses and cute puppies to sell beer. The connection? The connection must be created between a felt sense and the product using emotions and the appeal of charismatic animals, particularly young animals who are neotinized. "The object of a dream, like that of an advertisement, is to awaken desire by association" (Forest, 2016, p. 340). Advertisements depend on stimulating pleasure that "then awakens desire, and finally, via the product, offers a means of satisfying said desire" p. 30). Williams (1980, p. 185) supposed that

> [i]f we were sensibly materialist, in that part of our living in which we use things, we should find most advertising to be of insane irrelevance. Beer would be enough for us, without the additional promise that in drinking it we show ourselves to be manly, young at heart or neighborly. A washing machine would be a useful machine to wash clothes, rather than an indication that we are forward looking or an object of envy to our neighbors. But if these associations sell beer and washing machines, as some of the evidence suggestions, it is clear that we have a cultural pattern in which the objects are not enough but must be validated, if only in fantasy, by association with social and personal meanings …

This is similar to Freud's (1915/1994, pp. 150–151) dream analyses in which "special techniques have been evolved, with the purpose of bringing about such changes in the play of mental forces that would otherwise give rise to unpleasure may on this occasion result in pleasure; … as a rule the repression is only temporarily removed and is promptly reinstated."

Due to the influence of strategic marketing and advertising, consumers are increasingly reframing wishes as needs. Under consumer capitalism, these "needs" must be constantly created, re-created, and reinforced to desire, ever and always, the newest, the latest, the most exciting version.

Forest (2016) identifies several steps to accomplish this bypassing.

1. "Oniricization of the advertising" (p. 341). This is where the ad promises something, some qualities, some outcome (popularity, for example) that is staged. "The prevalence of sexual themes, or more broadly, themes linked to *encounters* is clear here since they are easy entry points to individual fantasies" (p. 341). Desire is stimulated for a thing, a service, an experience.
2. Better yet, to reach a *repressed* desire via a "metaphorical synthesis modeled on dreams" (p. 342). Logos and brand building are examples here where the associated feelings are transferred to a brand/image (athleticism, success, Nike).

The point is to surpass conscious thoughts that might interfere with the selling message and reach underlying desires through unrealistic promises (be popular, loved, handsome/beautiful, successful, forever young). Barthes (1964) in "Rhetoric of the Image," traces this process in an advertisement for Panzani products. The advertisement features a red background and a toppled-over net grocery carrier filled to overflowing with Pasta, fresh tomatoes, red bell peppers, onions shredded cheese, and other sauce-making ingredients. Barthes notes that there is in all visual communication linguistic meanings that are denoted (obvious such as product labels) and connoted (deeper level such as what the word Panzani connotes, which is Italianicity). There is also a symbolic message (connoted), these are nonliguistic carriers of meaning such as a what a full bag of ingredients means (successful shopping), red background, tomatoes, peppers Italianicity, culinary production, and the overall presentation as a still-life. Third is the literal meaning of the items, the objects as objects but as re-presentations: tomato image of a tomato.

The link becomes signifier (the real item) to signified (what it means) thus becomes concretized, channeled in the direction preferred by the advertiser. The meaning is no longer arbitrary. This perfume *will* make you sexy; this diet *will* make you more attractive; this car *will* make you popular. The male gaze is a theory that corresponds with Freud's theories of voyeurism and scopophilia (see Chapter 4). Briefly, this theory posits that much media, in particular advertising and film, are created by men and the way of looking at the subject of the view is created for male heterosexual pleasure, supporting heterosexuality as the norm. "This 'photographic contract,' like the 'cinematic contract,' appears to operate as a cultural mechanism for producing and securing a female subject who desires to be desired by men—the ideal, fully oedipalized, heterosexual woman" (Fuss, 1992, p. 713). Recent years have seen a shift in this, but it hasn't, by a long shot, gone away as the dominate gaze. This "'concealed' ideological project—to fashion female viewers to consume the product by (over) identifying with the image," has been the foundation of much advertising, no matter the product (p. 713).

If everything in Freud's view is connected to sex (although we know his theories are more expansive than that; see Berger, 2019), it is no surprise then that it is said in advertising that sex sells, and it is partly true. Research shows that if there is too much sex, the advertisement is too sexy, and audiences remember the sex, but not necessarily the brand (Wirtz, Sparks, & Zimbres, 2017). What explains this? Through a Freudian lens, we see that the part of our brain that registers this primal urge (id) will overwhelm the more mediating part of our brains (ego) and a viewer won't remember the product, only the sex, or rather the sexy feeling generated by the ad. It is this pleasure drive Freud described in theories of development (see Chapter 2) as fundamental to human beings as satisfying urges, particularly forbidden ones, resonates in the pleasure centers of the brain.

Fragrance to Foreign Policy: PR

> Years ago, Americans grabbed toast and coffee for breakfast. Public-relations pioneer Edward Bernays changed that.
>
> Spiegel (2005, para. 1)

In 1905 the world was changing rapidly and growing widely. In a special series, National Public Radio referred to it as "Science's Miracle Year." 1905 was Albert Einstein's "year of miracles" (Harris, 2005). He published papers (four *Annus Mirabilis* papers in *Annalen der Physik* [Leipzig]—March 18, May 11, June 30, and September 27) that changed the way we saw the nature of light, of the universe, of ourselves, and introduced the now-famous equation $E = mc^2$, which was foundational work for modern theoretical physics (Harris, 2005). It was also the year Freud's *Three Essays on Theory of Sexuality* were published. As noted in Chapter 1, Freud was fascinated with physics, with the exchange of energies and saw the human body and mind as similarly energized. Also at this time, the way products, ideas, and political powers were expressed also changed radically. Freud's many concepts such as repression, pleasure drives, longings in need of satisfaction, and so forth became the tools of public relations, which (like advertising) still uses these terms today.

Public relations, defined as "strategic communication process that builds mutually beneficial relationships between organizations and their publics" ("About Public Relations"), focuses on presenting a positive public image to target groups, coordinating information during crises, managing online, social media, and internal corporate communications, and community relations. The focus is on persuasion, directing or redirecting people's thoughts, beliefs, considerations, and eventually behavior to fall in line with corporate goals.

The origins of professional public relations are typically credited to one man: Edward Bernays, Sigmund Freud's nephew. In fact, Bernays "was Freud's nephew twice over, his mother being Freud's sister and his father's sister Freud's wife" (Justman, 1994, p. 458). Bernays spent summers with his uncle, who gifted his nephew a copy of *General Introductory Lectures* and a box of Havana cigars. He studied agricultural science at Cornell University but became fascinated by shaping and directing public views. He coined the term "public relations counsel" in 1923 (Weaver, Motion, & Roper, p. 7). The predominant vision of human beings at the time was that we are essentially rational beings. Freud, however, believed while we could appear rational, underneath there was the muck and mire of instincts, desires, and longings, that were suppressed and repressed for us to succeed in a so-called civilized society. Despite the greatest efforts, however, our essential humanness seeps out. Desire for sex, the need for security, and outlet urges are part of every human being. Bernays soaked up discussions he had with his uncle each summer. According to Ann Bernays, his granddaughter, he believed that if you want to persuade someone of something, get them to behave in a certain way, believe in certain things, or change their behaviors, you must connect with deeper emotions. An example of how he did this occurred in the 1920s, when one of Bernays' clients was the Beechnut company, whose primary product at the time was bacon. The company wanted to increase sales. Mass production was rolling, people were working, children were in school, and meals like breakfast were quick. As Alix Spiegel (2005) reported (see quotation at the beginning of this section), the average American breakfast changed due to the influence of public relations. The now-familiar bacon and eggs breakfast was "like so many things in America, systematically engineered by a public relations agent" (Spiegel,

2005, 01.38). Coffee, juice, and toast. How to generate an appetite for bacon? Whereas many campaigns at the time focused on putting a product on sale. Bernays created a campaign that appealed to the desire for comfort, for nourishment. He gathered expert opinions for arguments he crafted. For example, he surveyed doctors asking if they recommended a hearty or light breakfast. Hearty, they replied. Bernays ran with this, formulating an educational campaign for bacon and eggs for breakfast, "He redefined the whole way America thought about breakfast that persists today" (Spiegel, 2005, 04:58). Whereas appeals in advertising prior to this time had largely emulated journalism through reason-why statements full of information, Bernays' knowledge of the mind, of the unconscious, brought about an epochal shift in persuasion strategies.

Relating to the public, understanding the group mind (see Bernays, 1928) was central to Bernays' strategies. His book *Public Relations* (1952, p. 2) draws on his uncle's theories about how individuals in many ways have not adjusted to the requirements of modern life. Bernays there relates how "[s]ociety has become more complex, and its processes have been speeded up over the last few centuries. The rate of progress of the many forces that make up society has been uneven, with consequently increased maladjustment and tension" (p. 1). Using psychoanalysis, he "came up with a hypothesis that, by understanding the group's mind, it would be possible to manipulate human behavior without their realizing it. So, to test his hypothesis, he launched his most famous public relations campaign- convincing women to smoke" (Held, 2009, para. 5) and that smoking was a form of liberation.[7] Based on his understanding of people as most reachable through baser, more pleasure-oriented instincts, and bypassing critical thinking, they could be sold products, ideas, and political candidates. In 1929, women were not allowed to smoke in public, and those who did were considered sexually promiscuous. American Tobacco Company president George Washington Hill wanted to expand the market for his Lucky Strike cigarette brand. Bernays consulted with Dr. A. A. Brill, a fan of Freud who told him that, to women, cigarettes were a symbol of power, particularly male power. Thus came the "Torches of Freedom" campaign which premiered in New York on March 31, 1929, in the Easter Parade. Bernays convinced debutantes (provided by *Vogue* magazine) that they could demonstrate their liberation by lighting up in public places. The press was tipped off in advance that the parade would be coming down Manhattan's Fifth Avenue, and the event would be newsworthy. Women of course weren't freed at all and came to be addicted to smoking the same as men, but Bernays used the opportunity of frustration with sex-based restrictions to promote his client. Justman (1994, p. 459) describes Bernays' impact:

> Bernays got his start staging a media event in a campaign against venereal disease and sexual hypocrisy. He created a fashion for Spanish combs. He promoted Lithuanian independence and salad dressing, Cartier jewels and racial equality. He organized a moderation craze. Always he pulled strings. He was the one, it appears, behind the carving of Ivory soap in schools—he was the Oz behind the curtain. He orchestrated a celebration of Edison that has been called "one of the most astonishing pieces of propaganda ever engineered in this country during peace time" (Doob qtd. In Bernays, 1965). He agitated for measures to counteract the severe deflation of the early 1930s. In his work for the American Tobacco Company, his invisible hand got physicians to issue findings favorable to tobacco. He stage managed a Fifth Avenue demonstration under the banner of women's rights, and in the midst of the Depression got fashionable New York to go crazy over green, which happened to be the color of a pack of Lucky Strikes. Like an industrialist turned public benefactor, Bernays dedicated himself to noble causes in his middle years. Probably his dearest cause was that of public relations itself; he began promoting it, and not incidentally himself, in his writings of the twenties, and by old age saw it as one of the highest and most morally demanding of vocations.

Clearly there are ethical issues with Bernays' psychological approach. "Unlike Freud, who strove to allow people to better understand their condition, Bernays sought to impose on people a certain belief through his public relations skills" (Justman, 1994, p. 459).

According to Michael Hammelburger, CEO at The Bottom Line Group:

> When our id develops into superego, consumers are motivated to respond to public relations that impact their emotions and morals. Brands can take advantage of any issue and make the circumstances work for them. For instance, Calm app[8] just announced that it's willing to pay for athlete's fines if they decide not to participate in press conferences. It's a good way to promote one's brand too without hiring a celebrity to promote their brand directly. In our case, we do take advantage of the business issues and trends by using them as an example of what will happen to enterprises that fail to consider spend management strategies in their operations. It makes our PR campaign more relatable and relevant. (qtd. in "What Freud").

While manipulating a collective mindset could be done for positive reasons, such as public health issues, more often it is not, and raises ethical concerns. Hammelburger (2021, para. 6) notes that Bernays lacked a complete understanding of his uncle's theories, in particular concerning women and minorities:

> For instance, Bernays' propaganda work in the Guatemalan Coup of 1954 was a total success by American commercial standards but proved disastrous for future generations of Latin American people and contributed to the growing negative ethnosociological issues still experienced today.

Bernays advocated for licensure for public relations professionals, offered important organizational advice, but it is adoption of psychoanalytic theory, whether he called it that or not, that most influenced public relations strategies and tactics then and today. Freud, however, was not pleased with the use of his ideas in this way. He did not support commercialization of psychoanalytic theory. In fact, Bernays proposed ways to earn a quick buck to his uncle who saw so as very American and vulgar. "When Bernays sent Freud a copy of his first book, *Crystallizing Public Opinion* (1923), Freud's terse response was, "I have received your book. … As a truly American production it interested me greatly" (cited in Justman, 1994, p. 465). Bernays did help Freud get his works published in the United States and tried to interest his uncle in publishing popular press articles for magazines such as *Cosmopolitan*. Freud refused and was in fact disgusted by the idea.

While one can't control how others might use or interpret one's work, there is evidence that Nazi propagandist Joseph Goebbels used and applied Bernays' books. Of course this is not something the field is proud of, and Thompson (2017, p. 52) notes that "no papers have been offered on the topic during 7 years of the International History of Public Relations conferences," despite Bentele's (1997) model. "One explanation … is unease at the 'highly effective and catastrophic application and development of propaganda theory by Hitler and his Nazi propaganda chief' including the 'propagandist psychological manipulation' associated with Bernays and other US public relations practitioners" (Weaver, Motion, & Roper, 2006, p. 10). Communications used in this way is a darker side of the practice of persuasion, although many might argue, using psychological techniques to persuade is in and of itself unethical. As Weaver, Motion, and Roper (2006, p. 7) remark, "public relations, although widely practiced by corporations and governments alike, has monumentally failed to establish itself as of a positive social utility and benefit." However, that the field uses psychologically based strategies makes it worthy of interrogation. The connection between Bernays and Freud makes it an important aspect of media and communications to explore. Defenders say the public relations field is misunderstood, that it is more than propaganda or spin, and can be used legitimately. To propagandize, they argue, is not necessarily lying or manipulating what defenders say. Given that truth is a social construction one could argue untruths can be propagandized (for more on this see Foucault, 1980). Thus, "communication as terrorism" is a growing area of research (Thompson, 2017). This discussion of course situates the foundation of PR in the past, in its history. Do Freud's theories, or more broadly, a psychoanalytic approach, continue to appear as strategies in campaigns? Chapter 4 includes an example of this.

As discussed so far, several media platforms have used Freud's theories or psychoanalysis as a foundation for building storylines, slogans, and campaigns. Also relevant is how Freud himself has been presented in media content. Below are a few of these re-presentations.

Portrayals of Freud and Psychoanalysis

For decades, Freud and his ideas have been included in popular culture and media. Bainbridge (2011) studied media representations of psychoanalysis in the UK national press (400 articles) and changing attitudes toward it over a twenty-year period (1989–2009). They found that "'therapy culture' had become entrenched in the mediatization of everyday life" (p. 32), and practice and presentation of psychotherapy relate to consumers' inner worlds. Furthermore, Bainbridge (2011) found a generally negative view of psychoanalysis in the press, in fact the process of deep psychological inquiry presented as a threat:

> The negative dismissal of psychoanalysis in the press, then, can be seen to represent a symbolic destruction of this threat, killing off the object that threatens to engulf us in this way. As a new, highly mediated sensibility has emerged, however, the attendant emphasis on narcissistic structures of being reflected in the enthusiasm for new media technologies such as those linked to social networking ironically permits a turn inward and the domains of psychological and emotional experience come to the fore, as my case study analysis has indicated. (p. 53)

Broadcast media such as films and television shows have attempted to portray Freud's theories and even the man himself. The silent film *Blind Alley* (1939), for example, is "an important early work in which the psychiatrist is portrayed as a godlike figure" ("Sigmund Freud," 1998). *Freud: The Secret Passion* (1962), directed by John Huston, stars Montgomery Clift as Freud. Philosopher, screenwriter, and activist Jean-Paul Sartre (1905–1980) wrote two early drafts of the screenplay. "Clift's serious, respectful portrayal of Sigmund Freud avoids caricature and Susannah York artfully plays his attractive guinea pig, a fictional amalgam of several of Freud's female patients" ("Sigmund Freud," 1998). York's character is a composite patient that illustrates many of Freud's case studies. According to the Library of Congress, Huston's inspiration for the film came because he "saw firsthand how neurotic symptoms can be triggered by a traumatic event while making the documentary *Let There Be Light* (about WWII veterans recovering from what then called 'shell shock').

Hysteria: Or Fragments of an Analysis of an Obsessional Neurosis (Johnson, 1993) is a two-hour British comedy by Terry Johnson. The play fictionalizes an actual 1938 meeting between Salvador Dalí and Sigmund Freud.

Another film is *The Seven Percent Solution* (1976),[9] which is based on a 1974 novel by Nicholas Myer. Actors Robert Duvall and Nicol Williamson play Dr. Watson and Sherlock Holmes, respectively. Watson believes Holmes has become delusional due to cocaine use and believes a professor is actually a criminal mastermind, played by Laurence Olivier). Watson tricks Holmes into traveling to Vienna where he is treated by Freud (Alan Arkin). Various adventures are had, crimes investigated, and subconscious secrets revealed.

The ghost of Freud appears in the 1983 American romantic comedy *lovesick* (Brickman, dir.). Sir Alec Guinness plays the ghost of Sigmund Freud who visits psychoanalyst Saul Benjamin (Dudley Moore) offering advice and warnings.

A six-part 1984 BBC television serial, *Freud: The Life of a Dream*, begins in 1938 when the Freud family arrives in London after fleeing Vienna. Through a series of flashbacks, the episodes show important moments in Freud's life and profession, ending with his death in 1939. *The Death of Salvador Dali* (2005) is an 18-minute fantasy short in which Dalí consults Freud on how to best represent madness in his art.

Mahler on the Couch (2010) (German) is a historical drama that focuses on Freud analysis of composer Gustav Mahler.[10] The film focuses on the affair between Mahler's wife, Alma, had with Walter Gropius, a German/American architect and founder of the Bauhaus School.

A Dangerous Method (2011), directed by David Cronenberg, stars Viggo Mortensen (Freud), Keira Knightly (Sabina Spielrein), and Michael Fassbender (C. J. Jung). The screenplay was based on the 2002 play *The Talking Cure* which came from the 1993 non-fiction work *A Most Dangerous Method: The Story of Jung, Freud, and Sabina Spielrein*. The film takes place in 1904, when Spielrein, becomes a patient at the Swiss psychiatric hospital Burghölzli. Spielrein's "hysteria" is the symptom in need of treatment by a young Dr. Carl Jung and she is helped through dream analysis and word association. The film mostly focuses on the dynamic between Jung and Spielrein but features Freud when the two doctors travel to the United States. The film is a good example of the process of transference and explores the break between Jung and Freud.

"Freud," a 2020 Netflix show (Austrian German), came out just in time for pandemic lockdown binge viewing. Described by one reviewer as a "ridiculous coked-up mess" (Horton, 2020), "the legendary psychologist is recast as a coke-fiend witch hunter who uses hypnosis to solve crimes in 19th century Vienna because … why not?" This eight-part historical fiction series stars Robert Finster as Freud who practices his hypnosis on his housekeeper Lenore (played by Brigitte Kern). Without spoiling it, the series does enact the frustration Freud felt, having developed sophisticated theories that were not taken seriously by his colleagues. In the series Freud resorts to coaching Lenore to prove to disbelievers that they are wrong about his methods. The mutilated body of a prostitute is delivered to Freud, given his training as a physician. He embarks on an investigation of her murder, meeting all types of repressed individuals along the way. Freud attends a séance, becomes involved with the medium Fleur Salmone (Ella Rumpf), and goes on a number of adventures. "The main show is the slurp of creepy, disturbing manifestations of repressed psyches coalescing into, by the later episodes, a nonsensical yet amusing horror show" (Horton, 2020, para. 6).

News and New Media

Can a psychoanalytic lens be used to understand how news is reported and interpreted? It would seem so. The subject has barely been considered, perhaps a failing of both Freudian theory and journalism studies. Despite claims of "objectivity" in reporting, no doubt reporters' interests impact the stories they pitch to their editors, which stories editors assign, and which stories appeal to audience members. How about digital media? Johanssen (2018) used psychoanalytic theory to explore the concept of affective-digital labor. Drawing on Freud they describe how "affect can be understood as a subjective, bodily experience which is in tension with the discursive and denotes a momentary feeling of bodily dispossession" (p. 22). Affective experiences of persons with facial disfigurements were the subject of interviews.

In a special issue of *Communication and Media* (2016, p. 5), editors Krüger and Johanssen posit "that psychoanalysis offers a reservoir of conceptual and methodological tools that have not been sufficiently tapped. Psychoanalytic perspectives offer a heightened concern and sensibility for the unconscious, that is, the element in human relating and relatedness that crisscrosses and mars our best laid plans and reasonable predictions." This connects to a more recent, lesser studied focus in media studies which is the audience, or "implicit notions" of subjectivity (Dahlgren, 2013, p. 72). This argument suggests that audiences, in their preferences, choices, and interpretations, lean toward or intend to lean toward rational thinking and choices. But as discussed in the public relations section, other parts of psychological makeup exert as, if not more, powerful push toward pleasures and satisfying desires. Thus a call for using psychoanalytic theory to examine "communicative modes beyond the rational" (p. 82). Taking this approach beyond individual-level producer or consumer, consistent with Freud's argument of there also being collective repression, suppression, and libido. It is "the movement of information and communication technology ever closer to the human body and into each and every aspect of everyday life." Psychoanalysis is integral to, and thus subject of the next chapter.

Chapter 4 includes examples of using a psychoanalytic approach not only for what they say about theories but also to provide ideas for studies that future scholars might wish to undertake in several areas and across platforms.

Notes

1 Link to video: https://youtu.be/1dgLEDdFddk.

2 See Joseph Campbell's work on mythology and heroes. For example, in Campbell (1949/2008).

3 Ernst L. Freud's son, Lucien (1922–2011), became a famous artist in his own right. A painter Lucian's early work was in surrealism but he later gravitated to realism. His work can be found in a number of collections: http://lucianfreud.com/lucian-freud-archive---public-collections.html.

4 For an extensive discussion of fashion and psychoanalysis, visit London's Freud Museum web page for recordings from the conference Fashion and Psychoanalysis: An international

interdisciplinary conference @ https://www.freud.org.uk/2017/10/15/fashion-psychoanalysis-international-conference/.

5 For a long while there was belief that subliminal advertising exists and works. There is some evidence of course that we can be influenced outside of our awareness but that we act on that, without thinking, is debated. For more on this see Zimmerman (2014).

6 For a complete discussion of the use of the term "propaganda" see M. C. Miller's (2005) introduction to Bernays' (1928) *Propaganda*.

7 The US tobacco company American Tobacco Company was to build their brand identity on this for Virginia Slims.

8 Calm is a software company that produces sleep and meditation related products, including an app.

9 Description and access information available at https://www.imdb.com/title/tt0075194/.

10 Freud and Mahler did in fact meet. Freud and his wife were on vacation and normally would not have their time interrupted by his work. However, Freud was drawn to meet Mahler because of his fame. The men were similar in age, had similar backgrounds, and were interested in the writings of Dostoevsky. It is said that Mahler feared losing his younger wife, his libido was reduced, thus he sought out Freud. Also to help Mahler cope with his wife's affair with Gropius. Freud and Mahler's "therapy" session was conducted during a long walk in which they made an immediate connection. For more on this see Mahlerfoundation.org).

References

About public relations. Public Relations Society of America. https://www.prsa.org/about/all-about-pr

Ackerman, C. E. (2018). *Psychoanalysis: A brief history of Freud's psychoanalytic theory*. https://positivepsychology.com/psychoanalysis/

Anwar, F. (1994, 1 September). You must be out of your mind. *The Guardian*, T6.

Anzieu, D. (1986). *Freud's self-analysis* (P. Graham, Trans.). Madison, CT: International Universities Press. (Original work published 1975)

Bainbridge, C. (2011). From "The Freud Squad" to "The Good Freud Guide": A genealogy of media images of psychoanalysis and reflections on their role in the public imagination. *Free Associations: Psychoanalysis and Culture, Media, Groups, Politics*, 62, 31–59.

Bainbridge, C. (2019). Television as psychical object: *Mad Men* and the value of psychoanalysis for television scholarship. *Critical Studies in Television*, *14*(3), 289–306.

Bainbridge, C., & Yates, C. (Eds.). (2015). *Media and the inner world. Psychocultural approaches to emotion, media, and popular culture*. Basingstoke: Palgrave Macmillan.

Bancroft, A. (2012). *Fashion and psychoanalysis*. London: Bloomsbury Publishing. See also: https://www.bloomsburycollections.com/book/fashion-and-psychoanalysis-styling-the-self/introduction

Barthes, R. (1964/1977). *Elements of semiology*. New York: Farrar, Straus, and Giroux.

Berger, A. A. (2019). *Media analysis techniques*. Thousand Oaks, CA: Sage.

Bernays, E. (1928). *Propaganda*. New York: Horace Liveright.

Bernays, E. (1954). *Public relations*. Norman: University of Oklahoma Press.

Bevington, D. (2008). *Shakespeare's ideas: More things in heaven and earth*. New York: Wiley-Blackwell.

Braga, A., & Logan, R. K. (2013). Mind and media: Exploring the Freud-McLuhan connection. *Explorations in Media Ecology*, *12*(3/4), 159–170.

Brickman, M. (director). (1983). *Lovesick* [Motion Picture]. Warner Bros.

Brooks, P. (2000). Introduction. In P. Brooks & A. Woloch (Eds.), *Whose Freud? The place of psychoanalysis in contemporary culture* (pp. 1–12). New Haven, CT: Yale University Press.

Brown, B. R. (2012, March 15). *Lecture six: Fetishism and popular culture: Umberto Eco's Casablanca*. Cultural Studies Introductory Lectures. http://culturalstudieslectures.blogspot.com/2012/03/fetishism-and-popular-culture-umberto.html

Campbell, J. (1949/2008). *The hero with a thousand faces* (3rd ed.). Novato, CA: New World Library.

Cavell, R. (2002). *McLuhan in space*. Toronto: University of Toronto Press.

Crane, D. (2012). *Fashion and its social agendas: Class, gender, and identity in clothing*. Chicago: University of Chicago.

Cumming, V. (2004/2021). *Understanding fashion history*. London: Chrysalis Books Group.

Cumming, V., Cunnington, C. W., & Cunnington, P. E. (2010). *The dictionary of fashion history*. New York: Berg.

A dangerous method. (2011). D. Cronenberg (dir.). Lago Film.

Death of Salvador Dali, The. (2005). D. Bishop (dir.).

De Berg, H. (2003). *Freud's theory and its use in literary and cultural studies*. Rochester, NY: Camden.

De Lauretis, T. (1984). *Technologies of gender: Essays on theory, film, fiction*. Bloomington: Indiana University Press.

Doob, L. (1935). *Propaganda: Its psychology and technique*. New York: Henry Holt & Co.

Elsasser, T. (2009). Freud as a media theorist. Mystic writing-pads and the matter of memory. *Screen*, 50(1), 100–113.

Elliott, A. (2004). *Social theory since Freud: Traversing social imaginaries*. New York: Taylor & Frances.

Etcoff, N. (2000). *Survival of the prettiest: The science of beauty*. New York: Anchor.

Ford, R. T. (2022). *Dress codes: How the laws of fashion made history*. New York: Simon & Schuster.

Freud Museum. London, UK. https://www.freud.org.uk/

Freud, S. (1889). *The interpretation of dreams*.

Freud, S. (1905). *The joke and its relation to the unconscious* (J. Crick, Trans.). New York: Penguin.

Freud, S. (1906). *The complete psychological works of Sigmund Freud* (Vol. 9). London: Vintage.

Freud, S. (1908/1989). Creative writers and day-dreaming. In P. Gay (Ed.), *The Freud reader* (pp. 436–443). New York: W. W. Norton.

Freud, S. (1909/1988). Freud and fetishism: Previously unpublished minutes of the Vienna Psychoanalytic Society. *Psychoanalysis Quarterly*, *LVII*, 155–156.

Freud, S. (1910/1990). *Leonardo da Vinci and a memory of his childhood*. New York: W. W. Norton.

Freud, S. (1922). *Delusion & dream*. New York: Moffat, Yard, & Co.
Freud, S. (1923). Two encyclopaedia articles. *Standard Edition, 18*, 235–262.
Freud, S. (1914/1989). The Moses of Michelangelo. In P. Gay (Ed.), *The Freud reader* (pp. 522–539). New York: W. W. Norton.
Freud, S. (1915). *The unconscious*. New York: Penguin.
Freud, S. (1919/2003). *The uncanny* (D. Mclintok, Trans.). New York: Penguin.
Freud, S. (1927). *Miscellaneous papers, 1888–1938. Vol. 5 of Collected papers* (pp. 198–204). London: Hogarth.
Freud, S. (1928). Dostoevsky and parricide. In *Standard edition* (Vol. 21, pp. 173–196). New York: Vintage.
Freud, S. (1930/1989). Civilization and its discontents. In P. Gay (Ed.), *The Freud reader* (pp. 722–772). New York: W. W. Norton.
Freud, S. (1930/2017). *Civilization and its discontents*. Vienna: Internationaler Psychoanalytischer Verlag.
Freud, S., & Breuer, J. (1895). *Studies in hysteria*. Penguin Books.
"Freud's Self-Analysis." Press Release. Encyclopedia.com. Cengage. https://www.encyclopedia.com/psychology/dictionaries-thesauruses-pictures-and-press-releases/freuds-self-analysis
Fuss, D. (1992). Fashion and the homospectatorial look. *Critical Inquiry, 18*(4), 713–737.
Gabbard, G. O. (2020, July 31). Qtd. in D. Schwartz. *We asked psychiatrists if Tony Soprano's shrink is good at her job*. Vice. https://www.vice.com/en/article/ep4mqn/is-tony-sopranos-therapist-jennifer-melfi-good-at-her-job
Gabbard, G. O. (2002). *The psychology of The Sopranos: Love, death, desire, and betrayal in America's favorite gangster family*. New York: Basic Books.
Germov, J., & Williams, L. (1999). Dieting women: Self-surveillance and the body panopticon. In D. Maurer (Ed.), *Weighty issues: Fatness and thinness as social problems* (pp. 117–132). New York: Transaction.
Gornick, V. (2019, April 19). Five best: Lisa Gornick on Freud in fiction. *Wall Street Journal*. https://www.wsj.com/articles/five-best-lisa-gornick-on-freud-in-fiction-
Hall, S. (1973). *Encoding and decoding in the television discourse* (CCCS Stenciled Paper No. 7). Birmingham, UK: Centre for Contemporary Cultural Studies.
Hall, S. (1980). Encoding/decoding. In S. Hall, D. Hobson, A. Lowe, & P. Willis (Eds.), *Culture, media, language* (pp. 128–138). London: Hutchinson.
Hammelburger, M. (2021, June 28). *What Freud can teach entrepreneurs about public relations*. PRontheGo. https://medium.pronthego.com/what-freud-can-teach-entrepreneurs-about-public-relations-85bb6ca96ec4
Hampton, C. (2003). *The talking cure*. New York: Faber & Faber.
Harris, R. (2005, March 17). *Albert Einstein's year of miracles: Light Theory* (Morning Edition). National Public Radio. https://www.npr.org/2005/03/17/4538324/albert-einsteins-year-of-miracles-light-theory
Haughton, H. (2003). Introduction. In S. Freud (Ed.), *The uncanny* (1899). New York: Penguin.
Held, L. (2009). Psychoanalysis shapes consumer culture. *APA Monitor*. https://www.apa.org/monitor/2009/12/consumer

Hoffeld, J. (1973, March 11). The aesthetics of Freud. *New York Times*. https://www.nytimes.com/1973/03/11/archives/the-aesthetics-of-freud-a-study-in-psychoanalysis-and-art-by-jack-j.html

Hollander, A. (1993). *Seeing through clothes*. Berkeley: University of California Press.

Horton, A. (2020, March 23). Freud review—Netflix revisionist drama is a ridiculous coked-up mess. *The Guardian*. https://www.theguardian.com/tv-and-radio/2020/mar/23/freud-netflix-review-historical-fiction-thriller

Huston, J. (Director). (1962). *Freud: The secret passion*. Universal International.

Jhally, S. (1990). *The codes of advertising: Fetishism and the political economy of meaning in the consumer society*. New York: Routledge.

Johanssen, J. (2016). Media research and psychoanalysis: A suggestion. *The International Communication Gazette*, *78*(7), 688–693.

Johanssen, J. (2018). Towards a psychoanalytic concept of affective-digital labour. *Media and Communication*, *6*(3), 22–29.

Johnson, T. (1993). *Hysteria: Or fragments of an analysis of an obsessional neurosis*. London: Royal Court Theatre.

Jones, E. (1957). *The life and work of Sigmund Freud* (Vol. 3). New York: Basic Books.

Justman, S. (1994). Freud and his nephew. *Social Research*, *61*, 457–476.

Kenny, E., & Nichols, E. G. (2017). United States. In *Beauty around the world: A cultural encyclopedia* (pp. 319–321). Santa Barbara, CA: ABC-CLIO.

Krüger, S., & Johanssen, J. (2016). Thinking (with) the unconscious in media and communication studies: Introduction to the special issue. *Communication and Media*, *11*(38), 5–40.

LaForce, T. (2010, January 20). Bossing Freud around. *The New Yorker*. https://www.newyorker.com/books/page-turner/bossing-freud-around

Lear, J. (2005). *Freud* (2nd ed.). New York: Taylor & Francis.

Love Sick. (1983). M. Brickman (dir.). Warner Brothers.

Macaulay, S. (2005, February 3). The kid stays in the picture. *The Times*. Section 2: 11.

Mansfield, N. (2000). *Subjectivity: Theories of the self from Freud to Haraway*. New York: NYU Press.

Masi de Casanova, E. (2015). *Buttoned up: Clothing, conformity, and white collar masculinity*. Ithaca, NY: Cornell University Press.

Mayo Clinic. (n.d.). *Antisocial personality disorder*. https://www.mayoclinic.org/diseases-conditions/antisocial-personality-disorder/symptoms-causes/syc-20353928

McGrath, P. (2008). Introduction. In D. DuMaurier (Ed.), *Don't look now* (pp. vii–xiii). New York: New York Review of Books.

Menand, L. (2017, August 21). Why Freud survives. *The New Yorker*. https://www.newyorker.com/magazine/2017/08/28/why-freud-survives

Menkes, S. (2020, September 9). #Suzypod: In conversation with Valerie Steele, the "Freud of fashion." Creative Conversations. *Vogue*. https://www.vogue.co.uk/fashion/article/suzypod-valerie-steele-the-freud-of-fashion

Merskin, D. (2014). *Sexing the media: How and why we do it*. New York: Peter Lang.

Miller, M. C. (2005). Introduction. In E. Bernays (1928). *Propaganda* (pp. 1–33). Brooklyn, NY: Ig Publishing.

Mulvey, L. (1978). Visual pleasure and narrative cinema. *Screen, 16*(3), 6–18.

Poscheschnik, G. (2018). *Game of Thrones*—A psychoanalytic interpretation including some remarks on the psychosocial function of modern TV series. *International Journal of Psychoanalysis*, 99(4), 1004–1016.

Rank, O. (1914/1999). Der Doppelgänger. In J. M. Fischer (Ed.), *Psychoanalytische Literaturinterpretation* (pp. 104–187). Berlin: Verlag.

Reilly, A., & Barry, B. (2020). (Eds.). *Crossing gender boundaries: Fashion to create, disrupt, and transcend.* London: Intellect.

Saper, C. (1991). A nervous theory: The troubling gaze of psychoanalysis in media studies. *Diacritics, 21*(4), 32–52.

Sassatelli, R. (2011). Interview with Laura Mulvey: Gender, gaze, and technology in film culture. *Theory, Culture, & Society, 28*(5), 123–143.

Schwartz, D. (2020, July 31). We asked psychiatrists if Tony Soprano's shrink is good at her job. *Vice.* https://www.vice.com/en/article/ep4mqn/is-tony-sopranos-therapist-jennifer-melfi-good-at-her-job

Sigmund Freud: Conflict and Culture. Film Series. Library of Congress. https://www.loc.gov/exhibits/freud/film.html

Silverstone, R. (1994). *Television and everyday life.* London: Routledge.

Simpson, J. (2017, August 25). Finding brand success in the digital world. *Forbes.* https://www.forbes.com/sites/forbesagencycouncil/2017/08/25/finding-brand-success-in-the-digital-world/?sh=583cbf4626e2

Sopranos, The. (1997–2007). M. Weiner (dir.) HBO.

Spector, J. T. (2001). On the limits of understanding in modern art: Klee, Miro, Freud. *American Imago*, 58(1), 479–496.

Spellbound. (1945). A. Hitchcock (dir.). Selznik Productions.

Spiegel, A. (2005, April 22). *Freud's nephew and the origins of public relations* (Morning Edition) [Radio broadcast]. National Public Radio. https://www.npr.org/2005/04/22/4612464/freuds-nephew-and-the-origins-of-public-relations

Steele, V. (1997). *Fetish: Fashion, sex, and power.* New York: Oxford University Press.

Steele, V. (2000). *Fifty years of fashion: New look to now.* Yale University Press.

Steele, V. (2022). Definition of fashion. Love to Know. https://fashion-history.lovetoknow.com/alphabetical-index-fashion-clothing-history/definitionn-fashion

Stone, I. (1971). *The passions of the mind.* New York: Doubleday.

The, J. T., Magistretti, P., & Ansermet, F. (2018). The epistemological foundation of Freud's energetics model. *Frontiers in Psychology*, 9, 1861.

Thompson, G. (2017). Parallels in propaganda? A comparative historical analysis of Islamic State and the Nazi party. *Journal of Public Relations Research*, 29(1), 51–66.

Tilkakartne, W. (2022, June 25). Here's how Laura Mulvey changed film theory with the male gaze. MovieWeb. https://movieweb.com/laura-mulvey-changed-film-theory/

Weaver, K., Motion, J., & Roper, J. (2006). From propaganda to discourse (and Back Again): Truth, power and the public interest, and public relations. In J. L'Etang & M. Pieczka (Eds.), *Public relations: Critical debates and contemporary practice* (pp. 7–21). New York, NY: Lawrence Erlbaum Associates.

Webster, B. (2010, January 20). Qtd. in T. LaForce. Bossing Freud around. *The New Yorker*. https://www.newyorker.com/books/page-turner/bossing-freud-around

What Freud can teach entrepreneurs about public relations. PRonthego. https://medium.pronthego.com/what-freud-can-teach-entrepreneurs-about-public-relations-85bb6ca96ec4

Williams, R. (1960, July/August). Advertising: The magic system. *New Left Review*,*4*, 27–32.

Williams, R. (1980). *Problems in materialism and culture*. Verso.

Winnicott, D. W. (1953). Transitional objects and transitional phenomena: A study of the first not-me possession. *The International Journal of Psycho-Analysis*, *34*, 89–97.

Wirtz, J. G., Sparks, J. V., & Zimbres, T. M. (2017). The effect of exposure to sexual appeals in advertisements on memory, attitude, and purchase intention: A meta-analytic review. *International Journal of Advertising*, *37*(2), 168–198.

Zimmerman, I. (2014, June 9). *Subliminal ads, unconscious influence, and consumption*. Psychology Today. https://www.psychologytoday.com/us/blog/sold/201406/subliminal-ads-unconscious-influence-and-consumption

· 4 ·

WHAT WOULD A STUDY LOOK LIKE?

> Melancholy betrays the world for the sake of knowledge.
> But in its tenacious self-absorption it embraces dead objects
> in its contemplation, in order to redeem them …
> The persistence which is expressed in the intention of
> Mourning is born of its loyalty to the world of things.
>
> Walter Benjamin (1977, pp. 156–157)

> Schizophrenia may be a necessary consequence of literacy.
>
> McLuhan (1962, p. 22)

> Psychoanalysis and mass communication are two institutions that shaped the twentieth century.
>
> Braga and Logan (2013, p. 169)

How might one take the contextual and theoretical understandings of Freud's ideas and apply them to media, advertising, and public relations?[1] Previous chapters briefly described Freud's major theories (Chapter 2) and discussed how these theories have been, or could be, used to study media, communications and popular culture content, consumers, and creators (Chapter 3). This chapter presents examples of the application of some of the theories, including a few not amplified in Chapter 2. These are not complete studies; instead, what I offer her are suggestions for students and scholars regarding how this work might be taken forward.

The first section of this chapter discusses the historical and cultural underpinnings to the psychological state of melancholy/cholia and applies this to unpacking meaning in the Freudian rich film *Melancholia* (von Trier, 2011) with a view of what it might mean in terms of the director himself, the conceptualization and execution of the film, and the activities of the main character. This is the longest analysis in this chapter, which is fitting given that film studies is the discipline that has relied most extensively upon psychoanalytic theory. The second section considers advertising and how tools of persuasion to sell something are used with the most obvious and most often applied element of Freud's theories. In this section, I explore how sex can be put to use for advertising through a focused analysis of a recent ad campaign for Gucci. Many of Freud's theories could be considered when it comes to promotional appeals, but the prominence that Freud gives to sex in his explanations for human behavior (he also addressed the role of violence) makes it worthy of continued exploration. The third section focuses on public relations and how Donald Trump's campaign for president of the United States as well as his post-2020 appeals, rely on psychoanalytic techniques to appeal to supporters. In the fourth section of the chapter I outline some important areas for future research. While all media platforms are potentially rich in technologies and content to view through a Freudian lens (as well as the psyches of creators and audiences), some are studied less than others. Suggestions beyond the already rich cinema studies area include fashion, music, public relations, and advertising.

A Freudian analysis of Melancholia

> Watching a well-made film, we don't sit by as spectators; we participate.
>
> Alfred Hitchcock (1936/1995, p. 109)

What does it mean to be melancholy? Is it the same as being sad or depressed? The term originates in the Greek word μέλαινα χολή *melaina chole*. "Melancholia was recognized as early as the time of Hippocrates, and continued through Galenic medicine and medieval times" (Paykel, 2008, p. 279). Typically it refers to deep sadness, moroseness, or wistfulness. The *Merriam Webster* (n.d.) dictionary defines it as follows:

NOUN: 1. a. a. Depression of spirits.
ADJECTIVE: 1. A. Suggestive or expressive of sadness or depression of mind or spirit.

Melancholy can include physical problems, even hallucinations and delusions, and more, varying from darkness to almost an enlightened state. Up until the 18th-century physicians believed it was caused by a buildup of "black bile," linked to the spleen. In his 1621 text titled *The Anatomy of Melancholy*, Robert Burton wrote in detail (900 pages) about the malady in both humorous and medically precise terms. The book, whose full title is *The Anatomy of Melancholy, What It Is: With all the Kinds, Causes, Symptoms, Prognostickes, and Several Cures of It* was republished five times over the following 17 years. It first appears to be a medical textbook dedicated to what was then considered to be a problem of the humors (temperaments), of which there were four: Sanguin, blood (red) was linked to hopefulness Choleric (yellow) associated with anger, bile, Flegmat (phlegm), white, not easily exited, and Melanc (black) bile to melancholy. For more than 2,000 years this view dominated many fields of study including medicine but also philosophy and art (for more on this, see Ferber, 2006; Radden, 2002; Wilson, 2008). During the Renaissance, seen by cultural historians and literary scholars as the "Golden Age of melancholy" (Carrera, 2010, p. 2) with "sorrow and fear … the inseparable companions of melancholy" (p. 21). Yet melancholy was also acknowledged as a state of mind from which inspiration can be drawn. "People did not have melancholy, they *were* melancholic" (Lund, 2021, p. 17). Melancholy was in some quarters thought to "engender a certain kind of creativity born from a deep awareness of the mutability of life and the inevitable cycle of birth and death" (Holly, 2013). The state has been considered as severe mental illness but also as "a fashionable malady among intellectual and political elites" (Carrera, 2010, p. 2).

In the preface to *Anatomy of Melancholy* Burton (1621/1857, p. 18) wrote, "I write of melancholy by being busy to avoid melancholy" for the state of melancholy can also be motivating in an odd way for those who find the fortitude to push through toward the next state of being. Whether as "disposition or in habit," said Burton noted that

> disposition, is that transitory *Melancholy* which goes and comes upon every small occasion of sorrow, need, sickness, trouble, fear, grief, passion, or perturbation of the mind, any manner of care, discontent, or thought, which causes anguish, dullness, heaviness and vexation of spirit, any ways opposite to pleasure, mirth, joy, delight, causing forwardness in us, or a dislike. In which equivocal and improper sense, we call him melancholy, that is dull, sad, sour, lumpish, ill-disposed, solitary, any way moved, or displeased. And from these melancholy dispositions no man living is free, no Stoic, none so wise, none so happy, none so patient, so generous, so godly, so divine, that can vindicate himself; so well-composed, but more or less, some time or other, he feels the smart of it. Melancholy in this sense is the character of Mortality … This *Melancholy* of which we are to treat, is a habit, a serious ailment, a settled humour, as Aurelianus and others call it, not errant, but fixed: and as it was long increasing, so, now being (pleasant or painful) grown to a habit, it will hardly be removed. (p. 93)

Bell (2014, p. 116) posits there are four ways to understand melancholia/y, which serve as a framework for the following sections. These are:

1. "A temperament of humans" … "determined by the ratios of four basic bodily liquids (or four humours)" (p. 116). This thinking that can be traced to ancient Greek gained traction during the Renaissance (years) Lee argues because of the popular concept that "genius … emerge[s]" … and was "closely related to melancholia and [this thinking] became the source of a major European cultural tradition, feeding into works such Dürer's etching *Melancholia I* (1514), Shakespeare's *Hamlet* (c. 1601), and Goethe's novel *The Sorrows of Young Werther* (1774)" (2021, p. 116).
2. Constellations and planets—in the painting *Melancholia I*, Dürer depicts Saturn (have you heard someone explain an experience by saying a planet is in retrograde?) and comets that have long thought to affect people, in particular depressed individuals.
3. Psychological Depression, as medically defined and diagnosed. In *Mourning and Melancholia* (1917, p. 244), for example, Freud writes: "[T]he distinguishing mental features of melancholia are a profoundly painful dejection, cessation of interest in the outside world, loss of the capacity to love, inhibition of all activity, and a lowering of the self-regarding feelings to a degree that finds utterance in self-reproaches and self-revilings and culminates in a delusional expectation of punishment."

Cultural and philosophical way[s] to understand melancholia as "decadence" (Lee, 2021, p. 117) which the author traces etymologically to the French word decadence, "understood in conjunction with decay, decline, corruption, degeneration, and demoralization" (p. 117). But also the paradox of having "decadence, jollification, and downfall … mixed up" (p. 117). The pairing of opposite moods, temperaments, or the joy in destruction are seen in literature and media …. Or of joy or discoveries coming out of tragedy and loss, resilience, inner optimism, there is a fall but also a rebirth. Uses the music of Wagner as an example.
This thinking, although not perhaps the part related to bodily fluids, but that genius and madness are closely related hasn't entirely disappeared, writes Lee, who tells us to "think of Jimi Hendrix, Janis Joplin, Kurt Cobain, and Amy Winehouse. (2021, p. 116)

How Is Melancholy Understood Psychologically?

Today melancholy is typically classified as clinical depression. Therapists have clients but in the early times "they were patients or sufferers" (Lund, 2021, p. 17). It can be described as deep sadness, introspection, a "gloominess, a theatrical or aesthetic indulgence in reflective or maudlin remotion" (according to the *Oxford English Dictionary*). According to the DSM-5, Melancholic Depression "is a subtype of depression characterized by a severe loss of pleasure and prominent physical symptoms … include[ing] insomnia, weight loss, and psychomotor changes" ("Melancholic," 2021). This state can progress into nihilistic delusions, and it can be worse in the afternoon or evening.

The regard of melancholy in the present volume is interdisciplinary, as inspiration, and as the subject of curiosity. One can draw on physiology and psychology to explore it, but also on meteorology, theology, astrology, astronomy, and demonology. Greeks such as Aristotle, Galen, and Hippocrates considered the condition of melancholia, as do poetry and popular songs both ancient and modern. Some speak of a deep sadness, a longing, a despair, and desperation. Poets, artists, and writers have long considered this state, some drawing from their own experiences while others reach out in the interest of understanding. Poets such as John Keats ("Ode to Melancholy," "Hyperion"), Oscar Wilde ("Charmides," Humanitad"), Ralph Waldo Emerson ("Ode to Beauty"), and Edgar Allen Poe ("The Bells," "Annabel Lee") wrote of a state of melancholy, of sounds that were melancholic, or depths of sorrows. Music, classical, blues, and other genres, draw on melancholic emotions. For example, Tchaikovsky's "Serenade for Strings, 1st movement," Edward Elgar's "Nimrod," and the first movement of Beethoven's "String Quartet no. 14," are all contenders for the deep emotionality music can bring. Even Gilbert and Sullivan's (1879) otherwise rather silly *The Pirates of Penzance* includes "Ah, Leave Me Not to Pine Alone and Desolate." John Barry's theme from the movie *Somewhere in Time*, or practically any rendition of Leonard Cohen's "Hallelujah" can take one to a space of sadness, thoughtfulness, and contemplation.

The blues is likely the genre most closely associated with introspective and down-hearted emotions and yet, it is said, it also meant to be played and heard as a way out of the blues. This lyrical (rather than narrative) format of song is a way to express the singer's feelings. It can be joyful as well as deeply sad. Think "St. Louis Blues" by W. C. Handy, "A Change is Gonna Come" by Sam Cooke, "Georgia on my Mind," sung by Ray Charles, or Muddy Waters's

"Still a Fool." Here singing the blues as a way of getting out of the blues is a kind of homeopathic approach. The American blues tradition says that one gets out of that state by "rescu[ing] us from the despondency we may share with them by busying our brains" (Grovier, 2019). Burton (1621) proclaimed that "there is no greater cause of melancholy than idleness, no greater cure than business," while also insisting that "melancholy can be overcome only by melancholy."

Melancholy has been a clear theme in art (see Appendix 4.1). From Albrecht Dürer's woodcut, *Melancholia* (1514) shows a "sulking" and "lugubrious angel" angel "to murals" reputed to be by Banksy ("From this moment despair ends and tactics begin") (Grovier, 2019), there is a tradition of including a sense of forlorn, sadness, deep introspection, and medical consideration as well.

During the 18th and 19th centuries, melancholia/melancholy received the medical diagnosis of depression/mood disorder. Where originally the concept "included all forms of quiet insanity" (Paykel, 2008, p. 279), it later was regarded as an affective disorder, with a variety of manifestations, both psychological and physical. A classic late 19th-century textbook by German psychiatrist Emil Kraepelin (1856–1926) posed it as a combination of organic, pathological, neurological, and medical origins, systematizing the difference between "dementia praecox" (schizophrenia) "and manic-depressive psychosis" (Ebert & Bär, 2010, p. 191) (see also Gilbert, 2016). In Europe, psychoanalysts such as Freud developed a theory related to loss of love/attachment object. The term "depression" came into common use in the 19th century replacing the word "melancholy" (see Paykel, 2008).

Today depression is viewed as either short (not exceeding two months) or long term (clinical) presenting as a particular cluster of symptoms with diverse etiologies. Alternating states of melancholy and mania are now classified as bipolar/manic-depressive disorder. The DSM-II symptoms included loss of interest, loss of pleasure, and "decreased energy or fatigability" (see Tolentino & Schmidt, 2018). Thus, "a disorder of mood or affect" that can include changes in weight (gains or losses), fatigue, loss of confidence, inability to concentrate, and suicidal thoughts or attempts. Sometimes it presents as physical, mental, or a combination of symptoms.

The Experience

In *The Origin of German Trauerspiel*, Walter Benjamin (1928) averred: "Slowness is one characteristic of the melancholic temperament. Blundering is another, from noticing too many possibilities, from not noticing one's lack of practical sense. And stubbornness, from the longing to be superior—on one's terms" (qtd. in Sontag, 1978/1982, p. 391). Benjamin was melancholic: "I came into the world under the sign of Saturn," he wrote, "the star of the slowest revolution, the planet of detours and delays" (qtd. in Sontag, 1978/1982, p. 386). Benjamin (1892–1940) wrote extensively on the impact of media, technology, and society.[2] He was interested in states of being, particularly those of similarly Saturnine writers such as Kafka, Proust, and Baudelaire, and the artist Paul Klee. "Since the Saturnine temperament is slow, prone to indecisiveness, sometimes one has to cut one way through with a knife. Sometimes one ends by turning the knife against oneself" (Sontag, 1978/1982, p. 390). Further describing this temperament, Sontag (1978/1983) writes that "the self is a text—it has to be deciphered. The self is a project, something to be built. (Hence this is an apt temperament for artists and martyrs, those would court the purity and beauty of a failure,' as Benjamin says of Kafka. And the process of building a self and its works is always too slow. One is always in arrears to oneself" (p. 390).

Freud viewed depression as intimately connected to guilt and self-blame originating in early experiences and referred to it as a "disease" (1917, p. 256). Essentially, he saw the condition as the result of a collision between the unconscious and conscious resulting in conflict, as dis-ease. Urges, primitive drives, and desires (id) collide with one's sense of doing the right thing (superego) which would normally be balanced by the ego's mediation. In this case one can feel like a failure. In *Mourning and Melancholia* (1917), Freud wrote: "The most remarkable characteristic of melancholia, and the one most in need of explanation, is its tendency to change round into mania—a state which is the opposite of it in its symptoms" (p. 253). This doesn't happen in every situation but both melancholy and mania, Freud believed, "wrestl[e] with the same 'complex'" (p. 254), but in the former is a submission to it and the latter, a mastering of it.

In mania, the ego must have got over the loss of the object (or its mourning over the loss, or perhaps the object itself), and thereupon the whole quota of anticathexis which the painful suffering of melancholia had drawn to itself from the ego and 'bound' will have become available. … the manic subject plainly demonstrates his liberation from an object which was the cause of his suffering, by seeking like a ravenously hungry man for new object-cathexes. (p. 255). Trauma can induce this dynamic. According to Freud (1961, p. 275), trauma is "an experience which within a short period of time presents the mind with an increase of stimulus too powerful to be dealt with or worked off in the normal way." It can also be thought of as a "rupture in the subject, as something so profoundly life changing and threatening to the subject's coherence and well-being that the ego blocks images, memories or thoughts touching up that event from entering consciousness" (Krüger & Johanssen, 2016, p. 16). Some trauma victims describe leaving their bodies, or not being able to remember details. Even if the trauma is outside of or apart from us, witnessing it can bring about its internalization. If a child witnesses something traumatic, such as fighting or violence between trusted adults it can create at the least uncertainty, feelings of rejection. Rather than expression the feelings of betrayal or, in this view one might become depressed, feeling that the violence, even if purely verbal, is somehow the child's fault and that they are unlovable/bad. "Psychoanalysis understands depression as aggression that is too upsetting to manage or settle, so it is ultimately turned against the self (ego)," says psychologist Natalie Bernstein (2022).

The "self-reproaches" typical of depression is also something Freud identified as a common occurrence in the wake of the death of a loved one. "Such reproaches, he thought, might eventuate in hysteria, obsessions—or depressions, which he called, then and later, by the resonant, tradition-laden term 'melancholia'" (Gay, 1989, p. 584). In Freud's view, we punish ourselves and become highly self-critical. He compares mourning and melancholy as such:

> In mourning we found that the inhibition and loss of interest are fully accounted for by the work of mourning in which the ego is absorbed. In melancholia, the unknown loss will result in a similar internal work and will therefore be responsible for the melancholic inhibition. The difference is that the inhibition of the melancholic seems puzzling to us because we cannot see what it is that is absorbing him so entirely. (qtd. in Gay, 1984, p. 584)

Freud noted that it doesn't matter whether those around the melancholic see what they see, or agree with their self-criticism and denigration. "The essential thing … is not whether the melancholic's distressing self-denigration is correct, in the sense that his self-criticism agrees with the opinion of other people. The point must rather be that he is giving a correct description of his psychological situation. The analogy with mourning led us to conclude that he had suffered a loss regarding an object; what he tells us points to a loss in regard to his ego" (p. 585).

Film Analysis

An understanding of melancholia gives us a good starting point to unpack text using Freud's theories. The 2011 Lars von Trier film *Melancholia* is titled as such. It stars Kirsten Dunst (Justine), Charlotte Gainsbourg (Claire), Alexander Skarsgård (Michael), Charlotte Rampling (Gaby), Kiefer Sutherland (John), Stellan Skarsgård (Jack), and John Hurt (Dexter). Whether Freud would consider depression and melancholy to be the same thing is debatable. But the film clearly *is* about melancholia, the psychological state, about a planet, or a planet standing-in-for a psychological state, one impossible to escape.[3] A reviewer described it as "the greatest film about depression ever made" (Kaufman, 2021).

The story focuses on Justine (whom the BBC declares to be von Trier's "surrogate"), yet both Justine and Claire are melancholic, presenting in different ways: "They are not just in the state of depression that can be experienced by anybody at least once in life, but are in a state of extreme morbid melancholia to the extent that they cannot lead everyday life, like those who are paralyzed by scorpion venom" (Bell, 2014, p. 123). There are differences. For example, Justine "has capacity and is recognized in society. Claire has wealth and enjoys it, whether it is owned by her or any of her family members" (p. 123). But both become lethargic, both are not happy, despite what they have, or what they have lost. "The need to be solitary—along with bitterness over one's loneliness—is characteristic of the melancholic. To get work done, one must be solitary—or, at least, not bound to any permanent relationship" (Sontag, 1978, para. 49) such as marriage.

Critical Assessment

New York Times film critic A. O. Scott (2011, para. 2) described *Melancholia*[4] as "an excursion from the sad to the sublime by way of the preposterous" and quotes Freud's definition of the emotion "as a profoundly painful dejection, cessation of interest in the outside world, loss of the capacity to love, inhibition of all activity, and a lowering of the self-regarding feelings to a degree that finds utterance in self-reproaches and self-reviling's, and culminates in a delusional expectation of punishment." Scott (2011) takes a shot at director von Trier by saying audiences attend his films because of suffering—for the sadism of his sincere "tricks and provocations" (para. 4). This of course fits Freud's version of melancholy, by what the creative product reveals and those who attend it. Ultimately, "The world, Justine declares in her darkest moment of clarity, deserves its awful fate. The perverse achievement of *Melancholia* is how difficult it is to argue with her conclusion. Other critics, such as Peter Bradshaw (2011, para. 8) of *The Guardian* described von Trier as "that great maestro of facetious event cinema," and the film as "another instrument of torture." And yet, his critics say the film grows on the viewer:

> *Melancholia* is an absurd film in many ways, and yet it would be obtuse not to acknowledge those lightning bolts of visual inspiration. When Justine goes out into the fields to look at the awesome blue planet, and then takes her clothes off to bathe in its light—that really is powerfully erotic and strange. In some ways, for all its silliness and self-consciousness, this is the happiest experience I've had with Von Trier for some time. (para. 8)

Rolling Stone writer Peter Travers (2011) could not leave out von Trier's statement at Cannes, saying it overshadowed the film's premiere, which is a "potent beauty of a film." Travers describes Kirstin Dunst as "luminous" and "deservedly won the Best Actress prize at Cannes." "Her incomparable performance, a slow accumulation of moods from despair to euphoria, never strikes a false note (para. 3)."

Whether they liked, appreciated, or simultaneously condemned and condoned the filmmaker and the art, the movie got attention, even if for the discomfort many audiences felt. Too close to home? Too art-house?

A psychoanalytic critique of the film draws more upon the contents, the execution, rather than speculations about the state of mind of the director. However, given that von Trier (Brooks, 2018) is public about his own melancholia, it isn't a reach to say he is very much part of the film and the draw by audiences could be based on their attraction/repulsion to the topic. Part of what has been termed "the depression trilogy" of films, *Antichrist* (2009), *Melancholia* (2011), and *Nymphomaniac* (2013–2014), the films "follow[ed] von Trier's experience of clinical depression in 2006 and 2007" (Badley, 2022). Of course the film is stylistically beautiful as are the actors. However, for purposes of this section, the discussion focuses on the film itself, what happens and why using Freud's theory of melancholia primarily to unpack the actions of the main character Justine, but also with reflection on that of her sister, Claire and is organized as such. Other characters are also ripe for analysis (pun intended) such as Justine and Claire's parents, Justine's fiancé/husband, and Claire's husband.

The Film

For the first eight minutes of *Melancholia* (2011), viewers are invited to enter a sensory experience of visual and aural complexity. Reviewer Manohla Dargis (2011) describes it as "a masterpiece in miniature that is a palimpsest of literary, artistic and cinematic allusions." This opening is a set of 16 perfectly timed scenes, a mélange of images, some still photography, some slow motion, a melancholic scene set at a grand estate, the setting for the entire film. Whether a photograph, painting, or both the experience is dream-like. "The dream like stage, of surrealist nature of the film thus reflects the altered state, a desire dreaminess that the melancholic person is trying to control. Dreams reveal the structure of our unconscious desire that everyday life obscures with a series of contingent obstacles to that desire" (McGowan, 2015, p. 5). Something surreal *is* happening, something magical, something more-than as we are introduced to the film's characters. The only sound in the opening sequence is the prelude to Richard Wagner's opening to *Tristan und Isolde* (1857–1859). Marin (2018, para. 1) describes the opening sequence as

> a collection of gloomy, surreal, painting-resembling, slow-motion shots, is an insidious introduction to the themes of this compelling cinematic symphony of death and destruction. What completes the eerie dreamscape is the exquisite, haunting piece of music by Wagner—the Prelude to the tragic opera *Tristan und Isolde*, which magnifies the sorrow depicted in the shots and throughout the whole film. The film and the opera both exhibit the philosophical pessimism of Schopenhauer, revolving around unhappiness, death, and painful, unfulfilled human yearning. The nocturnal landscape, the Realm of the Night from Wagner's opera, symbolically stands for the realm of hidden truth; and the only escape or redemption from a world perceived as evil and relentlessly suffering, is spiritual release, death, hence Justine's morbid Ophelia moment and the early appearance of the destructive planet, Melancholia.

In his review, Roger Ebert (2011, para. 1) describes the opening as:

> mourning and apocalyptic, and disturbing images of a world not right. A woman dressed as a bride runs through a forest whose branches seem to grab at her in a Disney nightmare. She floats in a pond, holding flowers, like Ophelia. Another woman makes her way with a child over marshy grass that sucks at her. Looming in the sky is another planet, vast in size. The Earth is about to end.

Both Justine and Claire seem melancholy, if we draw on these descriptions. Lee (2021, p. 114) suggests they both experience it, from the perspective of decadence, because of "the loss of nature." In this case it is not so much they've lost the natural world, perhaps but themselves, of their true nature. Everything in the garden, golf course, and house is carefully manicured, controlled, and arranged. The lightning is unusual, adding a sense of loss of the natural—and the planet Melancholia's heading to end even that privileged world because, perhaps, of a loss of nature ... the garden, Garden of Eden, of innocence, naivety of privilege. Toward the end of the film (von Trier, 2011) Justine says the Earth is evil:

JUSTINE: The earth is evil. We don't need to grieve for it.
CLAIRE: What?
JUSTINE: Nobody will miss it.
CLAIRE: But where would Leo grow?
JUSTINE: All I know is, life on earth is evil.
CLAIRE: Then maybe life somewhere else.
JUSTINE: But there isn't.
CLAIRE: How do you know?
JUSTINE: Because I know things.
CLAIRE: Oh yes, you always imagined you did.
JUSTINE: I know we're alone.
CLAIRE: I don't think you know that at all.
CLAIRE: Well, perhaps. But what does that prove?
JUSTINE: That I know things. And when I say we're alone, we're alone. Life is only on earth, and not for long.

The following sections are character analyses of Justine and Claire using Freud's psychanalytic theory as a lens.

Part 1: Justine

The first half of the film focuses on the experiences of the film's main character, Justine. It is her wedding day, one meant to be the perfect presentation of possibilities of a future. She has everything going for her: a beautiful wedding, a reception at an extraordinary mansion, a successful career, the perfect husband. She is beautiful, creative, and works in the exciting world of advertising. The groom, Michael, is attractive, wealthy, successful, truly loves her, and is understanding of her ups and downs. Yet, she constantly and consistently self-sabotages looking like "Ophelia drowning: lying on her back in the water, holding a bouquet of flowers, veil flowing behind her head, against a natural green background (grass, lily pads, moss)" (Marso, 2017, p. 12).

Justine and Michael are late, very late, to the reception being held at her brother-in-law's estate (Tjolöholm Castle in Sweden). Being late is not unexpected of Justine, but in this case, it's not entirely her fault as the couple are arriving in a stretch limousine whose driver is having difficulty making the tight corners in the winding road leading to the opulent home. The driver, Michael, and Justine all try to drive the vehicle, arriving two hours late. When the couple finally do appear, the first thing Justine wants to do is visit her horse, Abraham, and introduce him to Michael. Everyone is there, ready, hungry, slightly irritated, and waiting. Justine is radiant in her traditional white wedding gown with a long train; Michael is glowing as well, proud of this moment.

The first to speak in a series of toasts is Justine's boss, Jack, from the advertising agency where she works as a copywriter. She is "a portrait of the modern artist" in that selling is everything and art is used to do so (Lee, 2021, p. 125). Jack honors her, promotes her to Art Director, and says she's more talented than the ad world deserves; at the same time, for the entire reception, Jack maneuvers for a tagline needed to complete a campaign. In fact Jack has "hired" his nephew to spend the reception hounding her for this tagline. Told she is better than the ad business, more creative than most, "melancholy is coiled at the root of her genius" (p. 125). Justine alternates between extremes of being productive and blocked. She can barely speak at this point; she cannot use her words. Justine might be searching in herself for her true/natural self, own feelings and stimulation, excitement, defying rules, and ignoring Jack's nephew's attempts at prying out a slogan. She urinates on the lawn, squatting in her wedding dress, has sex with another man, the nephew, and wears her wedding gown the entire day, cycling through stages of repression, depression, needing to produce, create, all leading to repulsion. She yearns to be independent, inspired, create genius and yet, in an advertising environment must create on demand. "It is characteristic of the Saturnine temperament to blame its undertow of inwardness on the will. Convinced that the will is weak, the melancholic may make extravagant efforts to develop. If these efforts are successful, the resulting hypertrophy of will usually takes the form of a compulsive devotion to work" (Sontag, 1978, para. 44).

Lee (2021) cites Nietzsche's criticism of Wagner "as someone who imitates the lives of others, refers to him as a 'monkey' who 'apes' others. Thus Justine isn't a writer per se, but a *copy* writer" (p. 133). That she moves slowly, and eventually not at all, is another indication of growing melancholy. Justine's parents, "who make mortifying speeches" (Pistelli, 2013) are, like many of the films characters, narcissistic opportunists. According to Sontag (1978, para. 48): "For the melancholic, the natural, in the form of family ties, introduces the falsely subjective, the sentimental; it is a drain on the will, on one's independence." Furthermore, "this wedding is accordingly meant to ensure Justine's future participation in the system: to usher her at last into the order of normality—jobs, kids, cars, and the rest" (Pistelli, 2013). Michael surprises her with a farm and orchard he has purchased on their behalf. Everyone has decided for her, about her, until Justine in fact, pulls the plug on everything. She does so at first, more passive aggressively: while guests wait for the cutting of the cake, Justine takes a bath. When it's time to throw the bridal bouquet, she just stands there. Eventually Claire steps in and tosses it for her as guests wait below the balcony. The sex she has with the nephew of her boss, climbing on top of him on the golf course could be meaningless, or it could be an act of power against her boss's pursuit of her for a tagline? These actions end her marriage. She tells her boss what she thinks of him, ending the dream job. This career-ending act is something Freud noted of highly successful individuals. Self-sabotage is not uncommon among highly successful people. We've seen this happen in politics and entertainment in the United States (Bill Clinton, Eliot Spitzer, Roman Polanski, Woody Allen, Harvey Weinstein) and in Great Britain, Hugh Grant. Freud recognized how "people often suffer breakdowns and explosions in their private lives not after a *failure*, but paradoxically, after a *triumph*" (Kahr, 2015, p. 12). Sometimes called imposter syndrome, this too-good-to-be-trueness, in fact can derail careers and lives that otherwise looked like they were perfect. Freud argued in part it has to do with becoming more successful than one's parent. In the case of men, their fathers, "as though the essence of success was to have gotten further than one's father, and as though to excel one's father was still something forbidden" (Freud, 1936, para. 5). Pistelli (2013, para. 6) situates this in the film:

> von Trier knows his Freud well enough to know that melancholia means an ego-wasting inability to let go of the lost object, which in this case is life itself. The melancholic is emphatically not a Buddhist or Stoic or monastic, one who has superseded her own attachment to the world; instead, the melancholic actually *loves the world more* than those who are successfully able to mourn, to bury the dead, to get married, to go to work, to efface themselves in the name of perpetuating things. The melancholic doesn't discipline herself to turn away from the world; she remains in the world and brings it down by the force of her own abjection.

The object is the life ahead for Justine. What she will be/come after this day is over. She is in mourning, as Freud (1917, p. 245) describes this as follows:

> [E]ach single one of the memories and situations of expectancy which demonstrates the libido's attachment to the lost object is met by the verdict of reality that the object no longer exists; and the ego, confronted as it were with the question whether it shall share this fate, is persuaded by the sum of the narcissistic satisfactions it derives from being alive to sever its attachment to the object that has been abolished.

Justine's horse, Abraham, plays an important role in several scenes, both in the Justine half and Claire half of the film, as do horses generally. Claire introduces Abraham to Michael, even though wedding reception guests are waiting. Abraham is a massive black horse, but for whatever reason, he will not cross the little footbridge that separates the estate from the village, that is, from the real world. Later in the film, Justine, out of fear and frustration, viciously beats Abraham with her riding crop when, once again, he won't cross.

At times Justine swings from melancholia to mania and back again, in bursts of what seems like recovery to resolve and back again. Roger Ebert (2011, para. 3) described it as "a desperate acting out." Freud (1917) reminds us of "the interdependence of the complicated problems of the mind forces us to break off every enquiry before it is completed—till the outcome of some other enquiry can come to its assistance" (p. 285). Planetarily what is happening, with Melancholia headed toward earth, is more than the others can process, but Justine seems relatively unfazed, as if she expected something like this. She is "Aunt Steelbreaker" to her nephew, "Better to be an artist than a politician. Better to be Ophelia than Hamlet, who may in the end have toppled the state" (Pistelli, 2013).

Part 2: Claire

The second half of the film focuses on Claire, or more precisely, we get let in on Claire and her relationship with Justine. Claire is the caregiver, the protector. No matter what Justine does, Claire is there to comfort her, excuse her to others, intervene. Despite what Justine might say to her, there is a deep connection between the two. Claire is the "good sister," the "normal one" presented in contrast to Justine who is "disorderly, irresponsible, indifferent, while being selfish, and showing paralysis" (Bell, 2014, p. 134). Claire "has it all," a different way than Justine. She is person of the world, with order, resources (via her wealthy husband), and a beautiful child. She is scheduled and precise. She is the confident head of the house, and yet she is also the one who is most fearful when it becomes clear that the deeply blue Melancholia is headed for a collision with Earth. She falls into the abyss here. Others comfort her, assure her, and if possible, explain away the inevitable. According to Ebert (2011, para. 5):

> In the cast of von Trier's characters, impending doom seems to have created a mental state of dazed detachment. They continue to act as if their personal concerns have the slightest relevance. Von Trier has never made a more realistic domestic drama, depicting a family that is dysfunctional not in crazy ways but in ways showing a defiant streak of intelligent individualism.

That is so of course until Claire's husband commits suicide. When others are weakening, Justine becomes stronger and heads toward the forthcoming catastrophe, helping her nephew process and prepare using shared fantasies about caves and protection, fully embodying his Aunt Steelbreaker image. Claire, however, is dragged into it, into space where the seemingly perfect and the perfectly seemly are colliding. Everything she has planned and organized for her sister is now about her. Claire has "saved" Justine from herself, in many ways, the roles shift. Again from Ebert (2011, para. 8):

> Violent death is often a shabby business in the movies. It happens in depressing bedrooms, bloody bathtubs, shattered cars, bleak alleys. Its victims are cast down empty of life. Here is a character who says, I see it coming, I will face it, I will not turn away, I will observe it as long as my eyes and my mind still function. Is it fair of me to speculate that von Trier himself regards death in that way? He tends to be grandiose, but if one cannot be grandiose in imagining one's own death, then when is grandiosity justified?

Melancholia is an illustration of Freud's theory of the melancholic in a variety of ways. Freud (1930) posited that depression could manifest as aggression toward the self. This instinct, or death wish (Thanatos), could be self or other directed, self-destructive, and exhibited primarily as repetition compulsions. As a defense mechanism, repression or other unfulfilled, unconscious desires include denial (failure to perceive the source of anxiety); rationalization (justification of an action by an acceptable motive; displacement (directing repressed feelings toward an acceptable substitute); projection (attributing one's own unacceptable impulse to others); and sublimation (transforming an unacceptable instinctual demand into a socially acceptable activity) ("Sigmund Freud," 2022). Or, in other words, "This is the suffocating aspect of

Nurse Ratched in *One Flew Over the Cuckoo's Nest.* Fully internalized, it's the logic of suicide" (Hartz, 2022). The ego moderates selfish, self-directed desires of the id while the superego focuses on idealism. "As the superego bears down too heavily, symptoms can emerge: paranoia, loss of reality, odd behaviors, despair. … This response is unlikely to be well-organized. More likely it will be impulsive, awkward and strange—a paroxysm of forbidden desires, gratifying but destructive" (Hartz, 2022).

In addition, "genetically and environmentally influenced aggressive tendencies contribute to depressive symptoms" (Haddad, Neiderhiser, Spotts, Ganiban, Lichtenstein, & Reiss, 2013, p. 515). Haddad et al. (2013) built on Freud's theory of depression as aggression doing what he had not—test it empirically. This is not a shortcoming of Freud's work, although many criticized him for focusing on individual versus generalizable findings. He focused on individuals and considered melancholia in multiple individuals, as in qualitative research, which revealed patterns. In a study "of 909 pairs of adult twins, their partners, and one adolescent child per couple," Haddad et al. (2013) found that

> an individual's unique, not shared, experiences and perceptions contribute to depressive symptoms and internally directed aggression reinforces the use of patient-specific treatment approaches implemented in psychoanalytic psychotherapy or psychoanalysis. (p. 515)[5]

Through this theoretical and clinical lens Justine's frustrations with life, with expectations for her and of herself, combined with whatever might have been "gifted" to her genetically (evidenced by portrayals of her parents in the film), show at the least a lack of will to live. Her depression is so deep that it becomes physically debilitating (sleeping, loss of appetite/taste, suicidal ideation), and the film offers us the perhaps metaphorical sense that her depression may cause the end of the Earth through planetary destruction. This end she does not appear to fear; in fact she welcomes it as a resolution to suffering. In terms of Freud's (1917) theory, the loss Justine experiences is clearly that of self, of identity, who, as a person, as an artist, has autonomy, and yet "the individual internalizes the lost object as a way of holding on to it." In the opening sequence, lighting bolts shoot from Justine's heaven-reaching hands. Is the power flowing out or into her? What it amounts to is that, in the formation of the superego, and the emergence of a conscience, innate constitutional factors and influences from the real environment act in combination" (Freud, 1930, p. 92).

A Freudian Analysis of Advertising

> To consume in America is not to buy, it is to dream.
>
> Don DeLillo

What would Freud say about contemporary advertising? No doubt, based on his assessment of American culture and his nephew's use of psychological strategies to sell ideas and products, he would not be pleased. Nevertheless, reaching consumers through ads is a massive industry that relies on bypassing critical thinking, unless of course the product is, for example, a technology. Even then, possessing the newest is part of the sale.

This section is a discussion of why advertisers use the particular appeals they do, why the appeals work in general, and why sex in advertising in particular, has been used to the extent that it has to sell everything from cigarettes to sofas. Freud's notion of totems (and taboos) is discussed as background for understanding the role things play in the social construction of desire in consumer cultures. A discussion of a 2021 Gucci campaign epitomizes many of Freud's theories about sex. This section is also included to demonstrate the connection media studies theories such as semiotics have to psychoanalytically interpreting content and reception, as a logical extension of that theory.

Forbidden Desires

The word "taboo" has been used primarily to describe that which is prized, afforded qualities and characteristics beyond the object, but also stood in for ways of being, particularly in relationship with the natural world. In the world of totems there are also taboos, prohibitions on certain acts, such as killing an animal that is the clan symbol. "Frazer (1911) distinguished between taboo acts (sexual relations with strangers, forbidden foods), taboo characters (kings), taboo substances (blood) and taboo words" (Manceu & Tissier-Desbordes, 2006, p. 11). The term totemism was invented to describe practices of adoration and worship assigned to a particular totemic object. Early theorists such as Durkheim (1912/1995, p. 84) saw among religions how totems can be explained in sociological terms, thus the famous distinction of sacred and profane, where the sacred involves the worship of certain objects and beings wherein the "thing" has no inherent value, and is not "inherently sacred" outside of the sacredness assigned to it. The social and moral order of a society is thus organized around attitudes, beliefs, and behaviors toward these beings or objects. In the modern world this might be associating a national symbol, such as a flag, with patriotism, a particular color with an attribute, or a brand name with a "tribe" such as brand logos. Freud's work in this area, in *Totem and Taboo* (1918), is a review of the ideas of Durkheim, Frazer and others. But he focuses on the psychological motivations behind totemism, whereas these anthropologists looked at the sociological. Taboos are intended to inhibit pleasures in Freud's view, which humans naturally are driven to transgress, often unconsciously. Forbidden acts and desires are primarily related to Eros (sex) and Thanatos (death, and the fear of death). Taboos such as exogamy, Freud argued, were manifestations of the Oedipus complex. Forbidding intra-clan marriages, in a patriarchal system, positions males as the central totemic figure, "which is worshipped as an alleviation of the guilt for the desires of males for patricide and sexual relations with mothers" (Osbaldiston, 2011, p. 1461). Manceu and Tissier-Desbordes (2006) examine whether, in the French cultural context, sex and death, traditionally taboo topics, are acceptable in advertising. In a survey of 760 French consumers they found that "women and seniors are particularly hostile to sex and death in advertising," whereas "young people find these themes more acceptable" (p. 9). Of course what is socially acceptable, considered polite, varies by culture, for example, public nudity, what ought to be kept private (affairs of presidents, credit histories, salaries, individual freedom versus collective good, public displays of affection). The researchers examined "taboos appearing in advertising: the advertisements on taboo topics, and the use of taboo themes and images as an advertising strategy" (p. 14). Examples of the first include AIDS-prevention campaigns or ads for funeral companies and for the second this could include the use of skeletons or images of death to sell products such as perfumes or clothing. They make the distinction that "provocation is an intent of advertisers to chock the audience, while taboos are topics that can be used to achieve this intent … taboo is a stimulus whereas provocation is a strategy" (p. 15). As mentioned in Chapter 3, research is clear that if there is too much sex in an ad, the consumer is likely to forget the product, even though attention is increased (Aaker & Bruzzone, 1985; De Pelsmacker & Van Den Bergh, 1996). One psychological explanation is found via Petty and Cacciopo's (1983) Elaboration Likelihood Model (ELM) which says that "sexual appeals stimulate a peripheral route for ad processing" (p. 16), in other words, bypassing critical thinking by stimulating primal sexual drives (see also Richert et al., 2001).

Marketing Desires

The similarity between dreams and advertising is pronounced. People, places, and things are idealized, as is the self should one purchase the necessary ingredients for making the perfect cake, buying the perfect car, or reforming one's body to the perfect size and shape. "For a long time advertisements represented an ideal universe based on dreams, harmony, and beauty" (Manceu & Tissier-Desbordes, 2006, p. 10). "Freud believed dreams were vivid representations of repressed urges" having two aspects, including "the manifest content or narrative," which "one is able to remember upon waking," and "the latent content or the underlying, largely symbolic message" ("Psychoanalysis," 2022).

In "Psychoanalysis as Marketing Theory," Cluely (n.d.) discusses how closely connected psychoanalytic theory has been to marketing. In fact, since the early days of persuasive commercial appeals, "psychoanalysis helped the discipline develop beyond economics" and understand consumer behavior. Citing Lazarsfeld's (1934) analysis of breakfast beverage drinkers, he found that some chose tea, and some chose coffee. He noted that there were extrinsic (advice of others, the experience of a trip) and intrinsic reasons (coffee is delicious) for one over the other. From this survey research Lazarsfeld concluded, according to Fleck (1998, p. 107), "that it is not enough merely to ask which <<object>> people preferred, but that the reasons for their choice, irrespective of whether or not they proved accurate or adequate when put to the test, were of strategic important … tea advertising ought to be based on detailed arguments for tea drinking, whereas coffee advertising could be based much more on the mere but continuous repetition of the brand name."

No doubt because of fear of association with subliminal advertising claims of the 1950s, there was a marked turn away from using psychoanalytic theory after the 1960s. Prior to this, "under the heading of motivation research, marketers were swept away with the notion of being able to identify hidden motives of consumers" (O'Shaughnessy, 2015, p. 17). Even though "marketing in its rawest, instinctual, most potent form is like the inner child, the savage, the id of Freudian theory" (Patterson, Bradshaw & Brown, 2008, p. 454), Cluley (n.d., para. 4) suggests that "marketing in its rawest form *is* a Freudian theory that repressed itself through its scientific aspirations." In other words, marketing is "repressed psychoanalytic theory" (para. 4). Increasingly, as noted in this chapter (and in Chapter 5), there is scientific evidence for using psychoanalytic principles in campaigns. "Psychoanalytic marketing theory" is rooted in critical theory such as that of Marcuse (1964), Packard (1957/

1970), and Lasch (1979). The symbols and archetypes found in advertising as widely understood are encoded, drawing on Hall (1973). Images and words connect with the collective unconscious permitting and inviting in fundamental drives such as "sexuality, passions, lust and hatred into the things they consume" (Cluley, para. 10).

Not only is Freud's model of personality described as an iceberg, with the most visible part above the surface (the conscious), so is advertising noted to be the tip of the marketing iceberg, with most of the structure and activity occurring below the surface.

In *White Noise* novelist Don DeLillo (1985, p. 270) writes:

> "How does a successful television commercial affect the viewer?"
> "It makes him want to change the way he lives."
> "In what way?" I said.
> "It moves him from first person consciousness to third person. In this country there is a universal third person, the man we all want to be. Advertising has discovered this man. It uses him to express the possibilities open to the consumer. To consume in America is not to buy; it is to dream. Advertising is the suggestion that the dream of entering the third person singular might possibly be fulfilled."

As mentioned in Chapter 3, Freud was *not* happy that his theories were being used the way they were in public relations via his nephew, Edward Bernays. It's not a stretch to say he would not have approved either of using psychological/therapeutic tools to persuade consumers to buy things. An interesting definition of advertising comes from a psychoanalytic study of it: "[A]dvertising can be defined as an essentially commercial technique of influence that acts without the intermediary of the vendor" (Forest, 2016, p. 338). Advertising messages come to potential consumers through a variety of traditional as well as new media, social media, and more interpersonal means of selling. The goal of course is to sell something—a product, service, idea, or even a candidate. Some of the most creative uses of images and words can be found in the limited time and space of an ad. A single page, a few words, 30 to 60 seconds. Yet, what must go into the creation of these words and images to motivate audiences to *do* something is complex and riddled with ethical issues. Referencing former president of the Institute of Practitioners in Advertising, Rory Sutherland "explicitly called for a return to psychological models of the human actor that are informed by psychoanalysis. He noted that many of our most enduring brands and successful advertising campaigns were built on a psychoanalytic model of consumer behaviour promoted by Dichter and others."

Dichter "turned ad agencies into psychology labs, bringing the social sciences into what were basically factories of communication" (Samuel, 2022). Using in-depth personal interviews, Dichter's research "provided advertising with a kind of radar to find its way through the darkness of the collective subconscious" (Blenstein-Blanchet, founder of Publicis, in Samuel, 2022).

Forest (2016, p. 339) posits that "attention is a perfect path to the unconscious mind. The unconscious is thus made to serve as a purchasing advisor, speaking on behalf of the products advertised. The advertisement is all the more effective because it does so unbeknownst to the subject." Ads engineer, they encode meaning and work mostly unconsciously, not in the way some have argued subliminal advertising works but rather like public relations, to bypass critical thinking, to prevent us from stopping and carefully critiquing what we are being "sold" and why.

As discussed in earlier chapters, it is the unconscious, what has been excluded from consciousness or repressed for later consideration, that makes advertising work so well. According to Freud (1915, p. 582), appeals to basic human pleasure centers are particularly powerful, begin early in life, and are aspects of drives that remain with us:

> The nucleus of the unconscious consists of instinctual representatives which seek to discharge their cathexis [psychic energy]; that is to say, it consists of wishful impulses. There are in this system no negation, no doubt, no degrees of certainty: all this is only introduced by the work of the censorship between the unconscious and the preconscious. The processes of the system Unc. Are timeless; i.e. they are not ordered temporally, are not altered by the passage of time; they have no reference to time at all. The unconscious processes pay just a little regard to reality. They are subject to the pleasure principle; their fate depends only on how strong they are and on whether they fulfil the demands of the pleasure-unpleasure regulation. (Freud, "The Unconscious," p. 582)

In the 1998 documentary *Advertising and the End of the World*, Sut Jhally posits that, "If an anthropologist from Mars were to look at this society, where messages are everywhere, they'd conclude that this society is dominated by a belief in magic." By "this society," Jhally is referring to industrialized, modernized, urbanized societies, yet the concept of "magic" has deep anthropological roots. Raymond Williams referred to advertising as "the magic system," where many of the qualities indigenous communities ascribed to objects (totems[6]) that have nothing to do with the objects themselves are similarly abstract with those modern societies attribute to goods and services today. Anthropologists such as Claude Levi-Strauss and others paid particular attention to this dynamic. Worshiping inanimate objects as stand-ins-for powers, abilities, guidance, authority is, in some views "unknowing worship of a social order" (Osbaldiston, 2011, p. 1461). Jhally (1998, p. 2) goes on to say:

> What goods promise in advertising is immense. They can capture qualities of the natural world. They can perform feats of bewitchment and transformation. They can bring instant happiness, and gratification. They act as a passport into a world of fantasy and desire. Some products can even capture lady luck in the flesh.

To do business in a global economy one has to find commonalities, particularly when creating marketing and advertising. Accessing the *collective* unconscious, made up of course of individuals socialized in a particular culture, is of tremendous value when the goal is to sell essentially the same product to vastly different people in vastly different parts of the world. Drawing on Douglas and Isherwood, "consumer objects that act like totems serve to connect others socially, as well as hold deep psychological meaning for the self" (Osbaldiston, 2011, p. 1461). To reach consumers, the appeal therefore, might not be rational. "Unconscious thoughts [are] as significant, frequent, and normal as conscious ones in the universe of psychoanalysis, making them just as valuable to marketers as to therapists in terms of understanding people's behavior" (p. 10). Freud said: "The conscious mind may be compared to a fountain playing the sun and falling back into the great subterranean pool of subconscious from which it rises."

Freud (1918) in *Totem and Taboo* looked at the anthropological work and the power of practices, including forbidden ones such as incest, to order a society. What is off limits (yet might remain desirable) is part of the psychological work of organizing individuals into social groups. The images that matter to them, the information conveyed is meant to support a dominant point of view. Desires must be managed and channeled if control is to be maintained, yet outlets for base desires are also needed. "Well behaved consumers must enjoy their lot and still find that their deepest selves lie somewhere behind these pleasures, so that they can still govern their desires," also known as "tamed hedonism" (Sassatelli, 2011, p. 1429). And these are deep-seated, life-long desires that appeal to pleasure centers of the brain, some offering the opportunity, through fantasy via purchase, to transgress as well. Ernest Dichter, mentioned earlier "showed that sex was often lurking in the darkness" (Samuels, 2022). Furthermore, "Man … is more strongly motivated by the pleasure principle than by the principle of reality," Dichter said, convinced that, when it came to human motivation, the libido ruled" (Samuels, 2022). Advertising gave consumers permission to indulge their deepest desires and longings and justification for gratifying often suppressed longings:

> No wonder then that advertising is so attractive to us, so powerful, so seductive, because what it offers us are images of the real sources of human happiness: family life, romance, and love, sexuality and pleasure, friendship and sociability, leisure and relaxation, independence and control of life. That is why advertising is so powerful. That is what's real about it in one sense. … The falsity of advertising is not in the appeals it makes, which are very real, but in the answers it provides. We want love, and advertising points the way to it through objects. (Jhally, 1998, p. 10)

While much of motivation research has changed over the years, it is still present. Simply put, what it is that motivates someone to want, like, choose, or refuse something, anything, an idea, product, or service? The way products are sold thus reflect this desire to "buil[d] into products the same traits that we recognize in ourselves" (Packard, 1957/1970, p. 40).

Selling Sex

No aspect of human beings is more primitive or more accessible to marketing manipulation than sex. Even aggression seems strangely less accessible for those in marketing and advertising. These two drives were what Freud said motivated adults and were learned early as infants. Sometimes aggression is simply competitiveness—the best at this or that, for example, be the most popular, good-looking, successful, or admired. It can also be experienced in infants as rage at being denied something they want, for example, during weaning. Aggression and sex are connected in terms of competition for mates. However, reproducing the species can also be experienced as pleasure and is a vulnerable impulse. That these drives are so accessible, fundamental, and available make them fertile fodder for manipulation.

What is curious, given the preponderance of sex to sell, the phrase "sex sells," as mentioned in Chapter 3, is that it actually isn't the best tactic given that if there's enough sex in an ad, consumers aren't likely to remember the product. As Gramazio et al. (2021, p. 716) point out:

> Our findings suggest that, at the marketing level, the use of female sexualization in advertising is counterproductive for women and useless for men as consumers and that the use of male sexualization is counterproductive both for women and men. Put differently, our findings show that "sex does not sell," a result that questions sexualization as a useful marketing strategy.

And, in the Gramazio et al (2021, p. 714) study, they found that "female sexualization in advertising has a negative effect on women's responses and has a null effect on men's responses and that the use of male sexualization is counterproductive both for women and men." "Hostile sexism," however, is "an overt hostility toward women that is composed of the drive forces of paternalism, gender differentiation, and heterosexuality (p. 704). They found that "men with higher hostile sexism showed more purchase intentions after viewing sexualized than neutral ads" (p. 701). Zawisza et al. (2018) found a positive association between hostile sexism and purchase intentions toward stereotypically feminine ads" (p. 714). This parallels findings in pornography research that argue it is not so much the sex in pornography that results in violence against women, but violence in pornography (Lipps, 2016; Malamuth & Check, 1985).

Studies of Freudian sexual symbolism in advertising by Ruth, Mostache, and Kramer (1989, 1985) concluded that "genital symbolism motivates consumers' behavior via the sexual arousal based on an unconscious recognition of the male and female genitalia and the act of sexual intercourse" (1989, p. 1131), meaning that when it comes to alcohol, sex might sell booze. Here we are dealing with dopamine-enhancing substances (like drugs) which might complicate the response to the stimulant.

As discussed in Chapter 3, symbolism is an important part of dream analysis. "Psychoanalysts are … interested in symbols in people's dreams and what they reveal about the dreamers" (Berger, 2018, p. 102). The study of symbols, semiotics, is ancient. The etymological roots of semiotics was found "in Ancient Greece (το ση μα 'sign'; σημαίνω 'to give a sign') where the presentation of signs (from the Latin, signum) and their interpretation were important to medicine, religion and warfare" (Litowitz, 1991, p. 81). Medieval semiotics, which draw on even older theories, is attributed to two philosophers: Boethius (480–528) and Augustine (354–430) and their doctrine of sign. Augustine (*De Dial*, 1975, p. 86) noted that a sign "is something that shows itself to the senses and something other than itself to the mind." What became the tripartite construction of a sign (Signifier + Signified) can be traced here as a sign always stands in for something the mind knows, meaning is not static but rather defined, at times challenged, or maintained. Peirce's model identified three types of signs: icon, index, and symbol. A tree, for example, is a physical being in the world. When we see an image, such as a photograph, that resembles an individual species of tree, we understand the reference of this icon. An index bears a resemblance to what is signified such as an image of smoke for fire, a leaf for a tree, a footprint signifies a foot. Language works this way too. For example, when we say the word "tree" each of us gets a different mental image, often reflecting our experience (or lack thereof) with trees or a particular tree and each language has its own word for the same physical object.

This philosophy and method is thus based on the premise that "man [sic] can only know the world indirectly" (Litowitz, 1991, p. 82). Although in media studies what we typically consider are written, photographed, spoken words and images, which are re-presentations, other "signs" are read.[7] For example, in medicine we find that "medical diagnosis has always been the reading of signs that indicate sickness or health" (Litowitz, 1991, p. 81). We "read" nonverbal communications of one another as well as those of other species to ascertain mood, intent, and states of mind. Sebeok (in Deely, 1982) identifies "two trails" when considering semiotics. The first "leads outward into the general culture, widening to become the grand boulevard of semiotic influence, with incursions into all the humanities, social sciences, law and medicine, the multiform arts, the life science in general, the participatory university of quantum theory …. Deeply penetrating into the very fabric of both modern and traditional philosophy." The second trail is "inward-turning, all but subterranean byway traveled by a handful of specialist practitioners of the *doctrina signorum* for its own sake."[8]

For theorists such as Peirce (1839–1914) what is essential in unpacking the meaning of a sign is interpretation: "I define a sign as anything which is so determined by something else, called its Object, and so determines an effect upon a person, which effect I call its interpretant, that the latter is thereby mediately determined by the former" (EP2, p. 478). Thus, there are three parts to a sign: the sign itself, what it signifies, and what signifies it (the referent). For example: "An example of a sign whose sign-vehicle uses existential facts is smoke as a sign for fire; the causal relation between the fire and smoke allows the smoke to act as a signifier" (Atkin, 2022). Like Freud, and most theorists, Peirce's idea of signs went through a variety of modifications and refinements, coming up with classes and divisions for analysis (for more on this, see Chandler, 2021: Deledalle, 2001; Peirce, 1991; Tejera, 1988). However, he brought a schematic organization to the study of signs and makes an obvious connection with the psychological nature of language and meaning formation.

Swiss linguist Ferdinand de Saussure (1857–1913) is also a founder of contemporary field of semiotics (see *Course in General Linguistics*, 1916). He viewed semiotics as a science. Others central to the development of semiotics as a philosophical area of interest and method of analysis include American Charles Sanders Peirce (1839–1914), Roland Barthes (1915–1980),[9] Roman Jakobson (1896–1982) and Umberto Eco (1932–2016). "Nothing is a sign unless it is interpreted as a sign," declared Peirce (Peirce, 1931, p. 308). Psychoanalyst Jacques Lacan (1901–1981) brought semiotics into the field of psychology. These theorists "engage[d] in a search for 'deep structures' underlying the 'surface features' of phenomena" (Chandler, 2021). While a complete discussion of the history of semiotics and the use to study media is beyond the scope of this book, a basic mention of its use to analyze texts is important to the discussion of advertising which follows. Eco (1976, p. 7) stated that "semiotics is concerned with everything that can be taken as a sign." Signs are comprised of signifiers and signifieds and are found in texts. A text as used here is defined as "an assemblage of signs (such as words, images, sounds, and/or gestures) constructed (and interpreted) with reference to the conventions associated with a genre and in a particular medium of communication" (Tran, 2017, p. 64). It refers to "a message which has been recorded in some way (e.g., writing, audio recording and video recording) so that it is physically independent of its sender or receiver" (p. 64). Why does semiotics matter? Chandler (2021) advises that understanding how reality is defined (via words, images, gestures) through the meaning attributed to is an important part of literacy, "studying semiotics can assist us to become more aware of reality as a construction and of the roles played ourselves in constructing it. It can help us to realize that information meaning is not 'contained' in the world or in books, computers, or audio-visual media. Meaning is not 'transmitted' to us—we actively create it according to a complex interplay of codes or conventions of which we are normally unaware."

Litowitz (1991, p. 82) discusses general principles of semiotics as they relate to psychoanalysis (and vice versa), applying this to "a reinterpretation of three critical concepts—symptoms, dreams, and discourse." Dreams, for example, included traces, re-presentations of words, images, people, and animals, in Freud's view, that we have encountered (or avoided) in everyday life. Dreams use symbols that we thus might try to interpret, never knowing for sure if this means that. In discourse (whether visual or verbal) we similarly see or hear a word or image that stands in for something else (and by doing so "implies all the others not chosen (absent)" [p. 85]). Psychoanalysis can be examined as "a semiotic enterprise" (p. 86) for "if we assume that psychoanalysis seeks to understand individual meanings, the relevance of semiotics to psychoanalysis should be clear" (p. 86). We know that knowledge is mediated, that individuals have perceptions of reality, of what to them is "true," and, based on personal experiences (direct, indirect, symbolic) they come to form perceptions that vary at different stages of development. "Every case study and clinical example in Freud's work is a testament to the primacy of the interpretation of signs in psychoanalysis: symptom as sign; dream as sign; and language as sign" (p. 86). He did not call his theories semiotics, but rather used his interpretive knowledge, through watching patients, listening to their descriptions, and noting gestures to conclude that the unconscious "speaks" in different ways that one can learn to interpret. Freud (1913, p. 178) shared his understanding of the communicative potential of the manifestations of mental illness:

> What an hysteric expresses by vomiting an obsessional will express by painstaking protective measures against infection, while a paraphrenic will be led to complaints or suspicions the he is being poisoned. These are all of them different representations of the patient's wish to become pregnant which have been repressed into the unconscious, or his defensive reaction to that wish.

These representations are thus signs that are standing in for a wish/desire. Thus the foundation of Freudian theory is "the same semiotic gap of mediation and representation that necessitates interpretation" (Litowitz, 1991, p. 88). Whatever our instinctual, fundamental needs are, which are often suppressed and repressed from expression because of the collective social mores, it can find an outlet in forbidden, indulgent, idealistic re-presentations in the world around us, often a blurring of needs and wants. As can be seen in the discussion of advertising below, however:

> The overriding point is that Freud's many examples depend upon a theory of knowledge as mediated by different signs out of which a new sign is created in compromise formations such as dreams, parapraxes, and symptoms. These new signs are always overdetermined in that: (1) they include both unconscious and conscious information; and (2) they are never the result of a simple equivalence or a single natural connection. Rather, these signs result from several elements intertwined and interconnected, arising out of the whole fabric from which they are woven. (p. 91)

Freud discouraged saying that a symbol had only one meaning, and he appreciated that meanings can be negotiated. The dreamer might be prompted to consider certain interpretations by the analyst but should be given room to explore their own possibilities. Similarly, in the interpretation of what a media maker intended, or an actor expressed, or an audience member got from a particular advertisement, book, or film must be viewed as polysemic.

In advertising research, studying sexual symbolism is proverbial low-hanging fruit. Industries such as fashion (Ford, 2008; Adzura, 2007; Merskin, 2013; Reichert, Lambiase, Morgan, Carstarphen, & Zavoinia, 1999; Rutherford, 2007), food (Poon, 2016), alcohol (B, Ruth, 1990) personal products (Gramazio, Cadinu, Guizzo, & Carnaghi, 2021; Rutherford, 2007;), and automobiles (Bellinson, 2006; Conley, 2016; Lezotte, 2012) have, almost since their inception, focused on appeals to consumers sense of self, particularly sex appeal. This fundamental urge when coupled with aggression (competition) are easy ways to bypass critical thinking (Goffman, 1976) and reach the reptilian brain. Yet, this is not to dismiss the importance of continued research that addresses how prevalent this type of appeal is, how it is used to reach different target groups, and why, to an extent, sexual appeals can be successful (Reichert & Lambiase, 2003).

Fashioning Fantasies

There are dozens, if not hundreds, of books and websites devoted to critically analyzing advertising based on sexual stereotypes. A Freudian lens helps us identify what motivations might be in the minds of the advertising agency creatives who made the ad, what they thought would most appeal to the target audience, and why. Suppositions of tall narrow buildings or vodka bottles resembling penises or exploding whipped cream cans or yes, cigars, as suggestions of ejaculation are noticeable everywhere. An interesting example that doesn't conceal its connection to psychology is the 2021 Gucci "Seductive and Secret" campaign:

> [A] "seductive and secretive" story photographed by Mert Alas and Marcus Piggott. Looking to London's Savoy Hotel, where Guccio Gucci worked as a liftboy in his youth, encountering many glamorous people that would go on to inspire his designs, the campaign imagines a fictitious club housed within the hotel's historic walls. (Brennan, 2021)

High fashion photography has long played with the unusual, the bizarre, the shocking, and the sexual. What this campaign adds is direct reference to cultural studies and psychoanalytic books. There are bare breasts, buttocks, unusual animals, whips, and various S&M tropes. In one ad a whip holding androgynous duo, dressed in rich red and puce velvet (accompanied by a white peacock) hold a copy of Judith Butler's *Bodies that Matter*. An oversized copy of Freud's *Three Contributions to the Theory of Sex* is held in one hand by a pierced nose with dangling chain and muzzled model draped in Gucci clothing and purse in the other. Behind them is an angular individual in skinny black leather pants, no shirt, lace gloves, kneeling on a chair, face concealed. Another ad has a model, wearing a leather visor with chin and head strap, open-bloused with one nipple exposed who is licking the top of a woman's foot whose loose strapped shoe is barely on, all implying a foot fetish (the model also holds a copy of *Three Contributions*). Other images include very young-looking girls in a bedroom of old-fashioned furniture and wallpaper, wearing horse-back-riding/S&M jackets and hats, holding again *Three Contributions*. Another ad in the series features leather-clad sexually fluid models on all fours, observed faintly by a disinterested metrosexual type, looked over by reading Jean-Luc Nancy's *Sexistence* while two white peacocks jump around the room. Walter Benjamin's *The Work of Art in the Age of Technical Reproduction* is on the lap of a model who is draped in Gucci necklaces, passed out against the wall, while redheaded childlike female similarly unconscious on his lap, as they sit in the hallway, peacock looks out of the frame. The hotel guests are also "caught" reading Baudrillard's *Simulacra and Simulation* and *Sexistence* by Jean-Luc Nancy. "Explaining the campaign's connections to these works, Gucci says: "Our erotic relationship with the world overwhelms everything: artefacts, dreams, clothes … Knowledge itself becomes an object of desire" (Brennan, 2021).

Similarly, in the accompanying 1:26 film titled *Aria* (that carries a disclaimer of viewers should be 18 years and older) an albino-haired, blond-lash guest arrives at the hotel. They hear dogs barking outside. The pace and sound become a repetitive soundtrack element, as the main character walks through the lobby, eyeing other guests, some who are reading the books in the still photographs. The individual ascends the stairs, passing other guests, and getting a peek into other rooms where guests are mingling, kissing, and other activities, all to the soundtrack of "I want you, to want me too … just like I want you … I want you. The right way" (a variation on the Marvin Gaye song). There are scenes of the models filming one another, of voyeurism, of S&M, of peeping through slightly open doors. Many of Freud's theories, of the appeal and motivation of voyeurism, scopophilia, and "the gaze" all feature in this series of advertisements. Acting out of repressed desires? Front and center. Catharsis? Potentially. Something that is relatively new in advertising, less so to high fashion advertising, is androgynous models. This raises the question of whether "the gaze" is only heterosexual or if looking at and/or presenting someone as purely and perhaps only a sexual being is less objectifying than the traditional male gaze that Mulvey (1975) articulated in the pivotal article on the film. In 1979 sociologist Erving Goffman (1976) asked us to consider why don't gendered ads, with their strange gazes, positioning of women, and odd articulations, look strange to us? That so many advertisements (more than 3,000 a day) pass by the average person with little to no critical evaluation, suggests that what really is quite strange in most cases (the dreamworld of advertising) is potentially having more of an effect than we realize. Often women are presented in lower positions than are men, on the floor, on their knees, or, as Goffman (1976) pointed out in *Gender Advertisements* (1979) and Jhally in the *DreamWorlds* (1995, 2008, 2016) series of documentaries, as childlike (and children as adult-like) what does this suggest as a normal order of power? "Advertising doesn't always mirror how people are acting, but how they're dreaming … In a sense, what we're doing is wrapping up your emotions and selling them back to you" (Nelson, 1983, p. 10). Jhally (n.d.) instructs us that "The job of the advertiser is to understand the world of the segmented audience, so that the stimuli that is created can evoke the stored information: it has to resonate with information that the listener possesses." Thus, a psychoanalytic interpretation of advertising, coupled with semiotics to determine what a symbol means (encoding and decoding), offers important areas for future scholarship. While sex in advertising is relatively easy to find, why it has been used so often relates to Freud's theories of the two primary human drives: sex and aggression. Future studies could examine aggression in advertising using these same tools.

A Freudian Analysis of a PR Event

Considering the history of public relations, as discussed in Chapter 3, the examples are endless as to how humans are persuadable though the use of particular phrases, images, or framing of issues. Although contemporary practitioners might not attribute some of the strategies to Freud or psychoanalytic methods, there is little doubt that he was among the first, then adapted (or some might say appropriated) by his nephew, to reach people through techniques that bypass critical reflection and get to core values, beliefs, and desires. Many public relations campaigns could be analyzed through a psychoanalytic lens. An example of how this might be accomplished comes from a recent publication in *The International Journal of Psychoanalysis* (Ziennert-Eilts, 2020), which considers the attraction by many U.S. voters to Donald Trump.

To many, that an outlier like Donald Trump could become president of the United States, was shocking, to say the least. In "Public Affairs in the Time of Trump," Bovim and Koski (n.d.) relate how "before he was elected president, Donald Trump the candidate was a public relations revolutionary." He could generate controversy and coverage, racking "up more free press than any of the candidates he ran against combined. Surprised? This was a candidate who spent more on those red "Make America Great Again" hats than he did on polling. Given all the political experience, campaigns, and insider knowledge of elections that Hillary Clinton had, one would think she would have one. Millions thought she would. Yet Donald Trump was able to use his lack of sophistication and public relations skills to win. According to Bovim and Koski (n.d., p. 2): "Trump's unique PR style has totally disrupted Washington, rewriting the public affairs ground rules in the process."

Outfoxing the Media

In the pre-Trump era, as in the presidential campaigns of George W. Bush or Barack Obama, lobbyists and public relations firms were the first to be hired. With PR firms "you raised a collective ruckus in the media—articles, websites, press releases, etc.—and you aimed that noise at decision makers" (p. 2). This cycle was repeated multiple times, working or not working, getting reelected or not. An important shift in the media in recent years has been a change from 24/7 news cycles to "concurrent" news cycles. Some also refer to this as the "Trump effect" (Lawless & Fox, 2017). In the past, the agenda-setting nature of media moved from one hot topic/story to the next, with the big story of the day appearing on most media platforms. A new story would come along the next day and the pack would follow. With the Trump machine, there are many news cycles, "perpetuated throughout the media bloodstream by accomplices in the mainstream press" (p. 3). No story is dealt with in depth. There's another tweet, another release, and attention is kept short and always moving, according to experts such as James K. Glassman, former Undersecretary of State during the Bush administration (in Bovim & Koski, n.d., p. 3). Tweets sometimes happen spontaneously, becoming a form of entertainment in some camps. He eschews, enrages, and insults traditional media, cultivating his own channel via Fox and Friends (Poniewozik, 2019; Stelter, 2020). News he liked? Truth. Others? Fake. In the report, Bovim and Koski (n.d.) via The

Signal Group offer an array of tips in this new publicity world to succeed such as "know the person who knows the president," "talk about winning," and "access the white house." Each of these is a discussion of new ways the world of DC and national politics is working and strategies of persuasion that have shifted in today's world. How then does one psychoanalytically look at the success of the unconventional strategies and tactics of this administration? This could potentially be accomplished by peering through the lens of group behavior.

Manufacturing Consent

Freud wrote about how dominant (and individual) cultures regulate individual behavior. Should the individual wish to belong to a particular group, to fit in, they thus will repress parts of their nature. The education occurs early as Fromm (1962) wrote, it is the family that is "the first agent of socialization" and "serves the dissemination of societal principles" (in Poscheschnik, 2018, p. 1004). Certain unconscious elements remain repressed, or they would disrupt the family order. This eventually comes to play in group and societal behaviors. Should these feelings rise to the level of consciousness they can be disruptive, even violent. The 2020 election was accompanied by "the rise of destructive, hateful, anti-liberal, anti-democratic, and partly neo-Nazi developments in liberal democratic societies in Europe and the USA—albeit democratically elected—populist or autocratic leaders" (Zienert-Eilts, 2020, p. 971). Zienert-Eilts (2020) analyzed Trump's 2016 and 2020 election campaigns as well as actions in the COVID-19 pandemic during its onset in 2020. The foundation for the study comes from interdisciplinary research into group behavior and populism. Much like the term "propaganda," "populism" didn't always have a negative connotation (see Kaltwasser, Taggart, Espejo, & Ostiguy, for more on global history of the term). However, in the United States, populism can be viewed as Mudde (2017, p. 1) notes, "fundamentally juxtaposed to liberal democracy." There is no settled definition but is "a political strategy employed by a specific type of leader who seeks to govern based on direct and unmediated support for their followers" (p. 4). It requires a "strong and charismatic figure, who concentrates power and maintains a direct connection with the masses" (p. 4). Relevant to the current discussion on techniques used by the Trump campaigns is that populism is "a thin-centered ideology that considers society to be ultimately separated into two homogenous and antagonistic camps, 'the pure people' versus 'the corrupt elite,' and which argues that politics should be an expression of the *volonté Générale* (general will) of the people" (pp. 5–6). Its thinness as an ideology is evident in how discourse is malleable, and concepts change over time to suit the goals of those espousing it. Mudde notes populism contains "three core concepts: the people, the elite, and the general will" (p. 9). Whoever constitutes "the people" is a construction. This configuration of "the people" does not include everyone, but instead includes exclusively those who can serve the interests of the leader. In the case of Trump, the people targeted were the everyday folk, particularly those who felt their voices had not been heard in Washington. The elite became those who believe something different from "the people," and this was almost always made out to be the Democrats. Finally, general will relates to the idea of common sense, the sense being those who agree with the ruler/leader's version of common sense. "Populists are dividers, not uniters," writes Friedman (2017, para. 5), in an interview with Mudde, who describes how these populist formations imagine "two homogenous and antagonistic groups: the pure people on the one end and the corrupt elite on the other," while also imagining themselves to be guided by the "will of the people." The only legitimate people in this view are the ones in their group, who share their values. The people feel unheard, unseen, and are vulnerable to conspiracy theories that say their candidate/ruler/choice isn't in power because of corruption. Although not economically one of "the people" Trump seems to advocate for, the power of political Trump is the moralism. "The moral dimension of populism explains why someone like Donald Trump, who clearly is not a commoner, can nevertheless pretend to be the voice of the people, he doesn't argue, 'I am as rich as you.' What he argues is, 'I have the same values as you. I'm also part of the pure people'" (Mudde qtd. in Friedman, 2017, para. 15). The media play an important role as well. Trump declared that the media were against him, and that the media could often be found intentionally portraying his crowd size as smaller than it was (the crowds were small).

Grouping Psychology

Zienert-Eilts (2020) applies Freud's theory of "psychoanalytic understanding of unconscious processes in groups" (p. 973), drawn from his 1912 *Totem and Taboo* and the concept of a "collective mind in which mental processes occur just as they do in the mind of an individual (Freud, 1912, p. 156). Later, in *Group Psychologand Ego-Analysis* (1921), Freud explored the relationship of individuals to objects, but which are compounded when in groups. Early libidinal attachments to love object (which can as an adult be a leader) connect to "*idealisation* of the father" (ital. orig., Zinert, p. 974). Individual sense of self is placed upon this idealized leader and the group who holds similar views comes together with common charge. Freud saw this applying in the military and churches and those who extended his theories such as Wilfred R. Bion and Melanie Klein extended collective behavior even further (for more on this, see Bion, 1961; Klein, 1946/1993). Loss of individual identity takes place, regresses, and the individual becomes less who they are and more identified with the group who collectively mass regresses. Zienert-Eilts (2020) combines these and other theories to a "perverted containing" in the process of destructive populism" (p. 978). The group comes together, made up of undifferentiated individuals with collective complaints against a powerful other/mother figure (Hillary Clinton, for example) and becomes more insular. Clinton's "basket of deplorables" comment about some Trump supported cemented this group identification (Roberts, 2021). The paranoid-schizoid members "redirect fear of annihilation into the aggression of annihilation of individuals and concentrates the hopes and aggressions of the masses on this person" (Zienert-Eilts, 2020, p. 980) (see Klein, 1946/1993, for more on this). The leader, in this case Trump, assures "the people," he sees and hears them. The container of their groupness becomes perverted. What originally might have brought the group together (feelings of alienation, misunderstanding, powerlessness) "is replaced by a *double omnipotent destructive group identity*: on the one hand, by the symbiotic identification with the destructive, paranoid-schizoid leader and the other, by the identification with the other group members, who also move in a similarly paranoid-schizoid mode" (p. 980). More specifically:

> A vivid example of the interplay between a destructive populist, who moves on a destructive-narcissistic, paranoid-schizoid level and offers himself as an alleged helpful but de facto destructive container on the one hand, and his followers, who have regressed to a paranoid-schizoid level, based on a destructive-populist fit, on the other, is Donald Trump and his followers. (p. 981)

Trump's anti-liberal, anti-pluralist messages that were aimed at an elite group, claiming moral violations, pitting good against evil, involved a "distortion of truth and lies, with denial of reality and with the idealization of narcissistic omnipotence, unbridled, brutal aggression, and a lack of a sense of guilt" (Zienert-Eilts, 2020, p. 981). All of this was evident through his campaigns as well as his encounters with the COVID-19 pandemic. In this study, the author notes Trump's states that he is a victim, claims to be the voice of the people, that good people are his followers (us), that others are bad (them), that he patronizes reporters, particularly women, and particularly women of color, such as NBC News reporter Katy Tur. Trump said, for example, "She's back there, little Katy, back there. What a lie, Katy Tur. What a lie from NBC. Total lie. Third class reporter, remember. Remember that. Third class" (p. 982). A similar thing happened when NPR (and former *New York Times*) reporter Yamiche Alcindor said to Trump: "[Y]ou've said repeatedly that you think that some of the equipment that governors are requesting, they don't actually need. You said New York might not need 30,000 .... " Trump immediately interrupted by blurting out: "I did not say that. I didn't say that." Alcindor said, "You said it on Sean Hannity's Fox News, you said that you might .... " Cutting her off again Trump said, "Come on, come on ... you know, why don't you people act—why don't you act a little more positive—it's always trying to getcha getcha." To get a response to their original question, Alcindor asked again, to which Trump replied, "And you know what, that's why nobody trusts the media anymore. Let me tell you something. Be nice. Don't be threatening." After this a White House aide too away Alcindor's microphone (Emmrich, 2020). A clash had happened before when Alcindor asked Trump about his self-labeling as a nationalist, which he told her was a racist question.

Racist comments, mocking of people with disabilities, talk about "illegals," and lack of guilt or responsibility typify these encounters. The Fake News narrative was another tool of this administration's discourse to discredit, disavow, or distance from real issues, such as the seriousness of the Covid virus. Calling it "the Chinese Virus," Trump pitted the United States as a victim. There are many more examples where a psychoanalytic lens can be used to investigate and explain the power behind the discourse, repeated in multiple media channels particularly social media. Social media outlets such as Instagram and Facebook took unpredicted steps once the power these outlets to incite violence, following the January 6, 2021, attacks on the U.S. Capitol building (Colarossi, 2021; Etherington & Hatmaker, 2021). As Ziennert-Eilts (2020) explains, in part, the sometimes-inexplicable reasons followers of a charismatic leader follow, and the persuasive tactics that care used to distract his true believers from real threats and redirect them toward "phantasised threats (left-wing radicals, chaos, violence in the streets, loss of security), only to offer himself once more as the people's savior" (p. 988). In 1932–1933, Einstein and Freud exchanged letters titled "Why War?" In his July 30, 1932 letter, Einstein explored questions of what it is in humans that persists in waging war, and why there is such a nationalist bias. Einstein proposed a solution that would require compromise and acquiescence on the part of all nations. Einstein notes that what drives this is often a small group, "the so-called 'intelligentizia' [sic]" who motivate groups to states of "hate and destructiveness":

> The craving for power which characterizes the governing class in every nation is hostile to any limitation of the national sovereignty. This political power-hunger is wont to batten on the activities of another group, whose aspirations are on purely mercenary, economic lines. I have specially in mind that small but determined group, active in every nation, composed of individuals who, indifferent to social considerations and restraints, regard warfare, the manufacture and sale of arms, simply as an occasion to advance their personal interests and enlarge their personal authority.

Freud responded by essentially stating that, like other animals, humans are aggressive. What he misses, of course, is that almost no other species of animals engage in "wars" against their own species (Smith, 2019).

Ideas for Future Research

The examples in this chapter are meant as an introduction to how Freud's psychoanalytic theories can be used to study media. Most of the research using Freud's concepts has been in film studies, but any time scholars and students consider persuasion, perspective, or propaganda, Freud should be invoked. Using these theories, and those of his contemporaries who adopted and/or modified them, is an opportunity to deepen research by applying a psychological perspective to analyzing content, creators, or audiences. As concerns audience studies, this emphasis came later in the discipline known as Media Studies but is a natural companion; if you want to study preferences, choices, and interpretations, they are first of all psychological. After a few decades of focusing on content and creators, scholars turned to what brought audiences to content and how they decoded meanings. Semiotics, the study of signs, is a natural method to pair with psychoanalytic theory to unpack what is represented, how, and why.

Additional research is needed in on all areas of media and ancillary services through a psychoanalytic frame such as public relations and advertising using psychoanalytic theory to discuss and interpret responses, such as what makes certain content appealing and what does not, which audiences are drawn to it or not. "The experience of visual captivation" (Holly, 2013, p.

2), or, as Berenson (qtd. in Holly, 2013, pp. 1–2) says when, "the two become one entity; time and space are abolished, and the spectator is possessed by one awareness. The experience might be fleeting but also can be long-lasting. This is something discussed in art, that engagement between product and content (see above re: von Trier movie attendees and motivation). Similar to media effects, the impact of art, literature etc. can connect reader, viewer on a very primal level, reactivate a repressed longing, instigate a return to more innocent time. For example, seeing a particular photograph or work of art can "provoke a sad and romantic yearning for something that has long ago passed away" (p. 2). What type of audience is drawn to particular content and why? That is rich turf for future studies.

Music studies is another area where theory could be applied. Freudian theory could be applied to composers, performers, or the music produced. Imagine songs that have reached you on a deeply emotional level, reminded you of a particular place or time, or brought emotions you thought were over and done with. Consider what is considered appropriate or inappropriate for an occasion. "Melancholy is the condition of music," writes Steinberg (2014, p. 289), and, drawing on Freud, Steinberg asks: "[W]hat does music want? Music wants to speak and to speak importantly, and that unfillable wish is the source of its melancholia" (p. 290). Stories of loss, longing, betrayal, despair, and even emergence from that state are examples of psychology operating as a reflection of the artist's interests and resonating with audiences. Listening alone is a practice called "absolute music" (Dahlhaus (1977) qtd. in Hermand & Gilbert, 1994, p. 259); this "melancholy music, we might be hard pressed to distinguish diagnoses of its mood and meanings from occasions—in song, opera, or indeed dance—where we can infer the mood and meaning from accompany words, gestures, and personifications" (Steinberg, 2014, p. 288).

The preceding chapter was intended to give a sense of a few of the many ways Freud's theories can be used to unpack media content, consider the psychology of the creators of that content, and audience responses to it. How can those now intrigued by psychoanalytic theory and Freud move this area forward? Is Freud still useful as we move forward in the 21st century? That is the subject of the next chapter.

Notes

1 The term "media" is defined as "communication industries and technologies that include newspapers, magazines, radio, television, and film" (Lull, 2000, p. 287) as well as the internet and social media outlets. (.

2 See Kang, J. (2014). *Walter Benjamin and the media: The spectacle of modernity*. New York: Wiley.

3 The planet Saturn, the furthest visible in our solar system, has long been connected to feelings of melancholy. It "is the sixth planet from the Sun and the second largest planet in our solar system," and is ringed with multiple (53 confirmed) and several (29 provisional) moons ("Saturn"). There is a certain nostalgia associated with Saturn (Saturnus), "Saturn was king of that longed-for mythical time" (Daly & Rengel, 2009, p. 131). The mid-December festival of Saturnalia was a time of celebration, feasting, and gift-giving (eventually becoming Christmas under Christianity). "The first direct reference to it is as relating to melancholia occurs in Arab astrology during the 9th century" (Ikkos, 2021, p. 613). Darkest of the planets because of the distance, early peoples attributed contradictions, imbalances, and unpredictability to the planet. The darkness of it leant the association with black bile of the humors, in early Greek and Roman culture.

4 Rotten Tomatoes gives it 80% and IMDb, 7.1/10.

5 For elaboration on the findings, see the original study. Important additional findings include: "shared environment does not influence the association between depressive symptoms and internally directed aggression weighs in favor of the trends in psychoanalytic theory, including Freud's 1930 reformulation, that consider constitutional factors and individual representations of events as contributing to depressive symptoms" (p. 535) and "the genetic and environmental pattern of influence on the association did not differ by sex and therefore undermined Freud's theory that women are more influenced by hostility. However, there were some moderate gender differences found" (p. 536). The researchers note that a possible explanation for the gender difference is that it is less socially acceptable for women to express aggression.

6 "The word *totem* is derived from the Ojibway, or Chippewa, tribes of North America, who utilized the term to identify the specific species of animals the clans were named after. They also serve as a spiritual tool for both the clan and the individual" (Osbaldiston, 2011, p. 1461). For more on this see Lévi-Strauss, C. (1973). *Totemism*. London: Penguin.

7 For more on this see Umberto Eco's series of lectures (June 1980) and (1998). *Serendipities: Language and lunacy*. W. Weaver (trans.). New York: Columbia University Press.

8 *Doctrina signorum* (doctors/teachers of signs) harkens back to the ancient origins of studying signs and sign relations.

9 See Barthes, R. (1957)/1972). *Mythologies*. New York: Farrar, Strauss, and Giroux for more on this.

References

Aaker, D., & Bruzzone, D. (1985). Causes of irritation in advertising. *Journal of Marketing*, *49*(2), 47–57.

Acland, C. R. (2012). *Swift viewing: The popular life of subliminal influence*. New York: Duke University Press.

Adorno, T. (1994). *German essays on music: Theodor W. Adorno, Ernst Bloch, Thomas Mann, and others*. New York: Bloomsbury.

Badley, L. (2022). *Lars von Trier beyond depression*. New York: Columbia University Press.

Barthes, R. (1957)/1972). *Mythologies*. New York: Farrar, Strauss, and Giroux

Bell, M. 2014. *The Western Malady*. Cambridge: Cambridge University Press.

Bellinson, R. L. (2006). *Theory in culture: Toward a psychoanalytic criticism of advertising*. Thesis. Georgia State University.

Benjamin, W. (1977). *The origin of German tragic drama* (J. Osborne, Trans.). London: Verso.

Berenson, B. (2013). Qtd. in M. A. Holly, *The melancholy art*. Princeton, NJ: Princeton University Press.

Berger, A. A. (2018). *An introduction to psychoanalysis or Freud if fixated: Sherlock Holmes is introduced to psychoanalytic theory*. Marin Arts Press.

Bernstein, N. (2022, March 29). In K. Vogel. *Freud's theory of depression and guilt*. PsychCentral. https://psychcentral.com/depression/was-freud-right-about-depression-and-guilt#freuds-theory

Bion, W. R. (1961). *Experiences in groups and other papers*. London: Tavistock.

Bovim, E., & Koski, C. (n.d.). Public affairs in the time of Trump. In *Signal* (pp. 1–8). Available at politico.com.

Bradshaw, P. (2011, September 29). *Melancholia*—review. *The Guardian*. https://www.theguardian.com/film/2011/sep/29/melancholia-film-review

Braga, A., & Logan, R. K. (2013). Mind and media: Exploring the Freud-McLuhan connection. *Explorations in Media Ecology*, *12*(3/4), 159–170.

Brennan, O. (2021, September 13). *See Gucci's "seductive and secretive" new campaign*. AnOther. https://www.anothermag.com/fashion-beauty/13537/see-guccis-seductive-and-secretive-new-campaign-aria

Brooks, X. (2018, December 3). Lars von Trier on filmmaking and fear: "Sometimes, alcohol is the only thing that will help." *The Guardian*. https://www.theguardian.com/film/2018/dec/03/lars-von-trier-on-filmmaking-and-fear-sometimes-alcohol-is-the-only-thing-that-will-help

Burton, R. (1621/1857). *The anatomy of melancholy*. London: J. M. Dent and Sons.

Carrera, E. (2010). Madness and melancholy in Sixteenth- and Seventeenth-Century Spain: New evidence, new approaches. *Bulletin of Spanish Studies*, *87*(8), 1–15.

Carroll, N. (1987). The nature of horror. *Journal of Aesthetics and Art Criticism*, 46, 51–59.

Chandler, D. (2021). *Semiotics for beginners*. http://visual-memory.co.uk/daniel/Documents/S4B/

Cluley, R. (n.d.). *Psychoanalysis as marketing theory*. http://docplayer.net/165802579-Psychoanalysis-as-marketing-theory-dr-robert-cluley.html

Colarossi, J. (2021, January 8). Banning Trump from social media makes sense. But beware the downside. *The Brink*. https://www.bu.edu/articles/2021/trump-banned-from-twitter-facebook/

Conley, J. (2016). *Car troubles: Critical studies of automobility and auto-mobility*. New York: Taylor & Francis.

Dahlhaus, C. (1978/1997). The idea of absolute music. In J. Hermand & M. Gilbert (Eds.). *German essays on music: Theodor W. Adorno, Ernst Bloch, Thomas Mann, and others* (pp. 252-269). New York: Bloomsbury.

Daly, K. N., & Rengel, M. (2009). *Greek and Roman mythology, A to Z* (3rd ed.). New York: Chelsea House.

Dargis, M. (2011, December 30). This is how the end begins. *New York Times*, https://www.nytimes.com/2012/01/01/movies/awardsseason/manohla-dargis-looks-at-the-overture-to-melancholia.html

De Pelsmacker, P., & Van Den Bergh, J. (1996). The communication effects of provocation in print advertising. *International Journal of Advertising*, *15*, 203–221.

Deledalle, G. (2001). *Charles S. Peirce's philosophy of signs*. Bloomington: Indiana University Press.

DeLillo, D. (1985). *White noise*. New York: Viking.

Dima, V. (2014). Ousmane Sembene's 'La Noire de …": Melancholia in photo, text, and film. *Journal of African Cultural Studies*, *26*(1), 56–68.

Ebert, A., & Bär, K.-J. (2010). Emil Kraepelin: A pioneer of scientific understanding of psychiatry and psychopharmacology. *Indian Journal of Psychiatry*, *52*(2), 191–192.

Ebert, R. (2011, November 9). *I see it coming, I will face it, I will not turn away*. RogerEbert.com. https://www.rogerebert.com/reviews/melancholia-2011

Eco, U. (1976). *A theory of semiotics*. Bloomington: Indiana University.

Einstein, A. (1932, July 30). *Why war?* https://en.unesco.org/courier/may-1985/why-war-letter-albert-einstein-sigmund-freud

Emmrich, S. (2020, March 31). President Trump seems to have a problem with Yamiche Alcindor. I wonder why. *Vogue*. https://www.vogue.com/article/yamiche-alcindor-donald-trump-feud

Etherington, D., & Hatmaker, T. (2021, January 7). Mark Zuckerberg announces Trump banned from Facebook and Instagram for "at least the next two week." *TechCrunch*. https://techcrunch.com/2021/01/07/mark-zuckerberg-announces-trump-banned-from-facebook-and-instagram-for-at-least-the-next-two-weeks/

Evans, D. (1996). *An introductory dictionary of Lacanian psychoanalysis*. London: Routledge.

Ferber, I. (2006). Melancholy philosophy: Freud and Benjamin. *E-Rea*, 4.1. https://journals.openedition.org/erea/413

Ferber, I. (2013). *Philosophy and melancholy: Benjamin's early reflections on theater and language*. Stanford, CA: Stanford University Press.

Fleck, C. (1998). The choice between market research and sociography, or: What happened to Lazarsfed in the United States? In. J. Lautman & B. P. Lécuyer (Eds.), *Paul Lazarsfeld (1901–1976): La sociologie de Vinne á New York* (pp. 83–119). Paris: Ed. L'Harmattan.

Ford, J. (2008). Fashion advertising, men's magazines, and sex in advertising: A critical-interpretative study.

Forest, F. (2016). Psychoanalysis in advertising. *International Journal of Applied Psychoanalytic Studies*, *13*(4), 338–350.

Frazer, J. (1911/2002). *The golden bough*. New York: Dover.

Freud, S. (1989). The unconscious. In P. Gay (Ed.), *The Freud Reader* (pp. 572–584). New York: W. W. Norton.

Freud, S. (1912). Totem and taboo. Some points of agreement between the mental lives of savages and neurotics. *S.E.*, *XIII*, 1–162.

Freud, S. (1917). Mourning and melancholia. *SE*, *14*, 239–258.

Freud, S. (1919/1971). *The uncanny* (J. Strachey, Trans.). London: Hogarth.

Freud, S. (1921). Group psychology and the analysis of the ego. *SE*, *XVIII*, 69–143. I.O. German: *Massenpsychologie und Ich-Analyse*. *GW XIII*, 73–161.

Freud, S. (1930). Civilization and its discontents. *SE*, *21*, 64–145.

Freud, S. (1933). Why war? Letter to Albert Einstein. September 1932. *S.E.*, *XXII*, 199–215.

Freud, S. (1936). *A disturbance of memory on the Acropolis* [Letter]. http://www.freud.org.uk/2000/12/30/a-disturbance-of-memory-on-the-acropolis

Freud, S. (1961). Fixation to traumas: The unconscious. In *The standard edition of the complete psychological works of Sigmund Freud. Vol. 16. Introductory lectures on psych-analysis* (Part III). London: Hogarth Press and the Institute of Psycho-Analysis.

Friedman, U. (2017, February 27). *What is a populist?* The Atlantic. https://www.theatlantic.com/international/archive/2017/02/what-is-populist-trump/516525/

Fromm, E. (1962). *Beyond the chains of illusion. My encounter with Marx and Freud*. New York: Continuum.

Glick, P., & Fiske, S. T. (1996). The ambivalent sexism inventory: Differentiating hostile and benevolent sexism. *Journal of Personality and Social Psychology*, *70*, 491–512.

Gramazio, S., Cadinu, M., Guizzo, F., & Carnaghi, A. (2021). Does sex really sell? Paradoxical effects of sexualization in advertising on product attributes and purchase intentions. *Sex Roles*, *84*, 701–719.

Grovier, K. (2019, November 7). What is melancholy in the 21st century? *BBC Culture*. https://www.bbc.com/culture/article/20191107-what-is-melancholy-in-the-21st-century

Haddad, S. K., Neiderhiser, J. M., Spotts, E. L., Ganiban, J., Lichtenstein, P., & Reiss, D. (2013). Depression and internally directed aggression: Genetic and environmental contributions. *Journal of the American Psychological Association*, *56*(2), 515–550.

Hall, S. (1973). *Encoding and decoding in the television discourse*. Paper for the Council of Europe Colloquy on "Training in the Critical Reading of Television Language." Birmingham, UK.

Hartz, A. (2022, August 07). Freud explains cancel culture. *The Wall Street Journal*. https://www.wsj.com/articles/freud-explains-cancel-culture-id-ego-superego-hypermorality-censorship-1960s-counterculture-implicit-bias-mental-illness-psychoanalysts-11659887354?mod=Searchresults_pos1&page=1

Hitchcock, A. (1936/1995). Why thrillers thrive. In S. Gottlieb (Ed.), *Hitchcock on Hitchcock Vol. 1: Selected writings and interviews*. Berkeley: University of California Press.

Holly, M. A. (2013). *The melancholy art*. Princeton, NJ: Princeton University Press. https://press.princeton.edu/books/hardcover/9780691139340/the-melancholy-art

Ikkos, G. (2021). *Saturn: Star of melancholy*. Cambridge: Cambridge University Press.

Jhally, S. (n.d.). What's wrong with a little objectification? http://www.sutjhally.com/articles/whatswrongwithalit/

Jhally, S. (1997). *Advertising and the end of the world* [Motion Picture]. Northampton, MA: Media Education Foundation.

Jhally, S. (1998). *Advertising and the end of the world* [Transcript]. Northampton, MA: Media Education Foundation.

Kahr, B. (2015). *Freud*. New York: Pegasus.

Kaltwasser, C. R., Taggart, P., Espejo, P. O, & Ostiguy, P. Populism: An overview of the concept and the state of the art. In C. R. Kaltwasser, P. Taggart, P. Ochoa Espejo, & P. Ostiguy (Eds.), *The Oxford handbook of populism* (pp. 1–24). Oxford, UK: Oxford University Press.

Keats, J. (1820). *Ode to melancholy*. The Poetry Foundation. https://www.poetryfoundation.org/poems/44478/ode-on-melancholy

Key, W. B. (1973). *Subliminal seduction: Ad media's manipulation of a not so innocent America.* New York: Signet.

Klein, M. (1946/1993). Notes on some schizoid mechanisms. In. M. Klein (Ed.), *Envy and gratitude and other works, 1946–1963*. London: Karnac.

Kotler, P. (1965). Behavior models for analysing buyers. *Journal of Marketing, 29*, 37–49.

Kraepelin, E. (1883). *Compendium der Psychiatrie: Zum Gebrauche für Studirende und Aerzte (Compendium of Psychiatry: For the Use of Students and Physicians)*.

Krüger, S., & Johanssen, J. (2016). Thinking (with) the unconscious in media and communication studies. *Communication and Media, 12*(38), 5–40.

Lazarsfeld, P. F. (1934). The psychological aspect of market research. *Harvard Business Review, 13*(1), 54–71.

Lee, S. J. (2021). *Melancholia and decadence:* The film *Melancholia* (2011) by Lars von Trier. *Journal of Humanities, 81*, 113–145. https://doi.org/10.31310/HUM.081.04

Lezotte, C. (2012). The evolution of the "chick car" or: What came first, the chick or the car? *Journal of Popular Culture, 45*(3), 516–531.

Lipps, H. M. (2016). *A new psychology of women: Gender, culture, and ethnicity* (4th ed.). Long Grove, IL: Waveland Press.

Litowitz, B. E. (1991). *Semiotic perspectives on clinical theory and practice: Medicine, neuropsychiatry and psychoanalysis*. In B. E. Litowitz & P. S. Epstein (Eds.), *Semiotic perspectives on clinical theory and practice: Medicine, neuropsychiatry, and psychoanalysis* (pp. 81–11). Berlin: De Gruyter Mouton.

Lull, J. (2000). *Media, communication, culture: A global approach* (2nd ed.). New York: Columbia University Press.

Lund, M. A. (2021). *A user's guide to melancholy*. Cambridge: Cambridge University Press.

Malamuth, N. M., & Check, J. V. (1985). The effects of aggressive pornography on beliefs in rape myths. *Journal of Research in Personality, 19*(3), 299–320.

Manceu, D., & Tissier-Desbordes, E. (2006). Are sex and death taboos in advertising? *International Journal of Advertising, 25*(1), 9–33.

Marcuse, H. (1955). *Eros and civilization: A philosophical enquiry into Freud.* Boston: Beacon Press.

Marin, D. (2018, September 12). Film sequence analysis: *Melancholia* (2011)—the surreal overature. https://dianamarin.com/2018/09/12/melancholia-2011-the-surreal-overture/

Marso, L. J. (2017). *Politics with Beauvoir: Freedom in the encounter.* Durham, NC: Duke University Press.

Martin, G. N. (2019). (Why) do you like scary movies? A review of the empirical research on psychological responses to horror films. *Frontiers in Psychology, 18*, 1–22.

McGowan, T. (2011/2016). Psychoanalytic film theory. In *Oxford bibliographies*. https://www.oxfordbibliographies.com/view/document/obo-9780199791286/obo-9780199791286-0052.xml

McGowan, T. (2015). *Psychoanalytic theory and The Rules of the Game*. New York: Bloomsbury.

McLuhan, M. (1962). *The Gutenberg Galaxy*. Toronto: University of Toronto Press.

Meek, A. (2010). *Trauma and media: Theories, histories, and images*. London: Routledge.

Melancholic depression. (2021, February 27). PsychDB. https://www.psychdb.com/mood/1-depression/melancholic

Merriam-Webster. (n.d.). Melancholy. In *Merriam-Webster.com dictionary*. Retrieved June 3, 2023, from https://www.merriam-webster.com/dictionary/melancholy

Merskin, D. (2013). Where are the clothes? The pornographic gaze in mainstream American fashion advertising (pp.). In T. Reichert & J. Lambiase (Eds.), *Sex in consumer culture: The erotic content of media and marketing*. New York: Routledge.

Mudde, C. (2017). *Populism: A very short introduction.* Oxford, UK: Oxford University Press.

Nelson, J. (1983, April 16). When the brain tunes out the admen tune in. *Toronto Globe and Mail.*

Nolan, S. (2009). *Film, Lacan, and the subject of religion: A psychoanalytic approach to religious film analysis*. London: Continuum.

O'Shaughnessy, J. (2015). Note on the marginalizing of psychoanalysis in marketing. *Marketing Theory*, *15*(1), 17–19.

Osbaldiston, N. (2011). Totemism. In D. Southerton (Ed.), *Encyclopedia of consumer culture.* New York: Sage.

Packard, V. (1957/1970). *The hidden persuaders*. New York: Penguin.

Paykel, E. S. (2008). Basic concepts of depression. *Dialogues in Clinical Neuroscience*, *10*(3), 279–289.

Pierce, C. S. (1991). *Writings on semiotic*. J. Hoopes (Ed.). Chapel Hill: University of North Carolina Press.

Pistelli, J. (2013, April 26). Lars von Trier, *Melancholia*. https://johnpistelli.com/2013/04/26/melancholia/

Poniewozik, J. (2019). *Audience of one: Donald Trump, television, and the fracturing of America*. New York: W. W. Norton.

Poon, S. (2016). The function of sexual imagery and visual seduction in food advertising. *International Journal Advances in Social Science and Humanities*, 4(3), 22–27.

Poscheschnik, G. (2018). *Game of Thrones*—a psychoanalytic interpretation including some remarks on the psychosocial function of modern TV series. *International Journal of Psychoanalysis*, 99(4), 1004–1016.

Radden, J. (2002). (Ed.). *The nature of melancholy: From Aristotle to Kristeva*. New York: Oxford.

Reichert, T., & Lambiase, J. (2002). *Sex in advertising: Perspectives on the erotic appeal*. New York: Taylor & Francis.

Reichert, T., Lambiase, J., Morgan, S., Carstarphen, M., & Zavoina, S. (1999). Beefcake or cheesecake? No matter how you slice it, sexual explicitness in advertising continues to increase. *Journalism & Mass Communication Quarterly*, 76(1), 7–20.

Roberts, R. (2021, August 31). Hillary Clinton's 'deplorables' speech shocked voters. *The Washington Post*. https://www.washingtonpost.com/lifestyle/2021/08/31/deplorables-basket-hillary-clinton/

Ruth, W. J., & Mostache, H. S. (1985). A projective assessment of the effects of Freudian sexual symbolism in liquor advertisements. *Psychological Reports*, 56, 183–188.

Ruth, W. J., Mostache, H. S., & Kramer, A. (1989). Freudian sexual symbolism: Theoretical considerations and an empirical test in advertising. *Psychological Reports*, 64(3).

Rutherford, P. (2007). *A world made sexy: Freud to Madonna*. Toronto: University of Toronto Press.

Samuel, L. R. (2013). *Freud on Madison Avenue: Motivational research and subliminal advertising in America*. Philadelphia: University of Pennsylvania Press.

Samuel, L. R. (2022, April 9). *How Dichter brought psychology to business*. Psychology Today. https://www.psychologytoday.com/us/blog/psychology-yesterday/202204/how-ernest-dichter-brought-psychology-business

Sassatelli, R. Tamed hedonism. In D. Southerton (Ed.), *Encyclopedia of consumer culture* (pp. 1428–1430). New York: Sage.

"Saturn." NASA Science Solar System Exploration. https://solarsystem.nasa.gov/planets/saturn/in-depth/

Scott, A. O. (2011, November 10). Bride's mind is on another planet. *The New York Times*. https://www.nytimes.com/2011/11/11/movies/lars-von-triers-melancholia-review.html

Sebeok, T. A. (1982). Foreword. In J. N. Deely, *Introducing Semiotic*. Bloomington: Indiana University Press.

Sigmund Freud. (2022). In J. L. Longe (Ed.), *The Gale encyclopedia of psychology* (4th ed., Vol. 1, pp. 474–476). Gale. https://link.gale.com/apps/doc/CX8273700321/HWRC?u=euge94201&sid=bookmark-HWRC&xid=ffa6568a

Smith, D. L. (2019). *The most dangerous animal: Human nature and the origins of war*. New York: St. Martin's Press.

Sontag, S. (1978, October 12). The last intellectual. *The New York Review*. https://www.nybooks.com/articles/1978/10/12/the-last-intellectual/

Sontag, S. (1978/1982). Under the sign of Saturn: Essays. In *A Susan sontag reader* (pp. 385–401). New York: Farrar/Straus/Girioux.

Steinberg, M. P. (2014). Music and melancholy. *Critical Inquiry*, 40(2), 288–310.

Stelter, B. (2020). *Hoax: Donald Trump, Fox News, and the dangerous distortion of truth*. New York: Atria.

Tejera, V. (1988). *Semiotics from Peirce to Barthes*. New York: Brill.

Tolentino, J. C., & Schmidt, S. L. (2018). DSM-5 criteria and depression severity: Implications for clinical practice. *Frontiers in Psychology*, 9, 450.

Tran, B. (2017). The art and science in communication. In B. Christiansen & H. C. Chandan (Eds.), *Handbook of research on human factors in contemporary workforce development* (pp. 60–84). Hershey, PA: IGI Global.

Travers, P. (2011, November 10). *Melancholia. Rolling Stone*. https://www.rollingstone.com/tv-movies/tv-movie-reviews/melancholia-105725/

Vogel, K. (2022, March 29). *Freud's theory of depression and guilt*. PsychCentral. https://psychcentral.com/depression/was-freud-right-about-depression-and-guilt

von Trier, L. (Director). (2011). *Melancholia* [Film]. Zentropa.

Wilson, E. G. (2008). *Against happiness: In praise of melancholy*. New York: Farrar, Strauss, and Giroux.

Zawisza, M., Luyt, R., Zawadzka, A. M., & Buczny, J. (2018). Cross-cultural sexism and the effectiveness of gender (non) traditional advertising: A comparison of purchase intentions in Poland, South Africa, and the United Kingdom. *Sex Roles*, *79*, 738–751.

Ziennert-Eilts, K. J. (2020). Destructive populism as "perverted containing": A psychoanalytic look at the attraction of Donald Trump. *The International Journal of Psychoanalysis*, *101*(5), 971–991.

Appendix 4.1: Melancholy Art, Media, & Popular Culture

It is impossible to list all the uses of melancholy, broadly defined, in the arts and popular culture. However, below are some listings designed to provide food for thought and for discussion. Do you agree with what's listed? Disagree? What would you add to these lists?

It is a melancholy truth that even great men have their poor relations.

Charles Dickens (1896, p. 395)

In Art

Aertegen Van Leyden—St. Jerome in His Study by Candlelight (1520)
Domenico Fetti *Melancholia* (1619)
Artemisia Gentileschi—*Mary Magdalene as Melancholy* (1625–1626)
Domenico Fetti—The Repentant St. Mary Magdalene (1671–1621)
Louis Cranach the Elder *Melancholia* (1532)
Francisco Goyoa (1798) Gaspar Melchor de Jovellanos
Edvard Munch *Melancholy* (1894)
Frederic Lord Leighton—*Lachrymea* (1894–1895) (mourning near funerary monument)
Vincent Van Gogh—*Portrait of Dr. Gachet* (1896)
Paul Gauguin—*Nevermore* (1897)
Giorgio De Chirico Melancholy and Mystery of the Street (1914)
Louis-Jean-François Langrenée *La Mélancolie* (18th century)
Pablo Picasso—*Melancholy Woman* (1902)
Salvador Dalí—Uranium and Atomica Melancholia Idyll (1945)

In Music

Rolling Stone's The 10 Saddest Songs of All Time (2013)

1. Eric Clapton "Tears in Heaven"
2. Nine Inch Nails "Hurt"
3. R. E. M. "Everybody Hurts"
4. Harry Chapin "Cat's in the Cradle"
5. Nirvana "Something in the Way"
6. George Jones "He Stopped Loving Her Today"

7. Pearl Jam "Black"
8. John Prine "Sam Stone"
9. Alice in Chains "Nutshell"
10. Hank Williams "I'm so lonesome I could cry"

In Film

1. von Trier *Melancholia* (2011)
2. Kauman *Synecdoche, NY* (2008)
3. McKellar *Last Night* (1998)
4. Coppola Lost in Translation (2003)
5. Beineix *Betty Blue* (1986)
6. Trier *Oslo, August 31* (2011)
7. Frears *High Fidelity* (2000)
8. Nicolli *Gattaca* (1997)
9. Scorsese *Taxi Driver* (1976)
10. Hamer *Kitchen Stories* (2003)
11. Scott *Blade Runner* (1982)
12. Cuarón *Children of Men* (2006)

References

30 films for a melancholic mood. IMDb. https://www.imdb.com/list/ls004310509/

Dickens, C. (1883). In F. G. De Fontaine (Ed.), *The fireside Dickens*. New York: G. W. Carleton.

Reader's Poll: The 10 saddest songs of all time. https://www.rollingstone.com/music/music-lists/readers-poll-the-10-saddest-songs-of-all-time-10875/10-hank-williams-im-so-lonesome-i-could-cry-209572/

· 5 ·

FREUD IN THE 21ST CENTURY

> We cannot fall out of this world.
>
> Freud (1929/2017, p. 7)

> Freud's brilliance was in recognising that disturbing memories don't just go away. His compassion lives to this day in the method he established for bringing them to light and reducing their negative and sometimes debilitating effects: psychoanalysis.
>
> Nicholson (2017, para. 19)

The preceding chapters illustrated many of Freud's central theories, particularly those that offer interpretative lenses applicable to media and cultural studies scholarship and broader interest. In addition, the chapters offered explanations that contextualized these theories within the historical periods within which they were first articulated, all with a nod to Freud's belief that scientific thinking is best tested, revised, and either abandoned or modified. Finally, in Chapters 3 and 4 we saw how and when psychoanalytic theories have been and could be used to study media and popular culture. In this chapter I discuss some of the criticisms of Freud's theories, as these criticisms are so prevalent in the literature that anyone considering using psychoanalytic theory should be aware of them. This is followed by a discussion of which disciplines are most likely to engage with Freud's theories, and an argument on behalf of the need for a multidirectional interaction between psychology, other social sciences, and the humanities. This is followed by a section that considers how his theories could be further incorporated in studies of media. Finally, the chapter concludes with a reflection on what Freud might have to say about today's world and our media production and use. Menand (2017, para. 10) speaks to the relevance for psychoanalytic approaches to interpreting media content, production, and consumption.

It is not a stretch to treat literary texts in the same way that an analyst treats what a patient is saying. Although teachers dislike the term "hidden meanings," decoding a subtext or exposing an implicit meaning or ideology is what a lot of academic literary criticism does. Academic critics are therefore always in the market for a theoretical apparatus that can give coherence and consistency to this enterprise, and Freudianism was ideally suited for the task. Decoding and exposing are what psychoanalysis is all about.

Criticisms and Challenges

While Freud is considered the "father" of psychoanalysis, he was not the only individual to consider this path to physiological healing. Freud inspired many others, including Alfred Adler, Carl Jung, Sándor Ferenczi, Otto Rank, Jacques Lacan, Karen Horney, Erich Fromm, Harry Stack Sullivan, and Melanie Klein. They took from his work what made sense to them and modified Freud's conceptual apparatus to reflect their own criticisms of the Freudian method. As the psychoanalytic practice grew, so did important modifications to his theories. Psychologists such as Melanie Klein (1882–1960) adapted Freud's work, particularly in their variation of psychoanalytic theory known as object relations. This theory focuses less on biologically based drives (id) and more on interpersonal relationships to help explain connection, loss, or fantasy development. The mother's breast, for example, or a symbol of this part of a person, is objectified by the infant, but can also become familiar as an image. Klein developed this theory to include unconscious fantasy and paranoid-schizoid and depressive positions. Klein stressed the first 4–6 months of a child's development as central (Freud saw 4–6 years as the crucial time), a nurturing mother (or primary caregiver) as "object." The father was less emphasized here, whereas Freud saw power/control of the male figure as a key part of psychological development. Human contact and relationships were primary to the Kleinian view, whereas libido (sexual energy) was central to Freud's theories (for more on this, see Klein; 1921, 1923, 1930, 1932).

A central concept related to object relations is splitting, which is mental separation of objects into good/bad categories, some of which become associated with anxiety and are repressed (for more, see Klein, 1932, 1935). Theorists such as Jacques Lacan expanded theories that originated in Freud's writings and practice. Both Freud and Lacan dealt with the human mind and saw the unconscious to be the origin of mental processes. However, Lacan expanded the theories to include language. He was a French philosopher who saw language as one of the definitive aspects of being human. He considered language to be the site wherein the self develops. "According to Lacan, the structure of the unconscious is similar to any other natural languages such as English, Spanish, Nepali, Hindi, or Chinese" (Pun, 2018, p. 52). Lacan identified three phases of development (see Vanheule, 2011): l'hommelette, mirror, and symbolic. In the first, a child has little self-knowledge and does not seem themselves apart from the mother (or primary caregiver). Then, as part of departing from this connection, a child might literally see themselves in a mirror and identify as autonomous. Lacan argued this happens at around 6–18 months, but that this is also a sort of false self. The realization of being separate is only part of development. Once separation, and incorporation of what is acceptable and what are taboo feelings toward parents are established, this then becomes a profound switch. Lacan also identified the desire one feels beforehand as the Oedipus complex. French psychoanalyst Jean LaPlanche (1924–2012), a student of Lacan, expanded Freud's theories of psychosexual development to include the seduction theory. LaPlanche broke with Lacan in 1964 believing that the unconscious is structured like a language, whereas Freud argued it precedes language. LaPlanche expanded Freud's theories in the realm of drives, the sexual unconscious, and repression.

In the field of philosophy, Jean-Paul Sartre (1943) dug into Freud's theory of the unconscious in *Being and Nothingness*. Paul Ricoeur, Theodor Adorno, Jürgen Habermas, Jean-François Lyotard, Jacques Derrida, and others, whose work is widely used in media and cultural studies, drew from Freud. As Mitchell & Black (1995) describe it:

> The startling reality is that very little of the way Freud understood and practiced psychoanalysis has remained simply intact. The major pillars of his theorizing—instinctual drives, the centrality of the Oedipus complex, the motivational primacy of sex and aggression—have all been challenged and fundamentally transformed in contemporary psychoanalytic thought. (p. xvii)

This would seem to be a normal phenomenon, wherein theories should be tested, revised, and perhaps reconsidered. And yet, as noted in previous chapters, there have been several criticisms of Freud as a person, as a psychologist, and as a scientist. Anyone of high profile no doubt experiences this. That Freud believed theories should be modified as the researcher learns more about their domain. This makes a great deal of sense today, but it opened him up to charges of being negligent, non-diligent, and wishy-washy (Shulman, 2021). These typically came from critics of psychotherapy as well as those who practice other forms of mental health work. Biographer Peter Gay commented: "They've convinced the convinced. Freud once had a sexy dream about one of his daughters, so they make him a pedophile. They love that sort of stuff" (in Fisher, 1995, para. 29). In fact, a 1995 Library of Congress exhibit, "Sigmund Freud: Conflict and Culture," was postponed in part because of criticisms (and budget issues) (Fisher, 1995, para. 1).[1]

The main controversies surrounding Freud and his theories fall into four main categories: (1) The Freud Wars, (2) lack of empirical rigor, (3) sexism, and (4) overemphasis on sex as an explanation for human behavior. These are discussed in the sections below.

The Freud Wars

Even though the focus in this book is on using Freud's theories to study media content and creators, it would be missing an important section were I not to address what has become known as "The Freud Wars," an even more impassioned philosophical battle over his person, ideas, and outcomes. John Forrester writes:

> The Freud Wars have been raging for some years now, with serious historical argument and abstract philosophical criticism neatly dovetailed with name-calling, ill temper, and vitriol. From television to the daily newspapers, from the weekly reviews to museum exhibitions, from books and articles published by scholarly presses to professional conferences and debates—all these open spaces for the public expression of opinion have become arenas of contestation. More private spaces are no doubt equally infused with sniping and surprise offensives, sometimes even the search for an armistice—at least they are in my experience. Leaving the necessarily more intractable private spaces to one side for the moment, how do questions as abstruse as different philosophical approaches to confirmation in the sciences or as gossipy as Freud's relationship with his sister-in-law become regular concerns of national newspapers? Why, in other words, do the Freud Wars matter to our culture at large? (1997, p. 1)

Philosophy departments have long pushed back against psychoanalysis. Tensions were reflected in 1993, when the *New York Review of Books* (NYRB) hosted a heated exchange on the topic of psychoanalysis. After having been a long-time believer in Freud's ideas, Frederick Crews wrote *The Unknown Freud* (1993), in which he charged Freud with articulating fraudulent ideas, taking advantage of a naive public to promote the techniques of psychoanalysis, and accusing Freud of a grandiose desire for psychoanalytic celebrity. Crews (1995/1997, p. 298) wrote, "Freud has been the most overrated figure in the entire history of science and medicine." Crews was not alone in criticism. Simón (2020, p. 86) aggressively argues that Freud's ideas should *not* be taught in psychology departments, that "the Freudian doctrine is a field populated by fantasies having little basis in reality" and that those who do not voice their opinions as the "dissenter" is viewed as "actually repressing and suppressing his motivations for criticism." Rather, Simón (2020) views Freud's ideas as belonging in philosophy perhaps, that their inclusion in psychology has cast doubt on the entire field of psychology. In a footnote, he says, "Goodbye Freud," and refers to "the cult of sycophants that Freud created" (p. 90).

It is the job of scholars to interrogate ideas, without deference to the author, regardless of that author's stature. In 2002, journalist Janet Malcolm published what's regarded as part comedy, part drama: *In the Freud Archives*, "a story of infatuation and disappointment, betrayal, and revenge" (book cover description). The book tells of an encounter between three men: "K. R. Eissler, the venerable doyen of psychoanalysis; Jeffrey Moussaieff Masson, a flamboyant, restless forty-two-year-old Sanskrit scholar turned psychoanalyst turned virulent anti-Freudian; and Peter Swales, a mischievous thirty-five-year-old former assistant to the Rolling Stones and a self-taught Freud scholar."[2]

Another example is the 2005 book *The Freud Wars: An Introduction to the Philosophy of Psychoanalysis*, in which British therapist (and object relations scholar) Lavinia Gomez critiques psychoanalysis with many of the same arguments mentioned above: lack of empirical rigor, too interpretive, and for various views of the unconscious. Besides focusing on the taboo, and therefore curiosity-arousing topic of sex, Freud's theories gained popularity in the United States, where they were medicalized. Both Hitler and Stalin actively drove psychoanalysis out of Europe. Lewis Menand described how psychoanalysis, a "product of Mittleuropa, once centered in cities like Vienna, Berlin, Budapest, and Moscow […] was thus improbably transformed into a largely Anglo-American medical and cultural phenomenon" (Menand, 2017, para. 5). While many Freudian analysts died at the hands of Nazis, some committed suicide, and about 50 immigrated to the United States. Menand describes the rise of Freudians in the United States:

> They took over American psychiatry. After the war, Freudians occupied university chairs; they dictated medical-school curricula; they wrote the first two editions of the *Diagnotist and Statistical Manual of Mental Disorders* (the *DSM*). … Most important, psychoanalysis helped move the treatment of mental illness from the asylum and the hospital to the office. (Menand, 2017, para. 5)

Psychoanalysis enjoyed a precarious popularity in the United States. In the United States there was widespread agreement that we hide our feelings, and that talking about our feelings can help bring psychological issues to light. Still there was pushback. As psychology and psychiatry became increasingly medicalized and insurance companies required certain diagnoses to provide the necessary imprimatur for billing, much of what was Freudian in the *DSM* (by the 3rd edition) was removed. In the 1970s, critics of Freud decried his theories of the unconscious as unoriginal. How might Freud respond? One might say that the veracity and vitriol of the attacks suggest that Freud's writings hit a nerve in these authors, tapping into some repressed material they would have preferred to remain submerged.

Lack of Empirical Rigor

Given that the American medical community evaluated Freud's ideas in the early 1900s from the standpoint of the natural sciences, it makes sense there would be this criticism. However, what Freud was doing, via self-analysis, reflection, and use of individual case studies, is consistent with what one conducting qualitative research might do. He also was very open about the need for theories to be modified as one learns more. Freud based his theories on self-analysis and work with individual patients, not on large-scale, generalizable studies, and yet some of his insights have proven to be quite applicable to the group level, particularly when it comes to sex in media. There has always been a tension, it seems, between quantitative research that produces generalizable statistics, and qualitative research that values individual or small-group experiences as knowledge. This criticism of Freud's work might in fact be more a product of that methodological divide than any actual shortcoming of his findings. Crews (1993, para. 3) states that "Freudian concepts retain some currency in popular lore, the arts, and the academic humanities, three arenas in which flawed but once modish ideas, secure from the menace of rigorous testing, can be kept indefinitely in play." Crews thus posits at least implicitly that one method of knowing (quantitative) is somehow better, and more sophisticated than others (qualitative) and is consist with these methodological battles. Despite our being taught that the best way to answer a research question is through triangulation, the quantitative/qualitative divide remains. I argue that this is what prejudiced many psychological researchers to turn away from Freud's work because it was mostly qualitative. In 2007, psychologist Jonathan Lear noted: Some of the most important things in human life are just not measurable, like happiness or genuine religious feelings. Freud, though, is particularly useful for gaining insights into questions of human existence. There will be the discovery of problems that the standard ways don't address," he said, and then "there will be a swing back to Freud" (in Cohen, 2007, para. 2).

Writing in *The American Journal of Psychiatry* in a review of Goldberg's (2004) *Misunderstanding of Freud*, Barlow (2005) suggests that

> psychiatrists who only write medicine prescriptions and have little or no interest in talking with patients should ignore this book. Those of us who continue to believe that sensitive emotional communication is crucial for understanding and facilitating clinical change (with or without the use of psychoactive agents) must give this book considerable careful attention. In grappling with these matters Goldberg defines the process of insight more extensively than any writer since Freud.

Sexism

Feminists have been highly critical of many of Freud's concepts, arguing that the assumptions and approaches of psychoanalytic theory are profoundly patriarchal, anti-feminist, and misogynistic. One could counter that Freud took women's concerns seriously, something that rarely happened back in that time. There are volumes of feminist pushback on Freud, such as Kate Millet's (1969) *Sexual Politics*, which was "one of the first attacks on the patriarchal dominance of psychoanalysis" (Balsam, 2016, p. 83). Did Freud see women as basically reproductive vessels? Hysterics? Or as something else? In a 2016 paper, "Freud, the birthing body, and modern life," Balsam (2016) reconsiders Freud's view of the female body and sexual pleasures and notes that, until he was 52 years old, he included female bodies in developmental theory. The "envy" that arose could indeed have been female patients pushing back on patriarchy, something that may have unsettled him. This includes some of the writings of his peers that might have influenced him (by Wittel and Ferenczi, for example). In *The Question of Lay Analysis* (1926/1990), Freud states: "We know less about the sexual life of little girls than of boys. But we need not feel ashamed of this distinction; after all the sexual life of adult women is a 'dark continent' for psychology" (p. 38) could be interpreted as either a more complex sexuality or recognition of neglect in the field. The pregnant female body was a source of childhood awakening, adolescent curiosity and comparison with other species, and, in his medical studies, "a relentless focus on the mind that took the sexed body as its bellwether" (Balsam, 2016, p. 66).

Juliet Mitchell (1974) argued Freud had been misread (see *Psychoanalysis and Feminism*).

Overemphasis on Sex As an Explanation

Freud's belief that, physiologically, human beings are comprised and motivated primarily by aggression and sex drive was controversial from the beginning. For example, on May 10, 1933, crowds of Nazi sympathizers in Austria publicly burned Freud's books chanting: "Against the soul-destroying overestimation of the sex life—and on behalf of the nobility of the human soul, we offer the flames the writings of Sigmund Freud" (Cohen, 2014, para. 16). Freud stated, in *Introductory Lectures* (1916/1917, SE 15: 22–23) that "society believes that no greater threat to civilization could arise than if the sexual instincts were to be liberated and returned to their original aims."

Freud argued that we struggle to fit our essential drives in to rules and obligations of "civilization." "Mechanisms of repression," based on sublimation, include "law, morality, culture, and the arts, and perhaps most important religion" (Bratlinger, 1983, p. 160). That sex, particularly psychosexual development during childhood, has such a powerful impact on ideas of the self has drawn a great deal of criticism. And yet, if we look at what it is that appeals to many people, clearly satisfaction of desires and drives are components of the "mechanisms" and appear in media content. The competition and aggression in sports, the appeal of sex in advertising, the bypassing of critical thinking skills in persuasive efforts, all speak to there being something to his idea that what motivates us as a species is as fundamental as drives. Too much of an emphasis on sex? Perhaps, but then again Freud always argued for a certain flexibility. Also, like social class, sex is a topic many aren't comfortable discussing let alone thinking about, and yet are an essential part of human makeup. "He inferred that sexual and aggressive fantasies were among the universal determinants of emotion, thought, and behavior … [proposing] that the human sexual drive influenced mental life in a developmental sequence" (Libido) (Hagan, 2017, para. 8). These theories were precursors to many of today's theories of personality.

Another criticism, less developed, is the Eurocentric tendency of his theories, that they may indeed only be applicable to Western cultures, given his own determining cultural experience. Critics argue that his "doctrine of psychoanalysis … was one of personality development and behaviors based on sexual perversion and aggression as being the universal norm" (Simón, 2020,

p. 85). Whether he proffered his ideas to be universal, other than fundamental human urges/drives is debatable. Based on his study and absorption of mythologies from many cultures and times it seems he was in fact setting the stage for what became the work of scholars such as Joseph Campbell (1949/2004) who saw universal monomyths as connecting human cultures.

Is Freud Taught in Psychology Programs?

Freud set out to help people. His was a calling of the medical profession in which he began his training and followed by the practice of psychology where he honed his understanding of mind/body/spirit connections. One would naturally think that a student could study Freud and his theories in departments of psychology at universities, right? Not so. Do traditional textbooks give weight to his writings and theories? No. "Freud is to the field of psychology, in many ways, as Newton is to physics. Courses in physics include Newton but don't stop there. Similarly, in psychology, Freud's ideas about the unconscious became the basis for later theories that built on his basic principles" (Whitbourne, 2012). Those who followed Freud are studied. For example, as mentioned previously, Klein (1921, 1923, 1930, 1932), Lacan (1966/2006), and Bowlby's (1988/2005) attachment theory arose from Freud's concepts of infant bonds. This same theory is now used to discuss adult relationships (Sable, 1992).

Another central concept is defense mechanisms. Rather than rely on self-reports, where people refuse to accept they are in denial, projective measures such as Rorschach inkblots are used to coax people to reveal unconscious fantasies and associations. Computer models of association and reactions also draw on early Freudian concepts. The Implicit Bias/Association test is an example in which quickly moving images are presented to the participant who then "unconsciously" responds based on deeply held assumptions and emotions that rise before critical thought is available. Word association, which draws on talk therapy, is a common tool in marketing focus groups. What is now referred to as psychodynamic methods of client engagement *is* taught in psychology programs, but is Freud credited? Rarely. "If you want to learn about psychoanalysis at the nation's top universities, one of the last places to look maybe the psychology department" (Cohen, 2007, para. 1). This is true in part due to modern U.S. psychology's emphasis on quantitative methods, measurable statistical, and evidenced-based approaches. However, as I have already argued, quantitative methods are not the only path to knowledge.[3]

Given how "Freud long ago became a metonym for psychoanalysis," there are ideas that are "absolutely necessary for a psychoanalyst to be familiar" as well as essential readings (Shulman, 2021, p. 1094). In a study of the database PEB-WEB in 2020, Shulman (2021, p. 1103) found terms such as "phallic," "narcissism," "anal," "obsessional," "sadism," "sadistic," "hysterical," and others of Freud-origin, having their "day." Apparently, "sadism," "sadistic," and "narcissistic" are enduring and durable (for a table documenting when terms were popular, see this study). Allen (1931/1959, p. 81) writes: "[N]ew words and phrases began to be bandied about the cock-tail tray and the Mah Jong table—inferiority complex, sadism, masochism, Oedipus complex. Intellectual ladies went to Europe to be analyzed; analysts plied their new trade in American cities." And Bair (2003, p. 414) describes how,

> [b]y 1935, psychoanalysis in general was "all the rage" in London, as it was throughout most of the world. Politicians were being psychoanalyzed by reporters in the daily newspaper, the literary world was entranced with the possibilities the new science offered for individual creativity, and critics in every field were busy applying and misapplying its doctrines to many disparate genres and disciplines.

While Freud may be marginalized in psychology programs, his ideas are used in many other disciplines. Cohen (2007, para. 1) discusses how Freud's theories "have spread to every nook and cranny of the culture from Salinger to *South Park*, from Fellini to foreign policy." Thus, English, comparative literature, media and cultural studies, cinema studies, and political science are majors in which a student might encounter a good doctor. Tufts University psychology student Jay Singh (qtd. in "Teaching," 2007) noted: "A lot of themes in literature fit really well with Freudian theories," Furthermore, "He explained that taking a psychoanalytic approach to studying a text allows the reader to approach not just the themes of the work, but to more deeply understand the author who wrote it" ("Teaching," 2007). Singh continues: "[S]cholars in the liberal arts have tended to use Freud as a springboard to examine issues and ideas never dreamt of in his philosophy—like gender studies, post-colonial studies, French postmodernism, Queer theory and so on" (Cohen, 2007, para. 14). This is not without its criticism, of course. Simón (2020, p. 90, n. 5) comments in a footnote: "One editor wrote to me: 'Many undergraduates taking psychology are disappointed to not be learning more about Freud; those we send over to the English department to revel in (gak!) Freudian analyses of literature.'"

Where to from Here?

I have throughout this book referenced studies in which psychoanalysts have considered media and communications content. However, some journals relate media and psychology as their focus. *Media Psychology*, for example, published by Taylor & Francis since 1999, is described in the Aims and Scopes, as being "an interdisciplinary journal devoted to publishing theoretically oriented, empirical research that is at the intersection of psychology and media/mediated communication." A quick content search on the journal's home page using "Freud" revealed six articles: a study of the appeal of tragedy (Goldenberg, Pysczynski, Johnson, Greenberg & Solomon, 1999), sitcom laugh tracks and behavioral norms (Rhodes & Ellithorpe, 2016), experiencing fictional characters (Konijn & Hoorn, 2009), "why people watch reality TV" (Reiss & Wiltz, 2004), "developing a typology of humor" (Buijzen & Valkenburg, 2004), and identification with television characters among young adults (Hoffner & Buchanan, 2005). However, in each of these publications, Freud is mentioned in most cases only once in concepts such as identification without applying or exploring his theories in the studies that followed. The more than three generations since Freud appear only as "launch[ing] point[s] and touchstone[s]" (Shulman, 2021, p. 1094).

Journal of Media Psychology, published by Hogrefe, is another venue that focuses "on how human beings select, use, and experience various media as well as how media (use) can affect their cognitions, emotions, and behaviors. Submissions must substantially advance the current state-of the art on a theoretical and/or an empirical level." A search of journal contents revealed nothing under the search terms "Freud," "psychoanalytic," or "psychoanalysis." The journal *Psychology of Popular Media Culture*, published by the American Psychological Foundation (APA), which first published in 2011, also resulted in no publications in which the term "Freud" was included, or "psychoanalytic," or "psychoanalysis." This could be an area of future study as there might be other terms that could yield theories that are attributable to Freud in these journals thus serving as touchstones for research.

Many theories used to study thought processes, popular culture, and media content had their origins in earlier times and have been modified and reworked to suit the present day. A new wave of research asks what, for example, Freud would make of social media and our behavior with it. Broyles (2018, para. 4) describes how

> the instantaneous nature of Twitter—or our "social id"—lends itself to both real-time moments of delight, humor, and shared event-driven experiences, but also gives voice to regrettable bursts and limited character shots of insults, sexism, racism, and other streams of consciousness that might have been better left unsaid (or at least, unwritten).

The "liking" on Facebook, fear of missing out (FOMO), professional support and connections via LinkedIn "are a 'social Super-Ego' that symbolizes our ideal self" (Broyles, 2018, para. 6). Williams (2018) analysis of Tumblr uses Freud's concept of repetition, engagement, trauma, and attachment to study "repeated viewing of GIFs and GIF sets on Tumblr for fan engagement" and "this platform's use as a mechanism for reassurance in the face of moments of rupture." Ray examines theories of seduction and trauma in films such as *Pillow Book* (2012b) and television programs such as *The Shield* (2012a), as well as human and animal divide and connection (2014).

In addition to this research, another outlet for interdisciplinary publishing is the "Psychoanalysis and Popular Culture" book series, published since 2009 by the Media and the Inner World research network. Rather than focus purely on textual analyses, "this [Taylor & Francis] series sets out to explore the creative tension of thinking about cultural experience and its processes, with attention to observations from the clinical and scholarly fields of observations" (Bainbridge & Yates, 2014, p. xiv). Titles include *Television and Psychoanalysis* (Bainbridge, Ward, & Yates, 2019), *The Inner World of Doctor Who* (MacRury & Rustin, 2019), *The Psychodynamics of Social Networking* (Balick, 2014), and *The American Dream and American Cinema in the Age of Trump* (Clarke & Clarke, 2022).

It is important not only to see the value of psychoanalysis at the individual, therapeutic level, but also as de Berg (2003) emphasizes, Freud's work is "a *critical theory of society*."

"What all of this shows is that we live in a time of enormous change and instability, where many of the ideas and values of the past have dissolved and scholars with open minds have to go back to first principles and renegotiate the ground upon which knowledge is based" (Tacey, 2007, p. 424). Stein (2020) argues that we should regard the practice of psychoanalysis and psychoanalytic theory as applicable in the wider world. This is something depth psychologists also do. Conditions such as trauma, repression, projection, and other states not only occur at the individual level but the collective as well. They ask:

> What can psychoanalyst and more narrowly, psychoanalyst who write, do today and tomorrow to have a more significant impact on human affairs beyond the profoundly important work analyst do with their patients do every day? What can we do outside the consulting room altogether? Where can psychoanalytic expertise be delivered and used to benefit society as a whole and, more specifically, to materially assist people in positions of authority, responsibility, and influence, people whose decisions and behavior are amplified by virtue of their leadership roles? (p. 142)

While Stein (2020) writes primarily to those who practice psychoanalysis (and defines the difference between them and "lay" persons as dictated by the medical community), their call is vital to media studies, to critiquing, unpacking, and explaining events on the part of media producers as well as to understandings media consumers might have as content is delivered to them. It also offers an interesting exploration in the field of journalism between professionals and so-called citizen journalists. Who creates content? Who has authority to interpret meanings?

All apply to media studies.

Are Freud's ideas still relevant to the worlds of psychology and the study of media? Without a doubt. In fact, the exchange should be multidirectional as Badenhorst and Rubitel (2021, p. 1145) note that "psychiatry has a long tradition of drawing on the humanities to understand mental functioning and individual experience" (see also Engle, 1980; Shlozman, 2017). It seems the social sciences beyond psychology such as those that serve as the interdisciplinary foundations for media and communication studies should be similar resources.

In their study of the impact of an introductory Freudian-psychoanalytic course in medical education, Badenhorst and Rubitel (2021) created a course in which 12 students "drew on literature, music, film, fine art, and broad cultural observation" to generate written reflections. Some students went beyond the assignment. In one case a student composed a piece of music and another, a short film (p. 1149). In the use of media and popular culture to generate doctor-patient empathy within the context of psychoanalytic theories, students, considering migrant theory, wrote on the following media and popular culture products (Table 5.1)

Table 5.1. Titles of Reflective Essays, Arranged by Genre

Cultural/anthropological observation
A Psychodynamic Approach to the Migrant Identity
Film
Charlie and the Chocolate Factory: A psychodynamic perspective
Psychodynamic analysis of Scorsese's *Taxi Driver*
Pain and Gain interpreted from a psychodynamic perspective
Can the film *Inside Out* turn Freudian-psychoanalytic models of the mind inside out?
Her: A reflection
Reflections on *Fight Club*
Literature
The Little Prince: A book of sadness, loneliness, and responsibility
Music
A reflection on Ludovico Einaudi's *Giorni*
Freudian viewpoint of Daniel Caesar's debut album
Fine Art
The Cholmondeley Ladies: Falling into the trap of looking without seeing
Music Video
A psychodynamic perspective on "The Trial" from Pink Floyd's *The Wall*

Source: Badenorst, W., & Rubitel, A. (2021). Freud and medical student education: Introducing an elective course. *Journal of the American Psychoanalytic Association*, 69(6), 1150.

In "What use is Freud?" Shulman (2021) articulates six elemental ideas that can/should be carried forth not only in psychology programs but have obvious connections to studying media content, creators, and consumers (italics orig., p. 1106):

1. Freud's work on the intentionality and meaningfulness of all mental life. See *Studies on Hysteria* (1895) and *The Interpretation of Dreams* (1900). His work, particularly in these volumes, "provides a set of lessons in unconscious intention, both expressive and defensive, and in unconscious forms of thinking in primary process" (p. 1108).
2. The decisive important of unconscious psychic reality, in contrast to material reality, as the reality that dominates patients and determines their particular suffering. This idea applies when considering creator motivations, creative output as well as interpretations of audiences. Creative work can be considered as "a symptom of the author who produced it, or as analogous to the relationship between the dreamer and

his or her dream, as if the work is a symptomatic reproduction of the author's infantile and forbidden wishes" (Peck & Coyle, 1993, p. 188).

3. Mind as a system of forces in continuous interaction, included forces of wish and instinct, of self-criticism, and of anxiety-triggered defense that often operates in the service of self-deception. This draws on Freud's topographic model (Id, Ego, and Superego) but reminds us that the relationship between these components is vibrant, pliant, and dynamic.
4. *Childhood as a time of maximal psychological vulnerability for a human being.* This foundational time is well known for how experiences can influence the quality of adult life. Media consumed during this time that have, according to theories of media effects, short- or long-term influences on self and others, in, of course, the context of other relationships.
5. *The intertwining of sexual sensations, wishes, and fantasies with each individual's search for love.* Every media product can be located in one or several genres. The stories we tell about ourselves, our myths, repeatedly appear in tales told orally or in representational forms. No wonder they resonate so well and are often comfortable and formulaic touching on fundamental human desires and dreams!
6. *The encounter of a patient and an analyst as replay of a botched story about the patient's search for love.* Transference has not been discussed so far in this book but merits a mention—that connection, sometimes an unhealthy one, between the therapist and patient in which the therapist becomes the source of strength and guidance for the client, "when patients transfer their feelings from parents or significant others to the therapist." This dynamic can be experienced by fan attraction to particular characters, to actors who might seem to audiences as the characters they play (parasocial interaction) or studied in different forms of content.

It is no longer possible to see a play or other work of art without drawing upon Freud's penetrating vision. No modern biography is without inquiry into the subject's childhood, family, and traumatic as well as beneficial early experience.

An illustration of how these six ideas fit into media studies can be found in the work of media scholar Arthur Asa Berger (2015) who has dedicated much time and attention to the application of psychoanalytic theories to media and cultural studies. In a video series for Sage Publishing as well as in several books and papers, Asa Berger argues that representational figures/images/illustrations can be read through a Freudian lens as male or female. For example, objects such as pens, knives, guns, sticks, and power tools are "male" symbols, whereas receptors such as ovens, bottles, cupboards, and other containers are "female." The male symbols penetrate; the female receives. The human psyche, which is in continual conflict, wishes satisfaction of desires and amelioration of guilt and Id, Ego, and Superego are always fighting for balance. As discussed earlier, this is evident in certain characters in stories and can be analyzed as such, most easily in superhero science fiction characters. Asa Berger reflects on the *Star Trek* series and three main characters playing out these dynamics: The doctor, McCoy, is an Id figure, he is emotional. Captain Kirk is superego and Spock, being absolutely rational, is the ego figure. All are in search of balance when seeking solutions to crises encountered by the Enterprise and its passengers. Cities, universities, entertainment venues, and monuments can be analyzed according to their roles and images. Similarly, television programs such as those relying on highly sexual images are Id events, whereas science programs are ego-oriented. Viewers don't necessarily know this, but rather that the program is appealing to a desire or need. These unconscious forces motivate them; they respond to material/genres that appeal to and potentially satisfy these cravings.

Conclusion

> Peeking into the nooks and crannies of psychotherapy allows us to see that Freud's influence lives on, even if it may be hard to recognize at times. Psychoanalysis circa 1910 was as much a cultural revolution as a scientific enterprise. Nevertheless, it is clearly a vital and evolving approach even in our highly empirical field today. Freud is dead, long live the king!
>
> Whitbourne (2012)

The world Freud left was one of full of violence and hate. He died, a refugee in London, three weeks after the start of World War II. Wars were seemingly endless in Europe; people were being killed based on nationality and religion. That was in 1939. What would Freud think of the world today? How best can media scholars use his ideas? Although "Freud was dismissive of radical politics," that "belief that social change could make people healthier or happier was deluded" (Menand, 2017), as in *Civilization and Its Discontents*, his ideas can be seen as liberatory (see Marcuse for example). In fact, according to a 2022 "real-life thriller" *Saving Freud* (Nagorski, 2022), *Freud* so believed that he was outside of politics, he had to be pushed to leave Vienna, believing things would right themselves (Hughes, 2022).

Despite critics, and there are many, "There is something irreversible about what Freud has done to twentieth-century culture," writes Forrester (1997, p. 2). Lists of "Eminent Freudians" would not only include Edmund Burke, Thomas Mann, and Jürgen Habermas, but also "any list should be capacious enough to include Claude Levi-Strauss and Woody Allen, Sir Aaron Klug and Brian de Palma, Richard Rorty, A. S. Byatt, and even the enigmatic French soccer player Eric Cantona" (p. 2). All times have their skeptics and all writers their critics. It's what we do as academics, as students, ideally as citizens—we question. I thus concur with Forrester (1997, p. 12):

> Not only does everyone know what Freud wrote and what everything Freudian 'really means,' everyone also knows what all the fuss is really about. So the process of writing about Freud must always be one of uneducating one's readers. I stand on common ground with some of Freud's critics on this issue, since at least some of them believe in reading and thinking closely about his work and its historical context. But, unlike these critics, it is my wager that the more one knows about Freud—the more one has unlearned what one was culturally hard-wired to know about him—the more interesting and surprising and thought-provoking he becomes. The final answer to Freud's critics is that many intelligent men and women—and maybe even children—have recognized and continue to recognize this.

Regardless of the criticisms of Freud, which are all worth considering, it important that we, as scholars, students, analysts, and analysands, remember that "we are explorers of a vast new world Freud opened, but could scarcely begin to explore himself" (Shulman, 2021, p. 1095). Freud's openness to new ideas, to modifying theories, to learning from the past, and taking individual experience seriously are all strengths we can carry forward. It takes a good amount of effort to dig deeply into Freud's theories, interpret them considering contemporary conditions, and potentially apply them. However, as media scholars, we regularly consider and reconsider many of our traditional media theories that have been modified, revised, disputed, and defended (agenda setting, uses and gratifications, magic bullet, spiral of silence). Debates about Freud's theories, the times in which they were articulated, and the relevance to today's individuals and cultures should seem like the normal rigor to which we regard all areas of inquiry. That his work was primarily qualitative is no reason to disregard them, rather should present an opportunity for further testing. That Freud studied people, what they did, felt, reasoned, wrote, and responded too makes it appropriate for considering media creation and consumption. In a review of the book *Why Freud Was Wrong* (Webster, 1996), Lawson (1995) writes:

> Popular anti-Freudianism resides in a strange perturbation of what is essentially a far from Freudian belief. Blaming Freud for his buck-passing, self-exonerating super liberalism is a strange misreading. No authentic Freudian would claim that we were helpless victims of our pasts. Rather Freud teaches one to recognize the past for what it is, so that one may understand, and therefore, if necessary, modify, one's actions in the present. Freudian psychoanalysis is not about casting blame, it is about taking responsibility.

Notes

1 The Library of Congress is the "repository of the world's largest collection of papers and artifacts from the father of psychoanalysis" (Fisher, 1995), thus making this cancellation significant. Both Oliver Sacks and Gloria Steinem protested it.

2 For more on Masson's criticisms see *The assault on the truth: Freud's suppression of the seduction theory* (1984). New York: Ballantine.

3 Freud is taught in Depth Psychology programs. In fact, that is where I first studied Freud in work on a second PhD at Pacifica Graduate Institute (https://www.pacifica.edu/). The institute offers "masters and doctoral programs in depth psychology, counseling, clinical psychology, mythological studies, and the humanities."

References

Badenhorst, W., & Rubitel, A. (2021). Freud and medical student education: Introducing an elective course. *Journal of the American Psychoanalytic Association*, 69(6), 1145–1152.

Bainbridge, C., Ward, I., & Yates, C. (Eds.). (2019). *Television and psychoanalysis*. New York: Taylor & Francis.

Bair, D. (2003). *Jung*. Boston: Little, Brown, & Company.

Balick, A. (2019). *The psychodynamics of social networking*. New York: Taylor & Francis.

Balsam, R. H. (2016). Freud, the birthing body, and modern life. *Journal of the American Psychoanalytic Association*, 65(1), 61–90.

Barlow, P. (2005, April 1). Misunderstanding Feud. *American Journal of Psychiatry*, *162*(4), 826–827. https://ajp.psychiatryonline.org/doi/10.1176/appi.ajp.162.4.826

Berger, A. A. (2015). *Psychoanalytic theory and media*. Sage Video. https://www.youtube.com/watch?v=ewR2GlKOPcU

Bowlby, J. (1988/2005). *A secure base*. New York: Routledge.

Bratlinger, P. (1983). *Bread and circuses: Theories of mass culture as social decay*. Ithaca, NY: Cornell.

Broyles, C. (2018, June 13). *Sigmund Freud and 21st century social media: Id, ego, & super-ego as social media platforms* [Blog post]. ACAP. https://acapnj.org/sigmund-freud-and-21st-century-social-media-id-ego-superego-as-social-media-platforms/

Buijzen, M., & Valkenburg, P. M. (2004). Developing a typology of humor in audiovisual media. *Media Psychology*, 6(2), 147–167.

Campbell, J. (1949/2004). *The hero with a thousand faces*. Princeton, NJ: Princeton University Press.

Clarke, G. S., & Clarke, R. (2022). *The American dream and American cinema in the age of Trump*. New York: Taylor & Francis.

Cohen, L. (2014, September 23). How Sigmund Freud wanted to die. *The Atlantic*. https://www.theatlantic.com/health/archive/2014/09/how-sigmund-freud-wanted-to-die/380322/

Cohen, P. (2007, November 25). Freud is widely taught at universities, except in the psychology department. *New York Times*. https://www.nytimes.com/2007/11/25/weekinreview/25cohen.html

Crews, F. C. (1993, November 18). The unknown Freud. *The New York Review of Books*. https://www.nybooks.com/articles/1993/11/18/the-unknown-freud/

Crews, F. C. (1995/1997). *The memory wars: Freud's legacy in dispute*. New York: Granta.

De Berg, H. (2003). *Freud's theory and its use in literary and cultural studies: An introduction*. New York: Camden House.

Engel, G. L. (1980). The clinical application of the biopsychosocial model. *American Journal of Psychiatry, 137*, 535–544.

Fisher, M. (1995). Under attack, library shelves Freud exhibit. *Washington Post*. https://www.washingtonpost.com/archive/politics/1995/12/05/under-attack-library-shelves-freud-exhibit/0dd66a76-fed1-4b1d-bdd6-e315cc29d19f/

Forrester, J. (1997). Dispatches from the Freud wars: Psychoanalysis and its passions. Cambridge, MA: Harvard University Press.

Freud, S. (1926). *The question of lay analysis* (3rd ed., J. Strachey, Ed.). New York: W. W. Norton.

Freud, S. (1930/1989). Civilization and its discontents. In P. Gay (Ed.), *The Freud reader* (pp. 722–772). New York: W. W. Norton.

Gay, P. (1995, December 5). Qtd. in M. Fisher. Under attack, library shelves Freud exhibit. *Washington Post*. https://www.washingtonpost.com/archive/politics/1995/12/05/under-attack-library-shelves-freud-exhibit/0dd66a76-fed1-4b1d-bdd6-e315cc29d19f/

Goldberg, A. (2004). *Misunderstanding Freud*. New York: Other Press.

Goldenberg, J. L., Pysczynski, T., Johnson, K. D., Greenberg, J., & Solomon, S. (1999). The appeal of tragedy: A terror management perspective. *Media Psychology, 1*(4), 313–329.

Gomez, L. (2005). *The Freud wars: An introduction to the philosophy of psychoanalysis*. London: Routledge.

Hagan, E. (2017, May 5). *Freud is everywhere*. Psychology Today. https://www.psychologytoday.com/us/blog/psychoanalysis-unplugged/201705/freud-is-everywhere

Hoffner, C., & Buchanan, M. (2005). Young adults' wishful identification with television characters: The role of perceived similarity and character attributes. *Media Psychology*, *7*(4), 325–351.

Hughes, K. (2022, August 18). *Saving Freud* by Andrew Nagorski review—a real thriller. *The Guardian*. https://www.theguardian.com/books/2022/aug/18/saving-freud-by-andrew-nagorski-review-a-real-life-thriller

Klein, M. (1921). Development of conscience in the child. In *Love, guilt, and reparation and Other Works 1921–1945: The Writings of Melanie Klein* (Vol. 1). London: Hogarth Press.

Klein, M. (1923). The development of a child. *International Journal of Psycho-Analysis*, *4*, 419–474.

Klein, M. (1930). The importance of symbol-formation in the development of the ego. *International Journal of Psycho-Analysis*, *11*, 24–39.

Klein, M. (1932). *The psychoanalysis of children* (International Psycho-Analytical Library, No. 22). New York: Hogarth.

Konijn, E. A., & Hoorn, J. F. (2009). Some like it bad: Testing a model for perceiving and experiencing fictional characters. *Media Psychology*, *7*(2), 107–144.

Lacan, J. (1966/2006). *Ecrits* (B. Fink, Trans.). New York: W. W. Norton.

LaPlanche, J., & Pontalis, J. B. (1974). *The language of psychoanalysis*. New York: Routledge.

Lawson, N. (1995, October 5). Why old Sigmund was right after all. *The Times of London*.

MacRury, I., & Rustin, M. (2019). *The inner world of Dr. Who*. New York: Taylor & Francis.

Malcolm, J. (2002). *In the Freud archives*. New York: New York Review of Books.

Masson, J. M. (1984). *The assault on the truth: Freud's suppression of the seduction theory* New York: Ballantine.

Menand, L. (2017, August 21). Why Freud survives. *The New Yorker*. https://www.newyorker.com/magazine/2017/08/28/why-freud-survives

Mitchell, J. (1974). *Psychoanalysis and Feminism*. New York: Basic Books.

Mitchell, S. A., & Black, M. J. (1995). *Freud and beyond: A history of modern psychoanalytic thought*. New York: Basic Books.

Nagorski, A. (2022). *Saving Freud: A life in Vienna and an escape to freedom in London*. London: Icon.

Nicholson, C. (2017, November 16). *Why Freud was right about hysteria*. The Conversation. https://theconversation.com/why-freud-was-right-about-hysteria-86497

Peck, J., & Coyle, M. (1993). Literary terms and criticism. In D. Lodge (Ed.), *Modern criticism and theory* (2nd ed., pp. 79–106). London: Longman.

Pun, M. (2018). The interpretation of the unconscious: From Freud to Lacan. *International Journal of Humanities and Social Science Invention*, *7*(1), 48–52.

Ray, N. (Ed.). (2012a). *Interrogating The Shield*. Syracuse, NY: Syracuse University Press.

Ray, N. (2012b). Seduction, receptivity, and the "feminine" in Peter Greenaway's *The Pillow Book*. *International Journal of Psychoanalysis*, 93(3), 517–538.

Ray, N. (2014). Interrogating the human/animal relation in Freud's *Civilization and Its Discontents*. *Humanimalia*, 6(1), 10–40.

Reiss, S., & Wiltz, J. (2004). Why people watch reality TV. *Media Psychology*, 6(4), 363–378.

Rhodes, N., & Ellithorpe, M. E. (2016). Laughing at risk: Sitcom laugh tracks communicate norms for behavior. *Media Psychology*, *19*(3), 359–380.

Sable, P. (1992). Attachment theory: Application to clinical practice with adults. *Clinical Social Work Journal*, *20*, 271–283.

Sartre, J. P. (1943) *Being and nothingness*. New York: Routledge.

Shlozman, S. C. (2017). Why psychiatric education needs the humanities. *American Psychiatry*, *41*, 703–706.

Shulman, M. E. (2021). What use is Freud? *Journal of the American Psychoanalytic Association*, 69(6), 1093–1113.

Simón, A. (2020). Goodbye Sigmund Freud. *Journal of Human Behavior*, *30*(1), 85–92.

Stein, A. (2020). Psychoanalysis in the public sphere: A call for taking analytic thinking, writing, and action into the broader world. *Psychoanalytic Perspectives*, *17*(2), 141–160.

Tacey, D. (2007). The gift of the unknown: Jung(ians) and Freud(ians) at the end of modernity. *European Journal of Psychotherapy & Counseling*, 9(4), 423–424.

Teaching of Freud slips in college psychology but thrives in other fields across universities. The Tufts Daily. https://tuftsdaily.com/archives/2007/12/05/teaching-of-freud-slips-in-college-psychology-but-thrives-in-other-fields-across-universities/

Vanheule, S. (2011). *The subject of psychoanalysis: A Lacanian perspective*. New York: Palgrave.

Whitbourne, S. K. (2012, May 15). *Freud's not dead; He's just really hard to find*. Psychology Today. https://www.psychologytoday.com/us/blog/fulfillment-any-age/201205/freud-s-not-dead-he-s-just-really-hard-find

Williams, R. (2018). Tumblr's GIF culture and the infinite image: Lone fandom, ruptures, and working through on a microblogging platform. *Transformative Works and Cultures*, *27*. https://journal.transformativeworks.org/index.php/twc/article/view/1153

APPENDIX 1: FREUD TIMELINE

1856 (May 6)	Born, Freiberg, Moravia (today Příbor, Czech Republic)
1860	Freud family moves to Vienna, Austria
1865	Began attending the Gymnasium
1873	Graduated *summa cum laude* from Gymnasium and begin study of medicine at the Vienna University
1878	Changed first name from Sigismund to Sigmund
1881	Received doctorate degree in medicine
1882	Employed as doctor at Theodor Meynert's psychiatric clinic
1884	Published monograph, detailed study of cocaine
1885	Worked with Jean-Martin Charcot at the Saltpetrier Hospital. Focus on hysteria and hypnosis
1886	Opened private practice
	Married Martha Bernays
1887	Mathilda born (1889–1967)
	Interest in hypnotherapy
1889	Friendship begins with Wilhelm Fleiss

1891	Oliver born (1891–1969)
1892	Move to Berggasse 19
1892	Freud and Josef Breuer describe the case of Anna O. in *Studies on Hysteria*
	Ernst born (1892–1970)
1893	Early formulation of seduction theory
	Anna (1895–1982) born
1896	First use of term "psychoanalysis" in *Zur ätiologie der hysterie*
	Father Jacob dies
1897	Begins self-analysis
1898	The Psychical Mechanism of Forgetting published
1900	*The Interpretation of Dreams* is published
1901	The Psychopathology of Everyday Life is published
	Begins analysis of 18-year-old Dora
1902	Founds the Wednesday Psychological Society
1903	Meets with Fleiss for the last time in Vienna
1905	Three Essays on Sexuality, Jokes, and their Relation to the Unconscious and Fragments of an Analysis of a Case of Hysteria (Dora) published
1906	Begins corresponding with Carl Jung
1907	Freud and Jung meet in person
	Delusion and Dreams published in W. Jensen Gradiva
1908	First International Psychoanalytical Congress on Freudian Psychology held in Salzburg
1909	Freud and Jung travel to the United States with Sándor Freenczi. Invitation by G. Stanley Hall to guest lecture at Clark University
1910	Founds International Psychoanalytical Association
1912	Founds journal *Imago*
1913	*Totem and Taboo* published
	Jung breaks from Freud
1916	First part of Introductory Lectures on Psychoanalysis appears
1919	Founds International Psychoanalytical Press in Vienna

1920	*Beyond the Pleasure Principle* published (introduces the death instinct)
1922	Grandson Lucian Freud born
	Works on A Seventeenth-Century Demonological Neurosis
1923	The Ego and the Id published
	Freud was diagnosed with Leukoplakia and jaw cancer
1925	Volume 1 of *Collected Works* appears
1929	Civilization and Its Discontents published
1930	Freud's mother, Amalia, dies
1933	Corresponds with Albert Einstein
	Public burning of some of Freud's books by Nazis
1938	Anna Freud arrested and interrogated by Gestapo
	Family moves to London to escape
1939	Freud dies of cancer in London on September 23

References

Cherry, K. (2018, July 1). *Sigmund Freud timeline*. Verywellmind. https://www.verywellmind.com/sigmund-freud-timeline-2795846

Sigmund Freud chronology. Sigmund Freud Museum Vienna. https://www.freud-museum.at/online/freud/chronolg/chrnlg-e.htm

APPENDIX 2: PUBLICATIONS OF SIGMUND FREUD

- 1884 On Coca
- 1891 On Aphasia
- 1892 A Case of Successful Treatment by Hypnotism
- 1893 Charcot
- 1893 On the Psychical Mechanism of Hysterical Phenomena
- 1894 The Neuro-Psychoses of Defence
- 1894 Obsessions and phobias
- 1894 On the Grounds for Detaching a Particular Syndrome from Neurasthenia under the Description "Anxiety Neurosis"
- 1895 Project for a Scientific Psychology
- 1895 Studies on Hysteria (German: *Studien über Hysterie*; co-authored with Josef Breuer)
- 1896 The Aetiology of Hysteria
- 1896 Heredity and the Aetiology of the Neuroses
- 1896 Further Remarks on the Neuro-Psychoses of Defence
- 1898 Sexuality in the Aetiology of the Neuroses

- 1899 Screen Memories
- 1899 An Autobiographical Note
- 1899 The Interpretation of Dreams (German: *Die Traumdeutung*)
- 1901 On Dreams (abridged version of The Interpretation of Dreams)
- 1904 The Psychopathology of Everyday Life (German: *Zur Psychopa_ thologie des Alltagslebens*)
- 1905 Jokes and their Relation to the Unconscious
- 1905 Fragment of an Analysis of a Case of Hysteria (Dora)
- 1905 Three Essays on the Theory of Sexuality (German: *Drei Abhandlungen zur Sexualtheorie*)
- 1905 On Psychotherapy
- 1905 Psychopathic Characters on the Stage
- 1906 My Views on the Part Played by Sexuality in the Aetiology of the Neuroses
- 1906 Psycho-Analysis and the Establishment of the Facts in Legal Proceedings
- 1907 Obsessive Actions and Religious Practices
- 1907 Delusions and Dreams in Jensen's Gradiva (German: *Der Wahn und die Träume in W. Jensens "Gradiva"*)
- 1908 The Sexual Enlightenment of Children
- 1908 Character and Anal Erotism (German: *Charakter und Analerotik*)
- 1908 On the Sexual Theories of Children
- 1908 "Civilized" Sexual Morality and Modern Nervous Illness (German: *Die "kulturelle" Sexualmoral und die moderne Nervosität*)
- 1908 Creative Writers and Day-Dreaming
- 1908 Hysterical Phantasies and their Relation to Bisexuality
- 1909 Family Romances
- 1909 Some General Remarks on Hysterical Attacks
- 1909 Analysis of a Phobia in a Five-Year-Old Boy (Little Hans)
- 1909 Notes upon a Case of Obsessional Neurosis (Rat Man)
- 1910 Five Lectures on Psycho-Analysis
- 1910 Leonardo da Vinci, a Memory of his Childhood (German: Eine Kindheitserinnerung des Leonardo da Vinci)
- 1910 The Antithetical Meaning of Primal Words
- 1910 The Future Prospects of Psychoanalytic Therapy
- 1910 "Wild" psychoanalysis
- 1910 The PsychoAnalytic View of Psychogenic Disturbance of Vision
- 1910 A Special Type of Choice of Object made by Men

- 1911 The Handling of Dream Interpretation in Psycho-Analysis
- 1911 Formulations on the Two Principles of Mental Functioning
- 1911 PsychoAnalytic Notes on an Autobiographical Account of a Case of Paranoia (Schreber)
- 1912 On the Universal Tendency to Debasement in the Sphere of Love
- 1912 Recommendations to Physicians Practising Psychoanalysis
- 1912 Types of Onset of Neurosis
- 1912 The Dynamics of Transference
- 1912 Contributions to a Discussion on Masturbation
- 1912 A Note on the Unconscious in Psycho-Analysis
- 1913 Totem and Taboo: Resemblances Between the Psychic Lives of Savages and Neurotics (German: *Totem und Tabu: Einige Übereinstimmungen im Seelenleben der Wilden und der Neurotiker*)
- 1913 The Claims of Psycho-Analysis to Scientific Interest
- 1913 On Beginning the Treatment (Further recommendations on the technique of psychoanalysis)
- 1913 The Disposition to Obsessional Neurosis
- 1913 Theme of the Three Caskets
- 1914 Remembering, Repeating and Working-through (Further recommendations on the technique of psychoanalysis)
- 1914 On Narcissism: An Introduction
- 1914 The Moses of Michelangelo
- 1914 On the History of the PsychoAnalytic Movement (German: *Zur Geschichte der psychoanalytischen Bewegung*)
- 1915–1917 Introductory Lectures on Psycho-Analysis (German: *Vorlesungen zur Einführung in die Psychoanalyse*)
- 1915 Observations on Transference-Love (Further recommendations on the technique of psychoanalysis)
- 1915 Thoughts for the Times on War and Death (German: Zeitgemäßes über Krieg und Tod)
- 1915 Instincts and their Vicissitudes
- 1915 Repression
- 1915 The Unconscious
- 1915 A Case of Paranoia Running Counter to the PsychoAnalytic Theory of the Disease
- 1915 Some Character-Types Met within PsychoAnalytic Work
- 1915 On Transience
- 1916 A Mythological Parallel to a Visual Obsession

- 1917 Mourning and Melancholia
- 1917 A Difficulty on the Path of Psycho-Analysis
- 1917 On Transformations of Instinct as Exemplified in Anal Erotism
- 1917 A Metapsychological Supplement to the Theory of Dreams
- 1918 From the History of an Infantile Neurosis (Wolfman)
- 1918 The Taboo of Virginity
- 1918 Lines of Advance in Psycho-Analytic Therapy
- 1918 Introduction to Psycho-Analysis and the War Neuroses
- 1918 On the Teaching of Psycho-Analysis in the Universities
- 1918 James J. Putnam
- 1919 A Child is Being Beaten
- 1919 The Uncanny (German: *Das Unheimliche*)
- 1920 The Psychogenesis of a Case of Homosexuality in a Woman
- 1920 Beyond the Pleasure Principle (German: *Jenseits des Lustprinzips*)
- 1920 A Note on the Prehistory of The Technique of Analysis
- 1920 Supplements to the Theory of Dreams
- 1921 Psychoanalysis and Telepathy
- 1921 Group Psychology and the Analysis of the Ego (German: *Massenpsychologie und Ich-Analyse*)
- 1922 Medusa's Head (German: *Das Medusenhaupt*)
- 1922 Dreams and Telepathy
- 1922 Some Neurotic Mechanisms in Jealousy, Paranoia and Homosexuality
- 1923 The Ego and the Id (German: *Das Ich und das Es*)
- 1923 A Seventeenth-Century Demonological Neurosis (Christoph Haizmann)
- 1923 Infantile Genital Organisation
- 1924 Neurosis and Psychosis
- 1924 The Loss of Reality in Neurosis and Psychosis
- 1924 The Economic Problem of Masochism
- 1924 The Dissolution of the Oedipus Complex
- 1925 The Resistances to Psychoanalysis
- 1925 Josef Breuer
- 1925 A Note upon the "Mystic Writing-Pad"
- 1925 An Autobiographical Study (1935 Postscript)
- 1925 Negation
- 1925 Some Psychical Consequences of the Anatomical Distinction between the Sexes

- 1926 Karl Abraham
- 1926 Inhibitions, Symptoms, and Anxiety
- 1926 The Question of Lay Analysis (German: *Die Frage der Laieanalyse*)
- 1927 The Future of an Illusion (German: *Die Zukunft einer Illusion*)
- 1927 Fetishism
- 1927 Humour
- 1928 Dostoevsky and Parricide
- 1930 Civilization and Its Discontents (German: *Das Unbehagen in der Kultur*)
- 1931 Libidinal Types
- 1931 Female Sexuality
- 1932 The Acquisition of Control Over Fire
- 1933 Sándor Ferenczi
- 1933 New Introductory Lectures on Psycho-Analysis
- 1933 Why War? (German: *Warum Krieg?* co-authored with Albert Einstein)
- 1936 A Disturbance of Memory on the Acropolis
- 1937 Lou Andreas-Salomé
- 1937 Analysis Terminable and Interminable
- 1937 Constructions in Analysis
- 1938 An Outline of Psycho-Analysis (German: Abriß der Psycho-analyse)
- 1938 Some Elementary Lessons in Psycho-Analysis
- 1938 The Splitting of the Ego in the Process of Defence
- 1938 A Comment on Anti-Semitism
- 1939 Moses and Monotheism (German: Der Mann Moses und die monotheistische Religion)

The Standard Edition

The Standard Edition of the Complete Psychological Works of Sigmund Freud. Trans. from the German under the general editorship of James Strachey, in collaboration with Anna Freud, assisted by Alix Strachey, Alan Tyson, and Angela Richards (24 Vols.). London: Hogarth Press and the Institute of Psycho-Analysis, 1953–1974.

- Vol. I. Pre-Psycho-Analytic Publications and Unpublished Drafts (1886–1899)

- Vol. II. Studies in Hysteria (1893–1895). By Josef Breuer and S. Freud
- Vol. III. Early Psycho-Analytic Publications (1893–1899)
- Vol. IV. The Interpretation of Dreams (I) (1900)
- Vol. V. The Interpretation of Dreams (II) and On Dreams (1900–1901)
- Vol. VI. The Psychopathology of Everyday Life (1901)
- Vol. VII. A Case of Hysteria, Three Essays on Sexuality and Other Works (1901–1905)
- Vol. VIII. Jokes and their Relation to the Unconscious (1905)
- Vol. IX. Jensen's "Gradiva," and Other Works (1906–1909)
- Vol. X. The Cases of "Little Hans" and the "Rat Man" (1909)
- Vol. XI. Five Lectures on Psycho-Analysis, Leonardo and Other Works (1910)
- Vol. XII. Case History of Schreber, Papers on Technique and Other Works (1911–1913)
- Vol. XIII. Totem and Taboo and Other Works (1913–1914)
- Vol. XIV. On the History of the Psycho-Analytic Movement, Papers on Meta-psychology and Other Works (1914–1916)
- Vol. XV. Introductory Lectures on Psycho-Analysis (Parts I and II) (1915–1916)
- Vol. XVI. Introductory Lectures on Psycho-Analysis (Part III) (1916–1917)
- Vol. XVII. An Infantile Neurosis and Other Works (1917–1919)
- Vol. XVIII. Beyond the Pleasure Principle, Group Psychology and Other Works (1920–1922)
- Vol. XIX. The Ego and the Id and Other Works (1923–1925)
- Vol. XX. An Autobiographical Study, Inhibitions, Symptoms and Anxiety, Lay Analysis and Other Works (1925–1926)
- Vol. XXI. The Future of an Illusion, Civilization and Its Discontents and Other Works (1927–1931)
- Vol. XXII. New Introductory Lectures on Psycho-Analysis and Other Works (1932–1936)
- Vol. XXIII. Moses and Monotheism, An Outline of Psycho-Analysis and Other Works (1937–1939)
- Vol. XXIV. Indexes and Bibliographies (Compiled by Angela Richards, 1974)

INDEX

A

Abraham, Karl 5–7, 177
Adler, Alfred 5–6, 148
Advertising 29, 51, 58, 66–67, 69, 81–86, 93–96, 99–100, 110–111, 116–129, 135
Aggression 28, 35, 38–39, 70, 106, 114–115, 122, 127, 129, 133, 149, 154
Ambivalence 2, 10, 31, 40, 45, 62
Anal Stage 45–46
Art x, 12–13, 25, 32, 62, 64–66, 79, 90, 101, 104, 108, 111, 136, 145, 159–161
Avoidance 40

B

Barthes, Roland 82–83, 125
Benjamin, Walter 99, 105, 128
Bernays, Edward 84–88
Black Swan 33
Breuer, Josef 5, 22–24, 41, 80
Brücke, Ernst 4, 11, 43
Bullitt, William C. 16

C

Bühler, Charlotte 42
Catharsis viii, 23, 128
Charcot, Jean-Martine 4–5, 23
Childhood x, 5, 23, 31, 37, 41–43, 48, 50, 58–61, 74, 80, 153–154, 161
  Development 50
  Repression during 44, 46
  Sexual development
Cigar (smoking) 1, 3, 6, 13–14, 26–27, 36, 51, 85, 127
Cinema (film) vii–viii, 31–33, 59, 73–79, 84, 100, 108–109, 156, 158
Collective unconscious 82, 119, 121
Condensation (*Verdichtung*) 30, 37
Connotative meaning ix, 82

Consciousness 5–7, 19, 22, 25, 29, 31, 35–38, 40–41, 45, 58, 73, 78, 106, 108, 119–120, 131, 158
Couch 5, 9, 13, 24–25, 51
Coulrophobi 32

D

Dalí Salvador 8, 12m 61, 90, 145
Dangerous Method 39, 90
Darwin, Charles 10
Day-dreams 61
Dead Ringers 33
Defense mechanism(s) 35, 40–41, 46, 62, 114, 155
dementia praecox (schizophrenia) 104
Denial 33, 40, 44, 62, 114, 133, 155
Denotative meaning ix, 82
Depression 19, 87, 100, 102–108, 111, 114–115
Depth Psychology 2, 9, 19–20, 51, 164
Displacement (*Verschiebung*)
Dopplegänger
Double Life of Véronique
Double, The
Dr. Jekyll and Mr. Hyde
Dramatization (*Dramatisierung*) 30, 37, 70, 114
Dreams x, 1, 5, 8, 10, 21, 24, 27–29, 31, 35, 37, 51, 60–61, 63–64, 66, 73, 81, 83, 109, 118, 123, 125–126, 128, 160–161, 170, 174, 176, 178
Dream Work (*Traumarkbeit*) 29, 66
Drives vii, 9, 28, 33, 36, 41, 44, 49, 74, 85, 105, 117, 119–120, 122, 129, 148–149, 154–155
Durkheim, Emil 116–117

E

Ego 8, 28, 33, 37–39, 44, 48–49, 71, 74, 81, 84, 105–107, 112–113, 115, 161–162, 171, 176–178
Eros 38–39, 117

F

Fantasy (phantasie) 9, 60–61, 70, 75, 82, 121, 148, 174
Fashion 66–69, 87, 92, 100, 127–128
Femme Fatale 33
Ferenczi, Sándor 5, 7, 148, 153, 177
Fetish(ism) 67–70, 74–77, 128, 177
fetishistic scopophilia 75
Film (cinema) vii–viii, x, 8, 25, 31–33, 50, 58–59, 61–62, 64, 66–67, 69, 73–79, 83–84, 89–91, 99–100, 107–115, 127–129, 135, 146, 156, 158–160
Fixation 40, 45, 48, 62
Fliess, Wilhelm 5
Fräulein Ann O. (Bertha Pappenheim) 5
Free association (*see also* Talking Cure) 5, 9, 21–23, 31, 39, 51, 63, 66, 90
Front Page, The 30

G

Gaze Theory 69, 73–78, 83–84, 128–129
Genital Stage 44–46, 49, 70, 123, 176
Graf, Max 6
Gucci 68, 100, 116, 127–128

H

Heterosexuality 49, 73, 78, 84, 123, 129
Homosexuality 49, 176
Hysteria 4, 6, 11, 23, 40, 72, 90–91, 106, 160, 169–170, 173–174, 178
Hysterical conversion 24
Humor/our vii, 26, 33–35, 46, 100–101, 157–158, 177
Humours 101–102

I

Id 8, 10, 38–39, 44, 47, 49, 71, 81, 84, 87, 105, 115, 118, 148, 158, 161–162, 171, 176, 178
Individuation 22
Instincts 10, 32, 37–39, 41–42, 44, 48, 50, 74, 85–86, 114, 118, 120, 126, 149, 154, 161, 171, 175
It 32

J

Jhally, Sut 76, 81, 120–122, 129
Jokes 1, 11, 20, 35, 170, 174, 178
Joker 32
Jolly Corner, The 33
Jung, Carl ix, 5, 7, 15, 22, 38–39, 42, 51, 82, 90–91, 148, 170

K

Kahane, Max 6

L

Latent Stage 29–30, 36, 44, 47, 66, 75, 118
Lazarsfeld, Paul 118
Levi-Strauss, Claude 120, 137, 163
Libido viii, 44, 47–49, 59, 74, 92–93, 113, 121, 148, 154

M

Manifest ix, 21, 24, 29–30, 91, 104, 114, 117
Man Who Haunted Himself, The 33
McLuhan, Marshall vii, 99
Mediatization 61, 89
Melancholia vii, 99–100, 102,
Melancholy 99–108, 110–112, 136–137, 145
Metaphor 10, 23–24, 38, 47, 63, 83, 115
Moll, Albert 42
Mulvey, Laura 73–78, 129
Music 65, 69, 100, 102–103, 109, 136, 145, 159–160

N

Narrative 23, 28, 62, 72, 74, 103, 118, 113, 134
Neurocognitive inhibition 23
News viii, x, 59, 67, 86, 91, 130, 134, 137, 150, 156
Novels (books) vii–viii, 12–13, 32–34, 58–59, 60, 62, 70–71, 76, 90, 102

O

Oral Stage 26, 44–45

P

Peirce 123–125
Phallic Stage 44, 46–47
Pleasure principle (*Lustprinzip*) 9–10, 38–39, 120–121, 171, 176, 178
Possession 33
Prestige, The 33
Projection 40, 62, 69, 80, 114, 159
Psychoanalysis 86, 89, 92, 99, 106, 115, 118–121, 125, 147–159, 162, 164, 170, 174–176
Psychoanaltyic criticism 63
  Psychoanalytic film theory 73
  Psychoanalytic media research 58
  Psychoanaltyic Movement 6, 175
  Puberty 41–42, 47–49
  Putnam, James Jackson 8, 50, 176

Public relations vii–viii, x, 58, 67, 84–88, 92, 99–100, 119–120, 129–130, 135

R

Rank, Otto 5, 33, 148
Rationalization 31, 40, 114
Reaction formation 40
Reality principle 10
Regression vii, 40, 62
Reitler, Rudolph 6
Repression viii, 8, 23–24, 33, 35–37, 39–41, 44, 46, 50, 62, 68, 71, 74, 82, 85, 92, 111, 114, 149, 159, 175
Rousseau, Jean-Jacques 43

S

Scopophilia 73–75, 77, 83, 128
Secondary Revision (*Bearbeitung*) 28, 30
Semiotics 116, 123–126, 129, 135
Sex
  Aggression
  Theory of
  Wishes (*Triebe*)
Shining, The 32
Sign 14, 123–126
Signifier 83, 123–125
Signified 83, 123, 125
Slips 20–21, 28, 33–35, 37, 64
Sontag, Susan 105
Sopranos, The 8, 79
Spellbound 8, 73
Stekel, Wilhelm 6
Stern, W. 42
Story telling 81
Sublimation 3, 154, 40, 50, 66–67, 114, 154
Suppression 3, 33, 37, 40–41, 49, 70–71, 92
Superego 8, 38–39, 48–49, 71, 87, 105, 115, 161–162
Symbols 26, 29–30, 38, 119, 123, 125, 162
Symbolization (*Symbolisierung*) 23, 29

T

Taboo 31, 44, 69, 74, 116–117, 121, 132, 149, 151, 170, 175–176, 178
Talking cure (*see also* Free Association) 5, 9, 21–23, 31, 39, 51, 63, 66, 90
Television vii, 8, 33, 58, 61–62, 67, 78–79, 89–90, 119, 137, 150, 157–158, 162
Therapeutic setting 8, 19, 21
Totem(ism) 74, 116–118, 120–121, 132, 137, 170, 175, 178
Transgression 68, 73
Trauma 5, 23, 28, 37, 41, 45, 58, 71, 90, 106, 158–159, 161
Trump, Donald 130–134, 158

U

Uncanny (Das Unheimlich) 27, 31–33, 64, 71, 174
Unconscious x, 5, 8, 11, 15, 20–22, 28–29, 31–41, 50–51, 57–59, 63–64, 66, 68, 74–76, 81–82, 86, 92, 105, 109, 114, 117, 119–121, 123, 126, 128, 131–132, 148–149, 151–152, 155, 160, 162, 174–175, 178

V

Vertigo 33, 73, 75

W

Wilson, Woodrow 12
Wish fulfillment 28

A CRITICAL INTRODUCTION TO MEDIA AND COMMUNICATION THEORY

David W. Park
Series Editor

The study of the media in the field of communication suffers from no shortage of theoretical perspectives from which to analyze media, messages, media systems, and audiences. One of the field's strengths has been its flexibility as it incorporates social scientific and humanist ideas in pursuit of a better understanding of communication and the media. This flexibility and abundance of ideas threaten to muddle the study of communication as it stakes out an interdisciplinary identity.

This series puts on center stage individuals and ideas whose importance to the study of communication can be reconfigured, reinvented, and refocused. Each of the specially commissioned books in the series shares a concern for the history of theory in the field of communication. Books provide sophisticated discussions of the relevance of particular theorists or theories, with an emphasis on re-inventing the field of communication, whether by incorporating ideas often considered to be 'outside' the field or by providing fresh analyses of ideas that have long been considered vital in the field's past. Though theoretical in focus, the books are at all times concerned with the applicability of theory to empirical research and experience and are designed to be accessible, yet critical, for students—undergraduates and postgraduates—and scholars.

For additional information about this series or for the submission of manuscripts, please contact:

David W. Park
park@lakeforest.edu

To order other books in this series, please contact our Customer Service Department:
(800) 770-LANG (within the U.S.)
(212) 647-7706 (outside the U.S.)
(212) 647-7707 FAX

Or browse online by series:
www.peterlang.com

www.ingramcontent.com/pod-product-compliance
Ingram Content Group UK Ltd.
Pitfield, Milton Keynes, MK11 3LW, UK
UKHW021839100926
8556IPUK00004B/435

9 781433 131202